P9-DCD-659

HOW TO PICK STOCKS
LIKE WARREN BUFFETT

HOW TO PICK STOCKS LIKE WARREN BUFFETT

Profiting from the Bargain
Hunting Strategies of the
World's Greatest Value Investor

Timothy Vick

McGraw-Hill
New York   San Francisco   Washington, D.C.   Auckland   Bogotá
Caracas   Lisbon   London   Madrid   Mexico City   Milan
Montreal   New Delhi   San Juan   Singapore
Sydney   Tokyo   Toronto

Library of Congress Cataloging-in-Publication Data

Vick, Timothy P.
   How to pick stocks like Warren Buffett : profiting from the bargain hunting strategies /
by Timothy Vick.
      p. cm.
   ISBN 0-07-135769-6
   1. Investments—United States. 2. Stocks—United States. I. Title.

HG4910.V528 2000
332.632'2—dc21

00-055015

McGraw-Hill

A Division of The McGraw·Hill Companies

   2 3 4 5 6 7 8 9 0   AGM/AGM   0 9 8 7 6 5 4 3 2 1 0

ISBN 0-07-135769-6

This book was set in Times New Roman by Patricia Wallenburg.

Printed and bound by Quebecor World/Martinsburg.

This publication is designed to provide accurate and authoritative information in regard to the subject
matter covered. It is sold with the understanding that neither the author nor the publisher is engaged in
rendering legal, accounting, investment, or other professional service. If legal advice or other expert
assistance is required, the services of a competent professional person should be sought.

—From a Declaration of Principles jointly adopted by a Committee
of the American Bar Association and a Committee of Publishers

McGraw-Hill books are available at special quantity discounts to use as premiums and sales
promotions, or for use in corporate training programs. For more information, please write to the
Director of Special Sales, Professional Publishing, McGraw-Hill, Two Penn Plaza, New York, NY
10121-2298. Or contact your local bookstore.

This book was printed on recycled, acid-free paper
containing a minimum of 50% recycled, de-inked fiber.

CONTENTS

PART 3
ANALYZING COMPANIES LIKE BUFFETT

PART 4
AVOIDING LOSSES

PART 5
CHICKEN SOUP FOR THE INVESTOR

ACKNOWLEDGMENTS

FROM THE DAY I BEGAN WRITING THIS BOOK, I willingly donned the robe of a disciple, not of a biographer. This book should be viewed as the latest in a body of literature that dissects Mr. Buffett's preachings. As such, it is impossible to complete a work on Warren Buffett without expressing my indebtedness to him for providing the world with his writings and anecdotes. No one who follows his methods and attains even a fraction of his successes can ever express their appreciation enough. There isn't an investor anywhere who cannot benefit from the folksy, utterly rational approach he espouses. It's ironic that, on the day I completed this manuscript, the Dow Industrial and Nasdaq indexes recorded their biggest single-day point drops in history. In the aftermath, investors again will be searching for philosophical direction. No great investor has left a clearer, more profitable set of tracks to follow than Mr. Buffett.

My deep thanks go to Rebecca for her encouragement and for showing patience through trying times. Also, to Mary Buffett for her insight and friendship. Her contributions to this book go well beyond what you will see in the printed pages. Additional thanks go to my colleague Kenneth Pogach, an instructor of finance at Purdue University, whose passion for investing and acute perspective on the markets have helped me improve my financial bowling score. I also thank Andrew Kilpatrick of Birmingham, Alabama, who, in my mind, deserves a lot more credit for his indefatigable efforts to unearth every piece of the Warren Buffett story. No one who writes about Buffett can go to press without relying on Andy's work. The same goes for Janet Lowe, who deserves accolades for her tireless devotion and writings on Buffett and Benjamin Graham. I extend gratitude to my editor at McGraw-Hill,

Jeffrey Krames, for his patience and devotion to the project. Jeffrey never wavered on the book, even as Mr. Buffett's methods came under intense media and public criticism.

I also wish to thank my agent, Wes Neff, for getting me back onto the playing field again and typesetter Patty Wallenburg of TypeWriting for creating the perfect-looking book you are about to read.

Finally, thanks to my children, Calvin and Natalie, for whom I do everything. May you both build on the legacy I am trying to leave.

Timothy Vick

P A R T

BECOMING A
BILLIONAIRE

How Warren Buffett Amassed His Fortune

It's not that I want money. It's the fun of making money and watching it grow.

Warren Buffett[1]

HOW DOES ONE ACCUMULATE $30 *billion*? It has been said that making your first million dollars is the hardest and that subsequent millions come much more easily. To a certain extent, that's true, just as it was easier, and considerably quicker, for the Dow Industrials to rise from 10,000 to 11,000 then it was for the Dow to rise from 2,000 to 3,000. As the numbers get larger, the percentage change needed to reach the next milestone contracts. Increasing money is not the same as, say, hitting 500 home runs, where it is just as difficult to strike the last 50 home runs as it is the first 50. Competitive endeavors such as sports make you earn every statistic. Finance hands you a Golden Goose—the power of compounding—and makes it difficult for you *not* to attain some measure of wealth.

Nevertheless, there's quite a difference between a mere millionaire and one who can tack three more zeros onto green ledger paper. The list of inductees into the compounding club drops exponentially as net worth increases. It's almost safe to say that there are one- one-thousandth as many billionaires in the world as millionaires. And there are probably one-tenth as many folks worth 11 figures ($10 billion or more) as are currently worth 10.

No mathematical formulas or bell curves, however, can make light of what Warren Edward Buffett, born August 30, 1930, in Omaha, Nebraska, has attained. There simply is no precedent for it in business history. The world's club of billionaires is replete with sheiks and kings, entrepreneurs, inventors, CEOs, those who struck it rich being in the right place, and those who merely came out of the right "heir womb." Warren Buffett mustered every ounce of horsepower his mathematically inclined brain could produce and created a career for himself exploiting the world's financial inefficiencies— over and over again.

No billionaire except Buffett has earned his *entire* fortune off Wall Street. Rather, most of his peers began with regular jobs and shepherded themselves up the business ladder through distinguished acts. Only later in life did they try to adapt their skill sets and compound their wealth by playing the quirky, schizophrenic world of Wall Street. Warren Buffett adopted finance and the trading of paper stock certificates as his bread and butter from the start (he bought his first stock at age 11). While his Omaha neighbors toiled for their families working in nondescript positions, the confident Buffett, then in his 20s, ran the world's most successful investment pool from a disarranged bedroom filled with annual reports, Standard & Poor's guides, and plenty of eight-packs of soft drinks.

For 45 years, Warren Buffett's business card could have read, simply, "capital allocator." His chief job description since the 1950s, one could argue, has been that of a fund-raiser. He scours the financial world for sources of cheap money, usually by purchasing a cash-generating company, and puts the money to use, typically compounding it at annual rates between 20 and 30 percent. Every dollar of value he adds to the process translates into a dollar of *intrinsic value* for a publicly traded entity called Berkshire Hathaway. The influx of dollars, which numbers in the billions these days, is sucked into Berkshire's perpetually bulging coffers and forms a stack of claim checks his shareholders are only too happy to have retained and reinvested on their behalf. His decision in the 1960s and 1970s to amass shares in this formerly antiquated textile company gives him and his wife, Susie, a nearly 34 percent stake in the same profits he takes pride in generating. Simply by thinking, he has generated billions of dollars of net worth for those who have entrusted him with their money.

This constant process of allocating and reinvesting shareholder dollars is done with such ease and confidence that Buffett accepts a yearly salary of just $100,000. Judging by the way he lives, a salary of more than $100,000 would probably seem an insult. Buffett is fully capable of finding profitable opportunities on his own and has never needed the buttress of a bimonthly payroll check. "I don't need three cars or three houses," he is wont to say. "That's just more things to take care of. I can't drive more than one car at a time, anyway."

Every description of Warren Buffett from friends, business associates, and shareholders carries the same tune, which is a remarkable testament to Buffett's mental, financial, and psychological constancy. He is, in essence, a grown-up version of the fun-loving, but cautious boy who wore a metal money changer around his belt, memorized the populations of cities, and was his classmates' emotional and practical auditor. Writings from his youth during the 1950s bear an incredible resemblance to his annual reports of the late 1990s. No amount of economic and political change over four decades has amended his dry wit, logic, and ability to detoxify data like a scientist conducting a control experiment.

Spend 5 minutes with Warren Buffett and you might walk away unimpressed by his physical appearance and his ostensible shyness around strangers. Despite his worldlywise demeanor, Buffett has spent nearly all of his 70 years circulating within a two-mile radius in central Omaha. Spend 20 minutes, enough time to let his synopses warm up, and you'll be treated to an encyclopedic recitation on topics ranging from college football to Coca-Cola's unit volume growth in Latin America or the balance sheets of major banks. Those lucky enough to get a 20-minute audience keep coming back for more. Some 14,000 investors spend an average of $1,000 each to descend on Omaha in May to hear a day's worth of his witticisms. If time and consistency build loyalty, Warren Buffett is the best consumer brand in finance.

THE STUFF THAT BILLIONAIRES COME FROM

The master investors of the past 60 to 70 years have all been mavericks. They shun convention, remain steadfastly devout to their pattern of thinking, and brush aside popular opinion. Had they not been so irreverent to Wall Street's formulaic patterns, they could not have attained their stature. "Group thinkers have not cracked the Forbes 400 in significant numbers for one simple reason: Doing the same thing in the same way as everyone else is decidedly not the way to overcome the leveling effects of competition," notes analyst and writer Martin Fridson."[2]

Legendary value investor John Templeton, who founded the fund family that bears his name, once took every nickel he owned and invested it in stocks just as World War II broke out. The nation was then gripped by ominous events in Europe and, still chilled by the experiences of the Depression, saw the war as a catalyst that would pull stocks lower. World War II, after all, didn't begin like the Civil War, where troops trotted off under the assumption the skirmish would conclude in two weeks. Investors sensed that the war in Europe could last years and take its toll on world economies and U.S. stock prices.

Templeton didn't see it that way. He was convinced the war would shake the U.S. economy out of its doldrums, cause an enormous increase in world output, raise employment to new heights, and spur wealth creation in the U.S. at rates not seen in decades. He went to local banks, borrowed as much money as he possibly could, and placed orders to buy $100 in stock of every publicly traded company on the New York Stock Exchange, or so the story goes. John Train wrote that Templeton walked out of the brokerage with shares in 104 companies, 34 of which were bankrupt.[3] It didn't matter to Templeton whether the market initially dropped after he invested his life savings. Templeton was confident that the powder keg lit under U.S. manufacturers would spur a stock market boom. He was right. Four years later, Templeton had disposed of nearly all 104 stocks, for which he initially paid $10,400. By that time, the shares were worth $40,000.

When legendary fund manager John Neff accepted the job of managing the Windsor fund in Philadelphia, he bought a home on a floodplain after being advised by real estate agents to avoid it. "I took the warning as an invitation to look inside," Neff wrote.[4] Undoubtedly, Neff calculated that the amount of possible flood damage the home could sustain over time was more than offset by the utility and appreciation potential the home offered. Neff lived in the home for 21 years "without regret."[5]

Like other money masters of the twentieth century, Neff displayed an ideal combination of frugality and intense profit motive. Before moving into his home, Neff lived in boarding houses and at the YMCA so he could stash half of his income into the bank. As a teenager, he caddied for local golf courses during the day and delivered newspapers in the evening. He mastered being value conscious by watching sign painters change the prices of produce daily at his aunt and uncle's grocery store chain. Always eager to compound money, Neff took a job as a shipping clerk for a jukebox company but would skip work to sell encyclopedias on the side for better pay.

Indeed, nearly every great investor has brought to the table a keen instinct for finding or adding value to an asset. In his early years, billionaire corporate raider Kirk Kerkorian would buy broken-down used cars from dealers, repair them (he cleaned engines for a living), and sell them for a $5 to $10 profit. After a stint with the British Royal Air Force, Kerkorian would buy used DC-3s for $7,000 to $10,000, convert them into commercial aircraft, and sell them for $60,000. As a 23-year-old, Laurence Tisch persuaded his parents to lease a run-down resort in Lakewood, New Jersey. They refurbished it, restored its appeal by providing live entertainment, and then bought the resort outright from the profits earned in the first two years. When the oil industry went bust in the late 1980s, Tisch bought drilling rigs for an average cost of $5 million and patiently waited for a rebound in crude oil prices. At their next cyclical peak, the same wells were producing $25 million a year in profits for Tisch.

Perseverance and confidence in their ability to make money separate ordinary investors from the truly great ones such as Templeton, Tisch, Neff, and Warren Buffett. By delving into their past, one can find almost identical character traits in all of them despite their growing up under unique—sometimes tragic—household circumstances, and living amid distinct social settings.

FROM $100 TO $30,000,000,000

Warren Buffett humbly, and often, comments that he owes his fortune to having been raised in a prosperous nation, one that happens to reward what he does. "When I was born, I had a 2 percent chance of being an American and a 98 percent chance of living in another country," he is fond of saying. "If I had been born in a jungle somewhere, I would eventually have been some animal's lunch. My skills wouldn't have been worth a damn. I am (wealthy) because of the tremendous society that surrounds me, and I happen to have adapted as best I could."

Being born an American carried Buffett to first base, just as it gives many natives a natural head start over the rest of the world. But inspiration for his career in finance most certainly drew from his father, Howard Buffett, who ran a brokerage house, Buffett, Sklenicka & Co., in Omaha and used the young Warren to post stock quotes on the blackboard. It was the late 1930s, and Wall Street's reputation as a deliverer of riches had been blackened years earlier by a chain of events that began right around the time Howard and his wife, Leila, conceived Warren. Howard, a pious man who held deeply conservative political views, struggled to make sure that his family never stood in soup kitchen lines as the sons and daughters of Nebraska's wheat farmers were doing. Times were difficult for the family after Warren's birth, but Howard righted the family finances as their young math prodigy was coming of age and taking to his grade-school classes.

WARREN THE HUSTLER

It must have been obvious from the outset that little Warren was on track to do special things. Anecdotes gathered from earlier biographers describe a boy fixated on money and counting; suspicious of things exotic, and deeply devoted to the few things—and people—he trusted. Midwest-sounding as it may be, it was nonetheless the perfect cocktail for spawning a professional investor who would beat Wall Street. Warren's interest in the stock market took root by the age of 10. By then he was posting quotes and filing stock and bond certificates at his father's office and charting price movements in his spare time. He was obsessed with deciphering patterns from what seemed to be random fluctuations and took to becoming an arm-chair "technician." He might have remained one to this day had it not been for his introduction to Benjamin Graham and his value-oriented methods.

It's one thing to be a math wizard. Buffett would put his nascent talents to practical use, looking for ways to exploit numbers for profit. The earliest story that emerges is that of a 6-year-old who would buy six-packs of Cokes for $0.25 and then sell each bottle for a nickel. This may have been the first of hundreds of *arbitrage* opportunities Buffett would exploit in his lifetime. At age 11, he and a friend developed a system for handicapping horses and would try to sell tip sheets, *Stable-Boy Selections*, at the racetrack. Everything worked fine until racing authorities put him out of business for not having a license. In another venture, Buffett would recruit neighborhood friends to dredge golf balls from creeks and ponds and then resell them. As the ringleader, Buffett would take a cut of the profits.

By his teenage years, there was no doubt to Buffett or his friends what he intended to do with his life: play the stock market. Bookish and reserved, Buffett was the type of youngster who was both admired and left alone, the type too timid to provoke a fight but who could get others to fight for him; the type whom everyone circled for answers to questions, yet left behind when the wild parties began. "I would not have been the most popular guy in the class, but I wouldn't have been the most unpopular either," he recounts. "I was just sort of nothing."[6] He read investment books incessantly and is said to have nearly memorized a favorite treatise, *A Thousand Ways to Make $1,000*. He read it on buses, on park benches, in his bedroom or any place that offered him the solitude to absorb the information. He would bring along the day's edition of *The Wall Street Journal* when playing basketball with friends. During rest periods, he would read.

And he was always scheming. While living in Washington, D.C. (Howard had won election to Congress in 1942 by running against Roosevelt's New Deal platform), he took on five newspaper routes and four competing dailies. When a customer canceled a subscription, which cut into his collections, Buffett would cross sell a competing paper and keeping the income flowing. "Collections were everything to him. You didn't dare touch the drawer where he kept his money," his mother once wrote. "Every penny had to be there."[7] Buffett later added a magazine route and kept mental track of every reader's subscription terms so he could hook them on a renewal.

More ventures followed. He and a friend, Don Danly, operated a pinball "route," as it's called in the business. They bought their first machine for $25 and placed it in a Washington barber shop. Finding they could earn their entire investment back within a few weeks,

Buffett and Danly expanded to seven machines that pulled in $50 a week. Warren would type monthly profit-and-loss statements for their enterprise. In 1947, Danly bought a 1928 Rolls Royce from a junkyard for $350, fixed it up, and the two of them rented it out for $35 a day. As Danly performed routine maintenance, Buffett stood nearby and read business books aloud.

At the age of 15, Buffett had saved enough money to buy a 40-acre farm in Nebraska from his father. By the age of 20, his fortune was an estimated $9,800—about $68,000 in today's inflated dollars.[8] Had Buffett simply let the $9,800 compound at 25 percent a year, he would have been worth $549 million by the end of 1999. But that wasn't enough. Confident he could grow his net worth at high rates, Buffett knew he had to find much more money to put to work.

THE INVESTMENT POOLS

Buffett needed a nudge from his father to attend college and chose the Wharton School of Business at the University of Pennsylvania in 1947. Two years of listening to professors who knew less than he about finance prompted the 19-year-old to leave Wharton and finish his degree at the University of Nebraska in Lincoln. During his senior year, Buffett read *The Intelligent Investor*, the latest book by money manager and Columbia University instructor Benjamin Graham, which would permanently fix Buffett's views on the financial markets. Buffett now longed to advance his business education and applied to Harvard Business School in 1950. After a 10-minute interview, Harvard rejected the 19-year-old awkward Nebraskan. Soon thereafter, Buffett applied to Columbia Business School—where Graham taught—was accepted, and graduated a year later with a master's degree in economics.

Buffett took to Graham's preachings with a passion and was, by all accounts, the best student Graham had ever taught. The two engaged in lively class debates while Buffett's classmates sat back, with mouths agape. The class was the catharsis Buffett had sought, the soothing method that wrapped around his persona like a security blanket. He had tried his hands at market timing, charting, and other forms of technical analysis. Graham's lessons—grounded on the premise that stocks should reflect the inner worth of a company and that superior returns could be experienced by buying undervalued securities—coursed through Buffett like a lightning bolt. In retrospect, Graham was Buffett's financial acupuncturist, the one who completed the circuit of knowledge and let Buffett fuse his analytical abilities, frugal tendencies, and business acumen to form a potent stock-picking system.

After graduating from Columbia, Buffett could scarcely wait to act out in practice what Graham theorized. Symbolically, he sought out Graham for his first financial job, but the elder professor refused to hire the lad. He returned to Omaha and worked as a stock salesman for his father until 1954. After three years of pestering, Graham hired Buffett to work at his investment management company, Graham-Newman. There, Buffett would learn the model for managing money he would take back to Omaha. Just two years later, Graham shuttered the company and retired. Buffett headed home. His net worth was an estimated $140,000, nearly all of it gained from buying and selling cheap stocks.[9] By this time, too, he had married Susan (Susie) Thompson of Omaha and had two of their three children.

Jobless but imminently confident, Buffett struck out on his own and formed Buffett Partnership, an investment pool that was no more than a shell organization on paper because Buffett ran the enterprise from his bedroom with scratch pads, a 49-cent accounting ledger, and a manual typewriter. Buffett invested $100 of his own money to start the partnership and persuaded family and friends to contribute $105,000. The ground rules were simple:

1. Buffett was free to invest their money in whatever security he deemed fit.
2. He would not charge them a penny in fees if he couldn't exceed a 6 percent return, roughly the yield on a government bond.
3. His yearly fee was 25 percent of the money earned over and above 6 percent.
4. Investors couldn't ask questions about his investments.
5. If they asked questions, Buffett would not answer.
6. He would allow new investments only once or twice a year.

Most money managers today take a flat fee, usually between 1 and 1.5 percent of asset under management. The fee structure is a self-neutralizing force and ensures some income to the manager even in down times. Buffett's compensation formula, borne of the confidence he could beat bond yields and the market, allowed him to compound his personal wealth much faster than a standard money management agreement permitted. If Buffett could earn 10 percent a year, his fee would amount to 1 percent (one-quarter of the 4 percent premium he earned over a bond yield). If Buffett could earn 20 percent on their money, his take-home pay would be 3.75 percent of assets under management. Table 1.1 shows what Buffett might have earned on the original $105,000 given him in 1957 (keep in mind that more new money flowed in every year). By the time he closed the partnership in 1969, his fees would have been more than four times those of a typical money manager's. His total compensation over 13 years would have constituted about 19 percent of the final assets under management.

The first list of investors included Buffett's aunt Alice, his sister Doris and her husband, Susie's father, and three family friends. Getting outsiders to trust this brash, young investor would take time, however, and Buffett needed to show a sterling track record before more well-

TABLE 1.1   Buffett's fee structure.

	Partnership Returns	Start with $105,000	Money Manager 1.25%	Buffett's Fees
1957	**10.4%**	$115,920	$1,381	$1,155
1958	**40.9%**	$163,331	$1,745	$10,114
1959	**25.9%**	$205,634	$2,306	$8,126
1960	**22.8%**	$252,519	$2,863	$8,637
1961	**45.9%**	$368,425	$3,881	$25,189
1962	**13.9%**	$419,636	$4,925	$7,276
1963	**38.7%**	$582,035	$6,260	$34,305
1964	**27.8%**	$743,840	$8,287	$31,721
1965	**47.2%**	$1,094,933	$11,492	$76,616
1966	**20.4%**	$1,318,300	$15,083	$39,418
1967	**35.9%**	$1,791,569	$19,437	$98,543
1968	**58.8%**	$2,845,012	$28,979	$236,487
1969	**6.8%**	$3,038,472	$36,772	$5,690
Total			**$143,411**	**$583,276**

heeled clients would open their checkbooks. One early skeptic was Don Keough, Buffett's neighbor in Omaha who ironically rose to become the president of Coca-Cola. Buffett offered Keough a chance to invest $5,000 early in the partnership's history to help him fund his children's education. Keough passed on the chance.[10] But as word spread of Buffett's miraculous year-after-year performance, winning new clients no longer was a problem. Investors from around the nation got wind of Buffett's prowess and wanted a piece of the pie. Laurence Tisch, the Chairman of Loews and CBS, invested $300,000 in the mid-1960s.

Buffett's form of money management was, to say the least, unconventional. Perhaps it was better that Buffett kept his clients in the dark about investments, because some wouldn't have been able to stomach the positions. A large chunk of their portfolios was being invested in arbitrage situations, where Buffett tried to capture price spreads in mergers and liquidations. Buffett also borrowed money (bought on margin) when using arbitrage to enhance portfolio returns. He invested the rest of their accounts in a small number of common stocks, sometimes concentrating portfolios in three to four companies. Ultimately, as assets under management swelled, he levered the asset base into a position of power and began taking controlling stakes in companies. Buffett found he could buy a significant position in an undervalued company, demand a board seat, take a leading role in righting the company's financial problems, and then assist management in selling the company for a higher price than Buffett paid. The most famous of these control investments was a textile mill called Berkshire Hathaway (see Chapter 2).

As assets grew and Buffett continued to pulverize the returns of the market (see Chapter 18 on how he did it), Buffett's personal wealth grew by leaps and bounds. His 25 percent yearly take, which he reinvested in the partnership, was compounding faster than the stocks in his portfolio. By 1964, Buffett's stake in the partnership's assets was $2,393,900, according to letters he sent shareholders. By 1966, it had grown to $6,849,936. When he closed the partnership in 1969, total assets under management were $104,429,431, of which Buffett's stake was an estimated $20 million to $25 million.

He clearly was on his way.

2

AMASSING A FORTUNE, PART II
Berkshire Hathaway: Buffett's Opus 1

WHEN HE CLOSED his investing partnership at the end of 1969, Warren Buffett, then a crew-cut 39-year-old with a net worth upward of $25 million, had seen enough. He had grown increasingly worried about valuation levels in the market and warned investors of his intent to pack it in. Like the markets of 1999 and 2000, Wall Street of 1969 had clearly fallen victim to momentum. Stocks with a sexy story were bid up to unprecedented premiums to their earnings and expected growth rates, while the rest of the market languished.

Bifurcated markets meant one thing to Buffett; the end of sanity. No longer could a diligent investment manager attain, let alone promise, decent returns for clients. No amount of research seemed to matter. Stocks with a good story were propped by institutional managers, who, like today, were probably about 30 years of age and had never known a bear market. In contrast, the market's underbelly was populated by

old-fashioned investments that kept falling in price despite the absence
of adverse news. In a word, overvalued stocks surged ahead, irrespective of fundamental principles: cheap stocks unraveled.

This was contrary to what Benjamin Graham had preached: A
stock trading below book value or liquidation value should eventually
rise back to its fair value. Nothing in the literature mentioned that a
cheap company would continue dropping in price. Although Buffett
continued to beat the Dow Industrials—he was completing his thir-
teenth consecutive year of doing so—the margin of outperformance
turned tenuous. The daily struggle to find stocks that could outrun the
market's high-growth rabbits slowly wore down most research-intensive money managers. Most would go "off model" and join the
momentum-hunting game to appease clients.

Buffett walked away, warning partners that the prospects for high
stock returns were fast fading. "We were lucky—if we had not been in
liquidation this year, our results would have been significantly worse,"
he wrote. "Ideas that looked potentially interesting on a 'continuing'
basis have, on balance, performed poorly of late. For the first time in
my investment lifetime, I now believe there is little choice for the average investor between professionally managed money in stocks and
passive investment in bonds."[1]

Liquidating $104 million in assets proved to be no quick task
because of the types of investments Buffett had made for clients. In
1963, he had bought 266,000 shares of Western Natural Gas, a exploration company that was liquidating assets and returning the proceeds
to investors. Buffett had hoped for a quick settlement and received the
majority of his investment when Western Natural Gas sold its gas
properties to Sinclair Oil. But by 1969, Western Natural Gas' assets
had still not been fully divested; the money owed shareholders
remained in a trust. Other arbitrage investments had yet to be
unwound. Buffett had to make a decision whether to sell the common
stock holdings or simply allocate the shares to partners.

One such investment was a textile mill, Berkshire Hathaway, in
New Bedford, Massachusetts. Buffett began accumulating shares for
the partnership in 1962, paying an average of $7 to $8 per share. The
idea to buy Berkshire came straight from the playbook of Graham,
since Berkshire sold for less than one-half its working capital. A rise
in the stock to at least Berkshire's balance-sheet value would give

Buffett a tidy triple-digit gain. Still under the spell of Graham and the pursuit of undervalued "turnarounds," Buffett aggressively hoarded what shares he could find. By 1965, Buffett and his clients controlled 49 percent of the stock. In May of that year, the inconspicuous money manager from Omaha seized control.

It's clear from his writings of the time that Buffett never intended to own a stake in Berkshire for very long, but the opportunity to merge his portfolio into Berkshire and create a vast investment conduit was too tempting to neglect. When he dissolved the partnership, Buffett gave clients the choice of accepting the Berkshire shares held on their behalf or to take cash. Buffett took the majority of his proceeds in stock and was only too happy to bargain for some of his partners' shares. When the liquidation settled, Buffett personally owned a 29 percent stake in Berkshire. He installed himself as chairman in 1970 and collected a modest $50,000 salary.

From that point forward, Buffett's fortunes were inextricably linked to Berkshire, and his career path was now on the runway awaiting takeoff. In one swoop, he greatly reduced his exposure to the public stock market and created the infrastructure to forward his investment plans. His fortune would now fluctuate with Berkshire's operating fortune, which he could mostly control. No longer was performance subject to the tug-and-pull of market gyrations. If he could continually increase the intrinsic value of Berkshire, he could ultimately enhance his own net worth.

The first move toward that end came in 1967, when Berkshire, by that time under Buffett's effective control, purchased National Indemnity, an Omaha insurance underwriter, for $8.6 million. Through the years, Buffett had developed an acute knowledge of the insurance industry and found National Indemnity's potential as an investment conduit mouth watering. Like most insurers, the company generated a significant yearly "float"—premiums collected today that didn't have to be paid as claims for years—that could be reinvested.

Berkshire Hathaway, the textile portion, generated virtually no excess cash Buffett could put to use, and, from all appearances, it never would. An insurer that was well capitalized and prudent with its underwriting could generate increasing amounts of free float through the years. From Buffett's point of view, it was better than soliciting for new money management clients. Thus the die was cast. For the next 30 years, Berkshire Hathaway would become the world's largest public investment pool, with quarterly profits from operations sent back to Omaha for Buffett to reinvest. The formula was straightforward:

1. Milk existing businesses within the holding company as well as possible for their cash flow and cut costs when necessary.

2. Use Berkshire's ever-increasing cash flow to acquire companies outright, making sure to buy cash-rich companies at prices cheap enough to generate a high return on Berkshire's original investment and increase its net worth.

3. Use cash flow from acquired companies to make public investments in stocks and bonds.

4. Acquire a portfolio of insurance companies with strong franchises to serve as conduits for the stock and bond purchases. Choose insurers capable of providing low-cost float to enlarge the potential pool of money from which Buffett could draw and leverage the returns on assets.

When Buffett buys a company such a General Reinsurance or Dairy Queen or invests in public stock such as Gillette, it is not his money put at risk. Usually, one of several insurance subsidiaries of Berkshire Hathaway makes the purchase, with Buffett or Lou Simpson, the co-CEO and investment manager of the auto insurer GEICO (which Berkshire bought outright in 1996), calling the shots. These purchases are made possible by the enormous amounts of money put at Buffett's disposal each year from the insurance properties. Insurers hold cash reserves to pay out projected claims but are free to invest these reserves until they must be paid. Profits from investing these reserves are generally taxed at a lower corporate rate, which gives Buffett a considerable rate-of-return edge over typical portfolio managers.

Berkshire's competitive advantage over other insurers lies in its strong balance sheet and superb track record of allocating capital, which, of course, go hand in hand. Its financial strength allows Berkshire to allocate capital much more aggressively than other insurers. The typical insurer invests its float in government bonds, which in recent years have yielded between 5 and 7 percent annually depending on market conditions. Many insurers, in fact, are limited to buying only investment-grade corporate and government bonds because regulators have historically not wanted companies to play fast and loose with policyholders' money. These companies also don't want to be caught holding equities that are declining in value when a catastrophe, such as an ice storm, hits a region and prompts thousands of immediate claims. State and local treasurers face the same investing restrictions as do many pension fund managers. In buoyant economies, these office holders can turn overly anxious and take excessive risks in pursuit of a few extra percentage points of annual gain.

Berkshire Hathaway, however, is not burdened with these restrictions. The Nebraska Insurance Department and ratings agencies give Buffett a wide latitude to put policyholders' surpluses to work in securities that can deliver much higher returns. Thus, Buffett is free to use the billions generated by Berkshire's insurance policies to buy common equities, bonds, or unconventional investments such as convertible preferreds (see Chapter 17). Moreover, he can use float to buy entire businesses, public or private, and bring them under Berkshire's tent. This degree of freedom, which a few other insurers such as Cincinnati Financial and Reliance Group have exploited as well, has allowed Berkshire to generate returns on its investment assets far superior to its competitors, even though its share of premiums written remains relatively small. Berkshire Hathaway writes a small percentage of the insurance industry's entire premiums, perhaps 2 percent or less, but it typically owns 20 to 25 percent of the common stock held by the entire insurance industry. Common stock holdings constituted 65 percent of Berskhire's insurance surpluses in 1999, a figure well above the industry average. Berkshire can typically earn a return of 20 percent or more on its investment assets, double what the rest of the industry posts.

Prudence has always been the hallmark of Berkshire's indemnity operations. The company has sufficient capital to underwrite billions of dollars more than it does in policies, but it has traditionally chosen to sacrifice market share for the sake of writing profitable policies. "People are always saying, 'Gee, why don't you write a lot more volume in relation to capital,'" Berkshire Hathaway Vice-Chairman Charles Munger said in 1993. "Everyone else is doing it. The rating agencies say that you can write twice as much in annual volume as you have capital. And they look at our $10 billion in insurance capital and say, 'That's $20 billion a year. What are you doing writing only $1 billion.' But then somebody else comes in and asks, 'Why did everybody get killed last year but you.' Maybe the questions are related."[2]

The ability to compound that competitive advantage over long periods has helped make Berkshire's stock the best performing in the insurance industry and is a major reason Berskhire can trade at large premiums to book value when other insurers don't. The company has a business model that simply can't be duplicated in the insurance industry.

The real power of Berkshire derives from its use of financial leverage, that is, the ability to invest amounts well in excess of the company's capital base. Let's say Berkshire has $100 million of capital on the balance sheet and receives $500 million a year in premiums. Buffett can invest the entire $600 million. If he earns 10 percent on the money at his disposal Berkshire would net $60 million, a 60 percent return on the original capital. Eventually Buffett must pay the $500 million back to policyholders to settle claims, but until he does, he has nearly free use of their money. If he can obtain a 20 percent yearly return on this float, Berkshire will rapidly grow its book value, which should lead to proportionate increases in stock price (see Chapter 10).

The trick is to obtain the float as cheaply as possible, and no insurer has done that better than Berkshire Hathaway. If an insurer can generate more in premium income each year than it pays in claims (an underwriting ratio below 100), the float is free because the company, in effect, is being paid to hold other people's money. If yearly claims exceed premiums, however, the float bears a real cost. For the insurer to break even, the investment manager must obtain a rate of return on the float that completely offsets the underwriting shortfall. When Berkshire bought National Indemnity, Buffett had $20 million in float at his disposal to reinvest. By 1999, that figure had swelled to $25.3 billion. More important, the aggregate cost of float has been negative the past 33 years.

In the 1970s, Buffett slowly increased his 29 percent stake in Berkshire. As the decade closed he and his wife, Susie, controlled 46 percent of the stock—the highest percentage they would obtain. Buffett owned roughly 520,000 shares, with a cost basis of $32.45 per share. Nearly all of his net worth was tied up in Berkshire stock. It was just a matter of keeping the company growing at rates to ensure high personal returns.

The fruits of his efforts are shown in Table 2.1 and Figure 2.1. From nebulous beginnings, Buffett has increased Berkshire's book

TABLE 2.1   Buffett's track record running Berkshire.

	Per Share		Berkshire Hathaway			$10,000 Invested	
Date	Book Value	% Increase	Dec. 31 Price*	Yearly Return	S&P 500 Return	With Buffett	With S&P 500
1965	$24	23.8%	$19		10.0%	$10,000	$10,000
1966	$29	20.3%	$17	–8.0%	–11.7%	$9,200	$8,830
1967	$32	11.0%	$20	15.7%	30.9%	$10,644	$11,558
1968	$38	19.0%	$37	82.7%	11.0%	$19,447	$12,830
1969	$44	16.2%	$42	13.5%	–8.4%	$22,073	$11,752
1970	$50	12.0%	$39	–7.1%	3.9%	$20,506	$12,211
1971	$58	16.4%	$69	79.5%	14.6%	$36,807	$13,993
1972	$71	21.7%	$79	14.3%	18.9%	$42,071	$16,638
1973	$74	4.7%	$71	–11.3%	–14.8%	$37,317	$14,176
1974	$78	5.5%	$40	–43.7%	–26.4%	$21,009	$10,433
1975	$95	21.9%	$38	–5.0%	37.2%	$19,959	$14,314
1976	$151	59.3%	$89	147.3%	23.6%	$49,358	$17,693
1977	$200	31.9%	$138	46.8%	–7.4%	$72,458	$16,383
1978	$248	24.0%	$152	13.8%	6.4%	$82,457	$17,432
1979	$336	35.7%	$320	102.5%	18.2%	$166,976	$20,604
1980	$401	19.3%	$425	32.8%	32.3%	$221,745	$27,260
1981	$526	31.4%	$560	31.8%	–5.0%	$292,259	$25,897
1982	$738	40.0%	$775	38.4%	21.4%	$404,487	$31,439
1983	$976	32.3%	$1,310	69.0%	22.4%	$683,583	$38,481
1984	$1,109	13.6%	$1,275	–2.7%	6.1%	$665,126	$40,828
1985	$1,644	48.2%	$2,430	93.7%	31.6%	$1,288,350	$53,730
1986	$2,073	26.1%	$2,820	14.2%	18.6%	$1,471,296	$63,724
1987	$2,447	19.5%	$2,950	4.6%	5.1%	$1,538,975	$66,974
1988	$2,976	20.1%	$4,700	59.3%	16.6%	$2,451,587	$78,091
1989	$4,298	44.4%	$8,675	84.6%	31.7%	$4,525,630	$102,846
1990	$4,614	7.4%	$6,675	–23.1%	–3.1%	$3,480,210	$99,658
1991	$6,437	39.6%	$9,050	35.6%	30.5%	$4,719,164	$130,053
1992	$7,745	20.3%	$11,750	29.8%	7.6%	$6,125,475	$139,937
1993	$8,854	14.3%	$16,325	38.9%	10.1%	$8,508,285	$154,071
1994	$10,083	13.9%	$20,450	25.0%	1.3%	$10,635,357	$156,074

continued on next page

TABLE 2.1   continued

| | Per Share | | Berkshire Hathaway | | | $10,000 Invested | |
Date	Book Value	% Increase	Dec. 31 Price*	Yearly Return	S&P 500 Return	With Buffett	With S&P 500
1995	$14,025	43.1%	$32,100	57.4%	37.6%	$16,740,051	$214,758
1996	$19,011	31.8%	$34,100	6.2%	23.0%	$17,777,934	$264,152
1997	$25,488	34.1%	$46,000	34.9%	33.4%	$23,982,434	$352,379
1998	$37,801	48.3%	$70,000	52.2%	28.6%	$36,501,264	$453,160
1999	$37,987	0.5%	$56,100	−19.9%	21.0%	$29,237,512	$548,323

Approximate year-end closing price. Berkshire used to trade on "pink sheets."

value and share price at annual rates in excess of 20 percent since taking over in 1965. In investment circles, this 35-year endurance record constitutes nothing short of miraculous in light of the stock market's roughly 11 percent return over the same period. His performance running Berkshire Hathaway is akin to Hank Aaron's hitting an average of

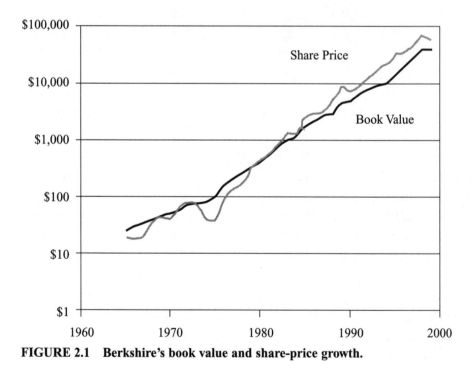

FIGURE 2.1   Berkshire's book value and share-price growth.

40 home runs for 35 years, Michael Jordan's leading the NBA in scoring 20 years in a row, or Jack Nicklaus' winning major tournaments at the age of 70. In a field where statistics say you must fail from time to time, Buffett kept shattering his own records.

BUILDING BOOK VALUE

The early years running the investment partnerships proved pivotal, for without the head start Buffett gave himself (recall that he was worth $25 million or so by 1970), he could not have attained billionaire status. The quirky investments made for clients in the 1950s and 1960s had just as much to do with his present fortune (by virtue of compounding) as have the later large-cap investments for which he is now famous. But Buffett's tone clearly shifted once he was at the helm of Berkshire. The overarching goal was to increase Berkshire's book value year by year, and by amounts large enough to push the stock up relentlessly. Taking small positions in workouts and turnarounds wouldn't cut it any more. Buffett had to graduate to the big leagues and take his chances, like all other great money managers, by buying Standard & Poor 500 stocks, the most heavily scrutinized companies in the world. "This is probably the most remarkable thing about Warren's performance," family friend and writer David Clark says. "He kept beating all the professionals buying the same stocks they were."

By the late 1970s, Buffett had rejected the most stern value-oriented tenets of Graham and had aligned his philosophy much more closely to that of money manager and writer Philip Fisher, Graham's contemporary. Graham represented the foundation—the Old Testament of finance—that approached stock investing with cynicism born from the 1929 crash and the Depression it helped spur. Fisher evolved out of those psychological trappings and saw the market as truly a mirror of the ever-growing U.S. economy. Continued growth in national output must concurrently lead to growth in corporate sales, earnings, and valuation, according to Fisher's new "growth-oriented" school. Continuing to pour money down the sinkhole of cheap stocks "with one good puff left in them," as Buffett called them, was the same as spending your money on a succession of run-down used cars. The vehicles may give you a good ride for awhile, but, eventually they bleed you dry.

Buffett's transformation from a "cigar butt" investor was logical. Building Berkshire Hathaway into a financial powerhouse could not be accomplished by loading up the portfolio with the likes of Rockwood Cocoa, Arcata, Sanborn Map, Western Natural Gas, Dempster Mill Manufacturing, Hochschild, Kohn & Co., and Blue Chip Stamps, seven of his early explorations. As Berkshire grew in size, Buffett's investments had to grow too. He only had to hope for occasionally manic-depressive markets to toss some great pitches at him.

WHAT LED TO BERKSHIRE'S FABULOUS STOCK PERFORMANCE?

Table 2.2 summarizes the major growth investments of Berkshire Hathaway over the past 20 years and calculates, as well as possible, Buffett's gain on these investments through September 1999. Profits had to be estimated because Buffett does not reveal his stock transactions until long after the fact. I had to determine an average sales price based on the price range for the stock during periods Buffett was selling. By 1999, the 14 stocks listed below had collectively accounted for an estimated $34 billion of pre-tax profits for Berkshire (subsequent chapters discuss how Buffett picks stocks for Berkshire's portfolio). Truly, these 14 golden investments account for a large proportion of the growth in Berkshire Hathaway's book value and of Buffett's net worth. On an after-tax basis, the profits equal more than 40 percent of Berkshire Hathaway's 1999 book value. Without the luxury of owning these common stocks, Berkshire Hathaway's stock price would trade at a fraction of where it does today.

Because Buffett holds a 33.7 percent stake in Berkshire, each after-tax dollar of profits he generates on the company's behalf is theoretically owed to him. That's another often-ignored asterisk to Buffett's fortune. Since taking over Berkshire in the late 1960s, he has increased his net worth from $25 million to $30 billion and *has paid relatively little capital gains taxes.* Because Buffett uses Berkshire Hathaway as a trading conduit, gains made on the sale of securities run through Berkshire Hathaway's income statement, not through Buffett's personal tax statement. Thus, gains made on the sale of securities enhance Berkshire's bottom line, making the corporation liable for taxes, yet serve to boost Berkshire's book value and intrinsic value. Through the years, the swelling portfolio has had a direct impact on Berkshire's share price,

TABLE 2.2   Berkshire Hathaway's investments over the past 20 years.

Stock	Shares Reported Owned in 1999	Cost Basis	Pre-tax Profits (mil.)
Coca-Cola	200,000,000	$6.50	$11,700
American Express	50,536,900	$29.09	$5,775
Gillette	96,000,000	$6.25	$3,360
Freddie Mac*	60,298,000	$5.11	$3,300
Wells Fargo*	63,595,180	$6.16	$2,535
GEICO (pre buyout)	34,250,000	$1.33	$2,348
Salomon/Travelers‡	Sold in 1998	$25.47	$1,400
Capital Cities/ABC/Disney*	51,202,242	$5.49	$1,311
Washington Post	1,727,765	$6.14	$930
USAir‡	Sold in 1998	$38.74	$550
General Dynamics†	7,693,637	$18.00	$450
Gannett*	4,261,300	$24.45	$300
M&T Bank	506,930	$79.00	$235
PNC Bank	Sold in 1995–97	$25.86	$150
Total major investments			**$34,344**

Includes profits from shares previously sold.
†*General Dynamics profits include a special dividend and profits from shares sold from 1994 to 1997.*
‡*Profits include dividends from convertible preferreds.*

which has had a proportionate impact on Buffett's net worth. Buffett is liable for taxes when he sells Berkshire shares, but he hasn't in more than 20 years. Occasionally, he will donate a modest amount of shares, but he and his wife Susie have held onto nearly all of the stock Buffett accumulated in the 1960s and 1970s.

The success of stock investments doesn't fully account for the rise in Berkshire's book value and Buffett's net worth. Remaining credit must be given to acquisitions. Berkshire Hathaway is an amalgam of disparate enterprises Buffett has cobbled together one at a time for the purpose of throwing off cash flow. Properties range from fine jewelers (Borsheim's), vacuum cleaner manufacturers (Kirby), and ice cream franchises (Dairy Queen) to jet leasing (Executive Jet), insurance (GEICO), and confectionery (See's Candies) (see Tables 2.3 and 2.4).

TABLE 2.3   Berkshire Hathaway's wholly owned businesses.

Insurance group—1999 revenues, $14.7 billion; assets, $84.2 billion

GEICO	Private auto insurance
Berkshire Hathaway Reinsurance	Catastrophe reinsurance
General Reinsurance	Property/casualty reinsurance
National Indemnity Co.	Multiline commercial insurance
Cypress Insurance	Worker's compensation
Central States Indemnity	Credit card insurance
Kansas Bankers Surety Co.	Reinsurance for banks

Manufacturing, retailing, service businesses—1999 revenues, $5.9 billion; assets, $4.0 billion

Adalet	Electrical accessories
Blue Chip Stamps	Marketing services
Borsheim's	High-end jewelry
Buffalo News	Daily newspaper
Campbell Hausfeld	Air compressors, washers, generators
Carefree	Recreational vehicle accessories
Cleveland Wood Products	Vacuum cleaner accessories
Dexter Shoe	Dress, casual, athletic shoes
Douglas Products	Vacuum cleaners
Executive Jet	Aircraft leasing
Fechheimer Bros.	Uniforms and accessories
FlightSafety International	Pilot training services
France	Ignition components
H.H. Brown Shoe	Work shoes and boots
Halex	Conduit fittings
Helzberg's Diamond Shops	High-end jewelry
International Dairy Queen	Licensing of ice cream chain
Jordan's Furniture	Home furnishings
Justin Industries	Concrete building products, shoes
Kingston	Appliance controls
Kirby	Vacuum cleaners
Lowell Shoe	Women's, nurses' shoes

continued on next page

TABLE 2.3   continued

Meriam	Pressure control devices
Nebraska Furniture Mart	Home furnishings
Northland	Electric motors
Powerwinch	Marine winches, hoists
Precision Steel Products	Steel service center
Quikut	Cutlery
ScottCare	Cardiopulmonary equipment
Scot Labs	Cleaning solutions
See's Candies	Boxed Chocolates
Stahl	Truck equipment
Star Furniture	Home furnishings
Wayne Combustion Systems	Oil and gas burners
Wayne Water Systems	Sump pumps
Western Enterprises	Gas fittings and regulators
Western Plastics	Molded plastics components
R.C. Willey	Home furnishings
World Book	Printed, multimedia encyclopedias

Financial products—1999 revenues, $846 million; assets, $24.2 billion

Scott Fetzer Financial
Berkshire Hathaway Life Insurance
Berkshire Hathaway Credit Corp.
BH finance
General Re Financial Products

On paper, this portfolio seemingly makes little sense. But each property possessed important characteristics at the time of purchase that Buffett uses when considering an acquisition:

1. They were profitable businesses with simple business models.
2. Each generated plenty of cash flow that could be forwarded to Omaha for Buffett to reinvest.
3. They were relatively unique businesses that held tenable positions in their markets.

TABLE 2.4 Berkshire Hathaway's operating earnings (losses) ($mil).

	1987	1988	1989	1990	1991	1992	1993	1994	1995	1996	1997	1998	1999
Insurance groups													
Reinsurance										(8)	128	(21)	(1,440)
GEICO										171	281	269	24
Other primary	(55)	(11)	(24)	(27)	(120)	(109)	31	130	21	59	53	17	22
Investment income	153	231	244	327	332	355	375	419	502	726	882	974	2,482
Buffalo News	39	42	46	44	37	48	51	54	47	50	56	53	55
Financial Services						20	23	22	21	23	28	205	125
Flight Services										3	140	181	225
Furniture	17	18	17	17	14	17	22	17	30	44	57	72	79
Dairy Queen												58	56
Jewelry									34	28	32	39	51
Scot Fetzer (includes Kirby, World Book, and Fechheimer)	92	97	98	102	97	110	111	121	110	122	119	137	147
See's Candies	32	33	34	40	42	42	41	48	50	52	59	62	74
Shoe Group					14	28	44	86	58	62	49	33	17
Accounting adjustments	(8)	(9)	(9)	(9)	(10)	(12)	(17)	(23)	(27)	(76)	(101)	(123)	(739)
Interest expense	(12)	(36)	(42)	(76)	(89)	(99)	(57)	(60)	(56)	(94)	(107)	(100)	(109)
Contributions	(5)	(5)	(6)	(6)	(7)	(8)	(10)	(10)	(12)	(13)	(15)	(17)	(17)
Other	29	57	37	71	90	68	29	36	37	73	60	60	33
Operating earnings	**282**	**418**	**393**	**483**	**400**	**461**	**643**	**839**	**815**	**1,221**	**1,721**	**1,899**	**1,085**
Capital gains from investments	**29**	**132**	**224**	**34**	**193**	**90**	**546**	**91**	**194**	**2,485**	**1,106**	**2,415**	**1,365**
Total earnings	**310**	**550**	**617**	**517**	**593**	**551**	**1,190**	**931**	**1,009**	**3,706**	**2,827**	**4,314**	**2,450**

4. They offered stable management. "We can't provide it," says
   Buffett. "My job is to keep a group of 15 to 20 managers enthused
   about what they are doing, because most of them are already
   wealthy beyond their belief."[3]
5. They were bought at prices that made mathematical and economic sense to Berkshire's bottom line. Buffett, for example, closed
   the purchase of Nebraska Furniture Mart in 1983 with a hand-
   shake. "He walked into the store and said, "Today is my birthday
   and I want to buy your store. How much do you want for it," the
   late owner Rose Blumkin recalled to a reporter. "I tell him, '$60
   million.' He goes, gets a check and comes back right away."[4]

The last point is perhaps most important to Buffett. Unless an
investment (a company or a stock) can be justified by mathematics, it
should be ignored until the right combination of price and value exists.
The following chapters probe more deeply into Buffett's reasoning and
stock-picking criteria.

P A R T

DEVELOPING A MATHEMATICAL MIND

3

BUFFETT MATH 101
The Power of Growth

THE FIELD OF FINANCE has evolved to the point that participants can analyze and solve virtually any problem. Thanks to advancements in mathematics made through the centuries, investors can reduce the task of personal finance to a series of logically derived equations. Indeed, a working knowledge of computation will take you a long way in finance. Mathematics is sterile, devoid of emotion or bias. Any time you can strip away irrationality from the oftentimes emotional realm of stock picking, your decisions—and results—will be that much better.

Financial planners believe that upward of 80 percent of all dilemmas we face involving money can be solved with routine mathematics. Using nothing more than simple algebra, for example, a consumer can calculate whether it's better to lease or buy an automobile, whether refinancing a mortgage will save money, whether it's better to buy term or whole life insurance, whether it's better to owe taxes on April 15 or to claim a refund, whether a fixed-rate mortgage is better than one with a variable rate, whether it makes more sense to pay a minimum balance on a credit card or pay the entire balance at once, and whether it's better to invest money on your own or through a 401(k) payroll deduction plan.

These decisions, along with hundreds of others you must make as a consumer, form a critical path to your long-term financial health. On the surface, the decisions might seem daunting, but they are all solvable within a few minutes. Successful investors such as Warren Buffett draw their inspiration from mathematics. But unlike so many other professional investors, Buffett doesn't believe in applied data mining. Anyone can juggle data and find ways to make an unsound investment appear safe or make an overvalued security appear cheap. It's deceptively easy, for example, to change a single assumption in an earnings forecast and turn a $25 stock into one worth $100 or more.

Nevertheless, in its essence, investing is a process of simplicity. One needs to understand basic algebra, at most, to conquer stock picking. By using tools taught to most eighth and ninth graders, a novice investor can achieve high returns over long periods. "If calculus were required, I'd have to go back to delivering papers," Buffett told an assembly of securities analysts in New York in 1994. "Essentially, you're trying to figure out the value of a business. It's true that you have to divide by the number of shares outstanding, so division is required. If you were going out to buy a farm or apartment house or a dry cleaning establishment, I really don't think you'd have to take someone along to do calculus. Whether you made the right purchase or not would depend on the future earning ability of that enterprise, and then relating that to the price you are being asked for the asset."[1]

In investing, mathematics should not be the end but rather the means. It should not consume your stock-picking methodology, Buffett believes, but should serve to reveal, very logically, whether a certain deal makes financial sense. Armed with some of the basic rules of finance, an investor can begin analyzing disparate securities with the same rigor as Buffett. If a project or buy-or-sell decision makes numerical sense, it should be carried out. If numbers don't justify the action, postpone the project for another day.

THE POWER OF COMPOUNDING

It goes without saying that to a person such as Warren Buffett, the power of compounding is paramount. No force exerts more influence on your portfolio than time. Time takes a bigger toll on your terminal wealth than do taxes, inflation and poor stock-picking combined. Time, you see, magnifies the effects of these critical issues. A poorly chosen stock may cost you only $2,000 in losses today, but over time that one suspect decision could cost $50,000 in lost opportunities. Trading frequently for short-term gains may net you strong gains periodically, but the overall result, validated by time, is to create an enormous tax burden that could have been avoided. Likewise, persistent inflation exacts a weighty toll on your portfolio because it destroys value at increasing rates. "Means and end should not be confused," Buffett once wrote to his partners. "The end is to come away with the largest after-tax rate of compound."

There's the old story that, if the Indians wanted to buy back Manhattan, they would have had to pay more than $2.5 trillion by January 1, 2000. That's what the $24 sale price in 1626 would have compounded into at 7 percent annual rates. And the clock keeps ticking. Next year, Manhattan's theoretical value jumps by $175 *billion* (7 percent of $2.5 trillion). The following year, another $187 billion is added. The year after that, $200 billion, and so on. Letting wealth accumulate and compound unfettered and, if possible, untaxed is a potent formula individuals should use to increase their standard of living.

Let time work to your advantage. Choosing good companies at fair prices seldom has produced losses for investors willing to wait patiently for the stock price to track the growth of the company. "Time is the friend of the good business, the enemy of the poor," Buffett has said many times. Strong enterprises see their intrinsic value rise consistently, lifting the stock every step of the way. Over a period of 5 years or more, there should be a very close correlation between the change in the value of the company and the change in the stock. Watching great companies increase their sales and earnings consistently is a dream come true for an investor. The power of compounding begins working its magic as the years progress and allows your net worth to gather momentum and increase (in dollar value) by greater and greater amounts.

Tables 3.1 and 3.2 show what happens to money that is allowed to sit and grow at different rates. Two principles should be readily apparent:

1. Time has a tremendous effect on terminal wealth. The longer that money can compound, the larger the sum will be.
2. The rate of return attained acts as a lever that magnifies or minimizes your ultimate wealth. Adding just a few extra percentage

TABLE 3.1 The gift of compounding: What $1 becomes over 50 years.

Growth Rate

Year	4%	6%	8%	10%	12%	14%	16%	18%	20%	22%	24%	26%	28%	30%
1	$1.04	$1.06	$1.08	$1.10	$1.12	$1.14	$1.16	$1.18	$1.20	$1.22	$1.24	$1.26	$1.28	$1.30
2	$1.08	$1.12	$1.17	$1.21	$1.25	$1.30	$1.35	$1.39	$1.44	$1.49	$1.54	$1.59	$1.64	$1.69
3	$1.12	$1.19	$1.26	$1.33	$1.40	$1.48	$1.56	$1.64	$1.73	$1.82	$1.91	$2.00	$2.10	$2.20
4	$1.17	$1.26	$1.36	$1.46	$1.57	$1.69	$1.81	$1.94	$2.07	$2.22	$2.36	$2.52	$2.68	$2.86
5	$1.22	$1.34	$1.47	$1.61	$1.76	$1.93	$2.10	$2.29	$2.49	$2.70	$2.93	$3.18	$3.44	$3.71
6	$1.27	$1.42	$1.59	$1.77	$1.97	$2.19	$2.44	$2.70	$2.99	$3.30	$3.64	$4.00	$4.40	$4.83
7	$1.32	$1.50	$1.71	$1.95	$2.21	$2.50	$2.83	$3.19	$3.58	$4.02	$4.51	$5.04	$5.63	$6.27
8	$1.37	$1.59	$1.85	$2.14	$2.48	$2.85	$3.28	$3.76	$4.30	$4.91	$5.59	$6.35	$7.21	$8.16
9	$1.42	$1.69	$2.00	$2.36	$2.77	$3.25	$3.80	$4.44	$5.16	$5.99	$6.93	$8.00	$9.22	$10.60
10	$1.48	$1.79	$2.16	$2.59	$3.11	$3.71	$4.41	$5.23	$6.19	$7.30	$8.59	$10.09	$11.81	$13.79
15	$1.80	$2.40	$3.17	$4.18	$5.47	$7.14	$9.27	$11.97	$15.41	$19.74	$25.20	$32.03	$40.56	$51.19
20	$2.19	$3.21	$4.66	$6.73	$9.65	$13.74	$19.46	$27.39	$38.34	$53.36	$73.86	$102.00	$139.00	$190.00
25	$2.67	$4.29	$6.85	$10.83	$17.00	$26.46	$40.87	$62.67	$95.40	$144.00	$217.00	$323.00	$479.00	$706.00
30	$3.24	$5.74	$10.06	$17.45	$29.96	$50.95	$85.85	$143.00	$237.00	$390.00	$635.00	$1,026.00	$1,646.00	$2,620.00
35	$3.95	$7.69	$14.79	$28.10	$52.80	$98.10	$180.00	$328.00	$591.00	$1,053.00	$1,861.00	$3,258.00	$5,654.00	$9,728.00
40	$4.80	$10.29	$21.72	$45.26	$93.05	$189.00	$379.00	$750.00	$1,470.00	$2,847.00	$5,456.00	$10,347.00	$19,427.00	$36,119.00
45	$5.84	$13.76	$31.92	$72.89	$164.00	$364.00	$795.00	$1,717.00	$3,657.00	$7,695.00	$15,995.00	$32,861.00	$66,750.00	$134,107.00
50	$7.11	$18.42	$46.90	$117.00	$289.00	$700.00	$1,671.00	$3,927.00	$9,100.00	$20,797.00	$46,890.00	$104,358.00	$229,350.00	$497,929.00

TABLE 3.2   Approximate years it takes an investment to grow.

Rate	Double	Triple	Quadruple	Rise 1,000%
4%	18	28	36	59
6%	12	19	24	40
8%	9	15	18	30
10%	8	12	15	25
12%	7	10	13	21
14%	6	9	11	18
16%	5	8	10	16
18%	5	7	9	14
20%	4	7	8	13
22%	4	6	7	12
24%	4	6	7	11
26%	3	5	6	10
28%	3	5	6	10
30%	3	5	6	9

points a year to your overall returns can have unfathomable consequences to your wealth. An investor who compounds $1 at 6 percent annual rates has $5.74 in his pocket at the end of 30 years. The same investor who can find ways to obtain higher returns (the purpose of this book) walks away with much more. If you can obtain a 10 percent annual return, your $1 compounds into $17.45 in 30 years. Compounding $1 at 20 percent annual rates compounds into $237.

The mathematics of compounding excited Buffett in his earliest years, and stories abound of how he memorized compounding and annuity tables to help him calculate an investment's merit and to keep his personal portfolio on a straight upward track. Biographer Roger Lowenstein, for example, tells the story of how a 7-year-old Buffett took ill suddenly and was hospitalized close to death. Forced to lie still in a hospital bed, Buffett entertained himself and, it seems, the nurses by scribbling a page full of numbers that projected his future net worth year by year.[2]

In Buffett's annual report to partners for the year ending in 1962, he broke cadence from his routine review of the market to discuss "The Joys of Compounding." Anyone reading this passage, even four decades after Buffett penned it, could see the raw-boned logic behind the 32-year-old Buffett's stubborn frugality. As he saw it, every dollar put to productive use magnifies the benefit to society by virtue of compounding. Wasting that dollar had serious long-term ramifications—for him, his partners, even for society at large. What if, Buffett mused in his letter, Spain had decided not to finance Christopher Columbus? The results would be staggering.

> I have it from unreliable sources that the cost of the voyage Isabella originally underwrote for Columbus was approximately $30,000. This has been considered at least a moderately successful utilization of venture capital. Without attempting to evaluate the psychic income derived from finding a new hemisphere, it must be pointed out that. . .the whole deal was not exactly another IBM. Figured very roughly, the $30,000 invested at 4% compounded annually would have amounted to something like $2,000,000,000,000 [two trillion].[3]

In financial terms, Columbus's four voyages to the Caribbean yielded very little for the crown, except to pave the way for generations of future navigators. Think how that $30,000, if spent more judiciously by Spain in the late fifteenth century, could have greatly increased the wealth of the Spanish people. By 1999, 37 years after Buffett made the analogy, Isabella's $30,000 expenditure could have compounded into more than $8 *trillion*, nearly the total annual economic output of the United States. Spain would be a world economic powerhouse today.

Postulating the value of assets five centuries into the future, of course, holds no practical meaning for investors who, if they're fortunate, can live only eight or nine decades. But Buffett's point is well taken. Letting money compound productively creates an enormous economic benefit, not only to investors but also to their benefactors and to society at large.

Buffett is occasionally criticized for not donating more of his wealth to foundations and charities, as many other tycoons have. Buffett's reasoning, however, is perfectly consistent with his investing philosophy. As long as he can continue to compound money at great rates, society would be better off if he didn't give away money now. He told Ted Koppel in a 1999 *Nightline* interview, for example, that if he had donated most of his money 20 years ago, society would have been $100 million richer. Because he chose not to donate, society will one day receive more than $30 billion. Had he given away $100 million in the 1970s, it's very doubtful that recipients could have produced $30 billion in economic benefits for society because few people alive can compound money as Buffett can. One day, the value of Buffett's foundation grants will certainly surpass $100 billion and then $200 billion, which would make Buffett's fortune the largest ever donated to charity.

On this topic, Buffett is behaving as any rational CEO would. If a company generates a high return on its assets, it should withhold dividends to investors and plow as much money as it can each year back into the business. Only when it can no longer generate a strong internal return should a company think about returning money to shareholders. It's very doubtful that recipients of his wealth could have compounded their largesse at the rate Buffett did. Isn't it better, Buffett believes, to conspicuous consumption today if it means leaving even larger amounts for society tomorrow?

"My money represents an enormous number of claims checks on society. It's like I have these little pieces of paper that I can turn into consumption," Buffett told *Esquire* magazine in 1988. "If I wanted to, I could hire 10,000 people to do nothing but paint my picture every day for the rest of my life. And the (Gross Domestic Product) would go up. But the utility of the product would be zilch, and I would be keeping those 10,000 people from doing AIDS research, or teaching or nursing."[4]

THE LINKS BETWEEN PRICE AND VALUE IN THE MARKET

No asset can outrun its own fundamentals forever. In the long run, there is perfect correlation between price and value. Eventually, the price of any asset seeks out, and finds, its true intrinsic value. This relationship holds for stocks, bonds, real estate, art, currencies, precious metals, even the entire U.S. economy—virtually any asset whose values fluctuate based on shifting perceptions of buyers and sellers. If you understand this basic mathematical relationship, you will have an advantage over most individual investors, for there are several truisms about price and value that an investor cannot ignore.

Between the mid-1920s and 1999, the Dow Industrials index grew at a compounded annual rate of around 5.0 percent (dividends provided the remaining return). Over that same period, earnings for the 30 Dow Industrials companies grew at 4.7 percent compounded rates. Interestingly, the book values of these same companies increased at around 4.6 percent annual rates. It's no coincidence the growth rates are so similar. Over long periods, the market value of a company's stock cannot outstrip its own internal growth rates by very much. Sure, technological gains can cause improvements in corporate efficiency and lead to *temporary* quantum leaps in earnings. But the competitive, cyclical nature of markets helps to maintain the direct relationship between sales, earnings, and valuation. In boom times, earnings growth can outstrip sales growth as corporations take advantage of economies of scale and better factory utilization. In recessions, earnings fall faster than sales (companies temporarily become less efficient) as companies find themselves overburdened with high fixed costs that cannot be covered by sales.

Figure 3.1 shows a chart for Abbott Laboratories, which juxtaposes the growth in share price and earnings between 1960 and 1995. You'll notice immediately how the trend line of earnings (represented by the continuous line) forms the basis of valuation. Over the 35-year period, Abbott's stock rose at around 15 percent annually. Abbott's earnings also rose at a roughly 15 percent rate. Growth in intrinsic value, as exemplified by growth in earnings and book value, should lead to identical growth in stock price. For much of Abbott's recent history, its share price and earnings have risen in tandem, most notably in the period between 1977 and 1989. During this period, investors rarely bid the stock beyond the company's presumed growth rate.

You'll notice a few periods in history when the market seemingly valued Abbott at prices far in excess of the company's actual, or presumed, growth rate. In the late 1960s and early 1970s, for example, Abbott's stock traded well above the earnings trend line. At its 1971 and 1972 peaks, Abbott traded for nearly 50 times earnings. Investors were willing to pay a much higher premium for a share of Abbott's future earnings than Abbott could, in fact, deliver. Abbott's shares were rising much faster than earnings, a phenomenon that cannot be sustained over time. A dislocation between price and value had occurred and had to be reconciled. After peaking at 50 times earnings, Abbott

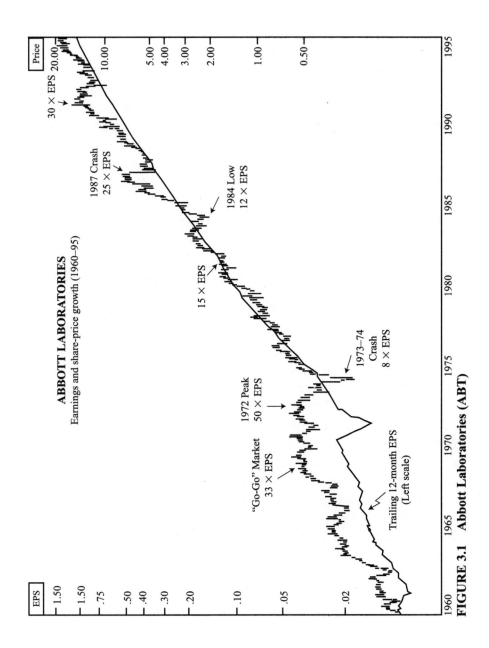

FIGURE 3.1 Abbott Laboratories (ABT)

41

plunged in a panic sell-off that left the stock trading at one-third of its peak value and at prices below the earnings trend line.

If investors were rational and had full information, a stock such as Abbott would perpetually be priced near the intrinsic value of the company. But in overheated markets, when investors seemingly will pay anything for a share of corporate earnings, prices become dislodged from reality. Wall Street begins to believe that companies such as Abbott can sustain uncharacteristic high growth rates and ignore the long, steady trend line of performance.

This relationship between price and value is important when putting market movements and trends in their proper context. Investors must never pay prices that cannot be justified by the company's long-term growth rate. More to the point, they should be leery of chasing stocks that are climbing well in excess of the growth in the company's value. Although it's difficult to pinpoint a company's exact worth, telltale signs can be found. For example, if a stock has been rising at 50 percent annual rates during a period in which earnings rose at just 10 percent rates, there exists a high probability that the stock is overvalued and destined to provide poor returns. Conversely, a stock that has been falling in price while earnings are rising should be scrutinized for possible purchase. If the stock plummets in price and trades at price-to-earnings (P/E) ratios below the company's presumed growth rate, a bargain situation may exist.

As the year 2000 opened, a huge disparity existed in the market between price and value. Dozens of high-technology glamour stocks were rising three to five times faster than their earnings as investors piled on and were willing to pay inflated P/E ratios for the chance to glom onto a winner. Central to this frenzy was the belief that old economic theorems had been invalidated, that U.S. companies had entered into a new growth phase that precluded a bust period. The irony was that none of the economic figures released by the government in recent quarters suggested that corporate performance has leaped onto a new, higher plateau as Wall Street wants us to believe.

If anything, the data suggest that companies are doing were performing or worse than could normally be expected nine years into an economic expansion. By 1999, profitability and asset utilization ratios were no higher than they were in the late 1980s, the only difference being that companies were using their capital structures more wisely to add value. But contrary to popular reports, cyclical risks had not been removed from income statements. Nevertheless, the investing public continues to salivate over the notion, still unproven, that the economy is immune from recession and that corporate earnings can be driven forever higher.

A wide dichotomy between facts and expectations can be dangerous in the financial markets. The public's desire to ignore evidence and unearth fast profits has fostered, in some industries, a giant pyramid scheme, where groups of investors seemingly sell stocks back and forth to each other, raising the price with each transaction, which occurred with Internet stocks. Pyramid schemes work only as long as both sides of the transaction remain dedicated to the game. When buyers begin dropping out, the remaining participants find out in a hurry how much the goods they traded were really worth. The spring 2000 declines in Internet stocks that took place as this book was being prepared showed how a pyramid scheme, when in reverse, swirls inward like a black hole.

PRICE AND VALUE COMPOUND TOGETHER

The forces that link price to value are inevitable and immutable. Over long time periods, earnings for Standard & Poor's (S&P) 500 companies cannot grow much faster than these companies' sales. S&P 500 sales can't grow much faster than U.S. economic output (if that occurred indefinitely, the S&P 500 companies would eventually *BE* the economy). Therefore, if stock prices are supposed to track earnings growth, and earnings track sales growth, and sales track output growth, *stock prices cannot be expected to grow much faster than the economy. B*ut they have. Between the fourth quarter of 1994 and the end of 1999, U.S. economic output grew by roughly $1 trillion. The value of common stocks, in contrast, rose $6 trillion over the same period. One cannot expect a company's stock price to rise faster than the enterprise's earnings for very long. Eventually, something has to give: either the stock plunges back to the trend line of earnings or earnings accelerate. By 2000, Wall Street clearly believed in the latter, leading to inexplicable levels of valuation. Investors were valuing Microsoft, Cisco Systems, and General Electric as if they were among the world's largest economies. A virtually unheard-of upstart company called Ariba was valued at $25 billion at its 2000 peak—more than Apple Computer—despite the absence of meaningful revenues or earnings. Qualcomm was being priced in the marketplace as if its sales could rise at nearly 47 percent a year perpetually.

When you think logically about these comparisons, you sense the folly. The total market value of the S&P 500 index should not exceed the size of the economy. This is a theorem Nobel Laureate James Tobin posited in 1969 when he devised a now-famous set of ratios that compared stock values to Gross Domestic Product and the replacement cost of assets. Applying Tobin's research, the market value of all U.S. equities surpassed Gross Domestic Product in the late 1990s—for the first time since 1929. Never before had the investing public been willing to pay such a huge markup for the economic inputs used to produce earnings. Investors who were willing to pay extraordinary prices for S&P 500 stocks were behaving no more rationally than the movie studio that paid its star actors $50 million to make a film that grossed only $20 million at the box office.

Eventually, prices must realign with value, a point Buffett has emphasized on numerous occasions. Back in the mid-1960s, analysts believed that IBM could grow 15 to 16 percent a year perpetually. Had that occurred, IBM's 1999 sales would have been $612 billion, 7 percent of U.S. output. Earnings would have been 15 times that of Microsoft's. Had Wal-Mart's sales grown at the rate analysts once projected, it would soon have absorbed 14 percent of every consumer dollar spent. In the 1980s, homeowners in California had to learn the hard way what happens when housing prices rise at thrice the rate of incomes for years on end. Eventually, prices for all investments must fall, or rise, back to their trend line level of value and affordability.

Benjamin Graham once commented that the biggest trap into which investors fall is to decouple price from value, to stray from the facts, and to base trading decisions on the actions of others ("I buy because others are buying," etc.) If you expect to get rich trying to predict the trading of others, "you must be expecting to try to do what countless others are aiming at, and to be able to do it better than your numerous competitors in the market," Graham wrote in 1949.

IGNORE WALL STREET'S PREDICTIONS OF PERFORMANCE

Most of the twentieth century's great investors shared a common belief that the sky was their limit, so to speak. They refused to accept "average" performance and strove to find ways to outperform their peers. In retrospect, their tales of success should serve as inspirations for what can be attained in the investment world when you set your sights higher than those of the general population. They attained 20 percent annual returns because they tried to. One cannot attain such a level of success by luck or complacency. The market doesn't reward fools for long.

For the better part of the 1990s, investors were told to expect 11 percent annual returns in the stock market. Seven decades of data, in fact, suggest that the market's long-term rate of return *may* be roughly this amount. To accept this benchmark is to put yourself on a course for mediocre performance. Too many investors fall prey to Wall Street's statistics and craft stock-picking strategies and portfolios that nearly guarantee them market-tying returns, at best. Some load their portfolios with too many stocks and, as a result, place statistical ceilings on their performance. Evidence shows that the more stocks one owns, the closer one's returns will mimic those of an index (see Chapter 4). Other investors limit their long-term returns by holding too many poor-performing stocks that offset the gains of their winners. Still others take excessive risks and pay high prices for their stocks. Such strategies work from time to time, but over long time periods, buying high ultimately weighs down your returns.

Brokers, financial planners, accountants, and money managers have all tried to convince investors to expect 11 percent annual returns from the market. The 11 percent figure has been recited so many times through the years it has become hardened in the lexicon of the bull market. The 11 percent figure wasn't pulled from thin air—it has historical backing: this is the compounded annual return an investor would have culled by buying a basket of large-cap stocks between 1926 and 1999. Because investors have little else to go on when trying to predict the direction of stocks (only a handful of the world's stock markets have operated continuously since the mid-1920s), they have had to rely almost exclusively on the 11 percent figure as their benchmark. But extrapolating stock-price trends is inherently dangerous, for many reasons. The stock market doesn't obey calendars and rarely behaves as predicted. Just before the last great bear market in 1973 and 1974, numerous articles claimed a new era had arrived, that stocks were destined to rise perpetually. Financial planners created glossy brochures showing how investors could compound their assets into a large retirement nest egg because of the market's tendency to rise consistently over time.

Today, many arguments have been made to support the thesis that the market's long-term trend line has been breached. Economists argue that the improvement in productivity experienced by U.S. manufacturers may usher in a new era of profitability. Others contend that the economy is virtually immune from recession and, by inference, immune from the types of bear markets that mute historical averages. Indeed, many market strategists have been relying on a quantum jump in growth. They want you to believe that market will continue to grow 11 percent a year *from present levels*, not from trend lines established decades ago. They are drawing new trend lines above and parallel to the old. It's a back-door way of saying, "the past is relevant, but only the good years."

Unfortunately, the market does not obey formulas. There is no guarantee that the recent past will be replicated. Just because the U.S. stock market has risen at 11 percent annual rates for 70 years doesn't mean the next 70 years will be the same. Certainly, the past says nothing of what we can expect over the next few years. By relying on dubious statistics—rather than focusing on companies and their performance, investors undermine their goals. They diversify too much, they demean the role of analysis, or they fail to monitor their portfolios properly. These three mistakes explain why most investors fail to achieve adequate returns.

To lay the groundwork for successful investing, you must first ignore the marketing scripts. It is wrong—and frequently risky—to link past returns to the future. Just because the S&P 500 index has risen at 11 percent annual rates does not mean it will return 11 percent over the next several decades. It may return 5 percent, or it may return 20 percent. According to Buffett, the market may post negative returns over the next several years before resuming an upward course. The good news is that once investors reject the sales utterances of Wall Street, they are no longer bound by limitations when setting goals. Buffett tells investors that it's possible to obtain returns far in excess of the market—whether the market rises 10 percent a year, 2 percent, or 20 percent.

As we showed in the section on compounding, the power of time works to the advantage of an investor who can keep ahead of the market. If you can obtain even minor improvements over the market's return, you will generate staggering long-term results due to compounding. Assuming the market rises 10 percent a year, an investor who begins with $10,000 and obtains 12 percent a year has 43 percent more money after 20 years than someone who merely kept pace with the market. After 30 years, the investor has earned 72 percent more money. The results explode when an investor can attain returns above 12 percent. By earning 14 percent, you would have 192 percent more money in 30 years. If an investor can attain 16 percent, he earns 391 percent more money by year 30.

Compounding also works in the opposite direction. The punishment for lagging behind the market is as substantial as are the rewards of beating it. After 30 years of 8 percent yearly returns, a portfolio lags behind the S&P 500 by 73 percent. It takes just a few major mistakes to keep your portfolio from attaining truly outstanding returns. Holding onto a poor-performing stock too long can put you years behind your long-term goals. So can selling a strong-performing company too early. A portfolio that is too large will ensure that you never generate a return above 11 percent. Conversely, a portfolio that is too small, with just a handful of stocks, forces you to be nearly perfect in stock picking. One disastrous holding could keep you behind the market for years.

The goal of trying to beat the market can prove to be quite worthy, Buffett noted in his 1988 annual report, because the long-term compounded returns of beating the market can be astounding. From 1926 through 1988, Buffett noted, the market provided a total return of 10 percent a year. "That means $1,000 would have grown to $405,000 if all income had been reinvested. A 20 percent rate of return, however, would have produced $97 million. That strikes us as a statistically significant differential that might, conceivably, arouse one's curiosity."[5]

WHAT DOES MATHEMATICS TELL US
ABOUT THE MARKET'S FUTURE?

Warren Buffett rarely comments on the stock market, and he rarely gives his opinion on the direction of the economy or interest rates. The world only learns of his purchases and sales when he must publicly disclose them, and that may not occur for months after the fact. Even when Buffett's dealings become public knowledge, he remains tight-lipped about his intentions and offers few clues about what led to his decisions. So, it was of great interest to investors when Buffett gave a series of speeches and public appearances in 1999 decrying conditions in the stock market. Not usually given to verbosity, Buffett dissected the performance of the stock market and the economy and laid out a compelling case that the market may provide unusually low returns in the coming years. The speeches, published in *Fortune* magazine in November 1999 and excerpted below, offer a compelling mathematical proof that investors cannot possibly get the same returns out of the stock market they have enjoyed in recent years.

Markets behave in ways, sometimes for a very long stretch, that are not linked to value. Sooner or later, though, value counts. To get some historical perspective, let's look back at the 34 years before this one—and here we are going to see an almost Biblical kind of symmetry, in the sense of lean years and fat years—to observe what happened in the stock market. Take, to begin with, the first 17 years of the period, from the end of 1964 through 1981. Here's what took place in that interval:

Dow Jones Industrial Average
Dec. 31, 1964: **874.12**
Dec. 31, 1981: **875.00**

Now I'm known as a long-term investor and a patient guy, but that is not my idea of a big move.

And here's a major and very opposite fact: During that same 17 years, the GDP of the U.S.—that is, the business being done in this country—almost quintupled, rising by 370%. Or, if we look at another measure, the sales of the Fortune 500 (a changing mix of companies, of course) more than sextupled. And yet the Dow went exactly nowhere.

To understand why that happened, we need first to look at one of the two important variables that affect investment results: interest rates. These act on financial valuations the way gravity acts on matter: The higher the rate, the greater the downward pull. . . .In the 1964–81 period, there was a tremendous increase in the rates on long-term government bonds, which moved from just over 4% at year-end 1964 to more than 15% by late 1981. That rise in rates had a huge depressing effect on the value of all investments, but the one we noticed, of course, was the price of equities.

Then, in the early 1980s, the situation reversed itself. You will remember Paul Volcker coming in as chairman of the Fed and remember also how unpopular he was. But the heroic things he did—his taking a two-by-four to the economy and breaking the back of inflation—caused the interest rate trend to reverse, with some rather spectacular results.

The power of interest rates had the effect of pushing up equities as well, though other things that we will get to pushed additionally. And so here's what equities did in that same 17 years: If you'd invested $1 million in the Dow on Nov. 16, 1981, and reinvested all dividends, you'd have had $19,720,112 on Dec. 31, 1998. And your annual return would have been 19%.

The increase in equity values since 1981 beats anything you can find in history. This increase even surpasses what you would have realized if you'd bought stocks in 1932, at their Depression bottom—on its lowest day, July 8, 1932, the Dow closed at 41.22—and held them for 17 years.

The second thing bearing on stock prices during this 17 years was after-tax corporate profits. Corporate profits as a percentage of GDP peaked in 1929, and then they tanked. But from 1951 on, the percentage settled down pretty much to a 4% to 6.5% range. By 1981, though, the trend was headed toward the bottom of that band, and in 1982 profits tumbled to 3.5%. So at that point investors were looking at two strong negatives: Profits were sub-par and interest rates were sky-high.

And as is so typical, investors projected out into the future what they were seeing. That's their unshakable habit: looking into the rear-view mirror instead of through the windshield. What they were observing, looking backward, made them very discouraged about the country. They were projecting high interest rates, they were projecting low profits, and they were therefore valuing the Dow at a level that was the same as 17 years earlier, even though GDP had nearly quintupled.

Now, what happened in the 17 years beginning with 1982? One thing that didn't happen was comparable growth in GDP: In this second 17-year period, GDP less than tripled. But interest rates began their descent, and after the Volcker effect wore off, profits began to climb—not steadily, but nonetheless with real power. . . .By the late 1990s, after-tax profits as a percent of GDP were running close to 6%, which is on the upper part of the "normalcy" band. And at the end of 1998, long-term government interest rates had made their way down to that 5%.

These dramatic changes in the two fundamentals that matter most to investors explain much, though not all, of the more than tenfold rise in equity prices—the Dow went from 875 to 9,181—during this 17-year period.

What was at work also, of course, was market psychology. Once a bull market gets under way, and once you reach the point where everybody has made money no matter what system he or she followed, a crowd is attracted into the game that is responding not to interest rates and profits but simply to the fact that it seems a mistake to be out of stocks. In effect, these people superimpose an I-can't-miss-the-party factor on top of the fundamental factors that drive the market. Like Pavlov's dog, these "investors" learn that when the bell rings—in this case, the one that opens the New York Stock Exchange at 9:30 a.m.— they get fed. Through this daily reinforcement, they become convinced that there is a God and that He wants them to get rich.

Today, staring fixedly back at the road they just traveled, most investors have rosy expectations. A Paine Webber and Gallup Organization survey released in July shows that the least experienced investors—those who have invested for less than five years—expect annual returns over the next ten years of 22.6%. Even those who have invested for more than 20 years are expecting 12.9%.

Now, I'd like to argue that we can't come even remotely close to that 12.9%, and make my case by examining the key value-determining factors. Today, if an investor is to achieve juicy profits in the market over ten years or 17 or 20, one or more of three things must happen. I'll delay talking about the last of them for a bit, but here are the first two:

(1) Interest rates must fall further.
(2) Corporate profitability in relation to GDP must rise.

You know, someone once told me that New York has more lawyers than people. I think that's the same fellow who thinks profits will become larger than GDP. When you begin to expect the growth of a component factor to forever outpace that of the aggregate, you get into certain mathematical problems. In my opinion, you have to be wildly optimistic to believe that corporate profits as a percent of GDP can, for any sustained period, hold much above 6%. One thing keeping the percentage down will be competition, which is alive and well.

So where do some reasonable assumptions lead us? Let's say that GDP grows at an average 5% a year—3% real growth, which is pretty darn good, plus 2% inflation. If GDP grows at 5%, and you don't have some help from interest rates, the aggregate value of equities is not going to grow a whole lot more.

So I come back to my postulation of 5% growth in GDP and remind you that it is a limiting factor in the returns you're going to get: You cannot expect to forever realize a 12% annual increase—much less

22%—in the valuation of American business if its profitability is growing only at 5%. *The inescapable fact is that the value of an asset, whatever its character, cannot over the long term grow faster than its earnings do* [emphasis mine].

I think it's very hard to come up with a persuasive case that equities will over the next 17 years perform anything like—anything like—they've performed in the past 17. If I had to pick the most probable return, from appreciation and dividends combined, that investors in aggregate—repeat, aggregate—would earn in a world of constant interest rates, 2% inflation, and those ever hurtful frictional costs, it would be 6%. If you strip out the inflation component from this nominal return (which you would need to do however inflation fluctuates), that's 4% in real terms. And if 4% is wrong, I believe that the percentage is just as likely to be less as more.[6]

4

BUFFETT MATH 201
Enhancing Returns with Little Effort

THE PREVIOUS CHAPTER SHOWED TWO WAYS in which average investors could take advantage of simple mathematical principles to enhance their portfolio returns. First, I showed how the power of compounding—letting time work in your favor—helps you capture the best possible gains from your favorite stock holdings. Second, I outlined how you can magnify the effects of time by aiming for higher returns. Investors should never accept average returns because that's the best they will ever attain. They should instead seek ways to further their yearly returns. Adding a few extra percentage points of gain each year compounds into huge amounts over time. As I have shown, it is possible to earn three times as much money over a 30-year period by improving annual returns a mere four percentage points.

Mathematicians and other academics like to believe that such prestidigitation is impossible to sustain over long periods. No investor, they argue, can consistently earn "abnormal" gains without taking undue risks or "striking it lucky." Buffett and generations of value investors before him have scoffed at that notion. Not only is it possible to attain market-beating results, but it can be done without taking excessive risks. In this chapter, I discuss three more strategies, all crucial to Buffett's success, for enhancing your returns. The wondrous thing about these three methods is that they really don't entail much blood or sweat—or good stock picking, for that matter—just a dose of rationality. Like dieting, where you attain your goal by doing nothing (you simply eat less), investors looking to pad their results can find solace in a few exercises that involve little or no effort.

STEP 1: THE MIRACULOUS ADVANTAGE OF BUYING LOW

I recall vividly a phone conversation with an elderly client in 1999 concerning America Online, a stock he was all too eager to buy.

> "I finally decided to bite the bullet," he explained to me. "I've been wanting to buy America Online for a year but it just kept going up."
>
> "Why did you buy it now, if you thought it was too expensive at half the price?" I asked.
>
> "It looked like it was going to keep going up," he explained. "I need a good return on my money, and there are not many stocks offering that."

What ever happened to the dictum "buy low–sell high"? These days, the manifesto seems to be "buy very high, hope to sell higher." I can appreciate the gentleman's desire for a high rate of return, but his strategy, of giving in to the crowd, is a fatal flaw that keeps most investors from maximizing the potential of their portfolio. Because high returns are the predominant goal of investing, it behooves individuals to gauge a stock's return potential before buying. Sadly, most investors place no hurdle rate on their stocks. They don't, for example, set a required return of 15 percent a year or screen for stocks that can rise a minimum 50 percent in 2 years. They simply buy at prevailing prices—no questions asked—hoping the price keeps rising, even though history shows that the highest rates of return are earned when you buy near price bottoms, not tops.

This applies to the overall market or individual stocks, such as America Online or Dell Computer. By virtue of their meteoric rally in the past few years, their rate-of-return potential going forward may be severely limited. Does anyone think Dell can rise 20-fold by 2002, let alone quadruple again? Most sensible analysts seem to think this stock will have a hard time even doubling over the next few years. But, alas, most investors use the recent past to extrapolate forward. They criticize themselves for missing the 6,000 percent rally in Dell between 1994 and 1998 and jump into the fray. To justify buying shares of Dell, they convince themselves that the stock can rise another 6,000 percent. The chances of that happening are slim to none.

It is no coincidence that most of the great money managers of the twentieth century—Buffett, Benjamin Graham, John Neff, Sir John Templeton, Philip Fisher, Laurence Tisch, Walter Schloss, Philip Carret, and others—are value oriented. Nearly all of them followed the investing game plan laid out in the 1930s by Graham, who taught hundreds of pupils over a 40-year period the merits of valuing companies and of buying stocks when the market underpriced the company. Buying a stock for $50 when the company was worth, say, $75 or more, Graham taught, was the latchkey that opened the doors to high returns. Almost by definition, an undervalued security must eventually rise in price, and an overvalued security must fall, Graham taught. The immutable laws of mathematics ultimately will bestow higher returns upon those stocks more apt to rise than fall.

Intuitively, what Graham preached, and what Buffett gleaned from Graham's teachings, makes perfect sense. If you wish to enhance returns, you must buy at the lowest possible price. The lower the price paid, the higher your expected returns. If you wish to double your money on a stock such as Intel, you stand a better chance buying Intel at $75 rather than at $90 or $100. Similarly, an investor who bought Dell Computer at a split-adjusted price of $8 necessarily will boast a higher percentage gain than the investor who bought at $18 or $38. Where Buffett differed from Graham was in insisting that price be linked to growth and quality. It wasn't enough that a stock was undervalued, at Graham exhorted, for hundreds of "cheap" securities linger in the market everyday. Buffett knew that the best returns would come from buying established growth companies, ones capable of growing faster than the market, but at reduced prices.

However applied, Graham's insistence on value became the tool many great managers have used to obtain stellar long-term returns. John Templeton combined Graham's value-oriented principles with a contrarian streak. When the masses were selling, Templeton wanted to buy, and vice versa. Neff practiced his own variation of contrarian investing that led him to emphasize financial ratios in his pursuit of market-beating gains. Schloss retained Graham's rigid balance sheet-driven style and sought out companies trading for less than their break-up or liquidation value. He beat the market handily over a 40-year period starting in 1956. Fisher made his mark by selecting a limited number of growth stocks that he would hold for decades.

From time to time, the great value investors have come under attack from academics who contend that Buffett and the others are aberrations or statistical flukes. Take any sample of 10 million investors, they say, and you're bound to find some who will beat the market regularly, just as you can assemble a crowd at a roulette table and find a few who spin "red" six times in a row. But what explains the fact that nearly all those investors who have beaten the market are value oriented, Buffett once asked:

> In this group of successful investors that I want to consider, there has been a common intellectual patriarch, Ben Graham. But the children who left the house of this intellectual patriarch have called their flips in very different ways. They have gone to different places and bought and sold different stocks and companies, yet they have had a combined record that simply can't be explained by random chance....The common intellectual theme of the investors of Graham-and-Doddsville is this: they search for discrepancies between the value of a business and the price of small pieces of that business in the market....Our Graham-and-Dodd investors, needless to say, do not discuss beta, the capital asset pricing model, or covariance in returns among securities. These are not subjects of any interest to them. In fact, most of them would have difficulty defining those terms. The investors simply focus on two variables: price and value.[1]

Over the past 70 years, numerous studies have validated the theorem that buying undervalued stocks leads to better gains than buying generously priced stocks. For these studies, it didn't really matter which criteria one used to dissect value. Buying within these undervalued parameters led to market-beating gains. Graham, for example, found that an investor could reap abnormal returns buying stocks priced below their net asset value. Subsequent studies found that buying stocks below their own book value led to strong returns over time.

Within the past 20 years, several studies have shown the effectiveness of "ratio" investing: selecting stocks based on their price-to-earning (P/E), price-to-sales (P/S), or price-to-book value (P/B) ratios. All these tests confirmed that investors do better selecting stocks in the bottom range of their ratios.

Whatever the methodology used, the act of being frugal generally enhances returns. Investors tend to be irrational and forever willing to overpay for glamour stocks and follow the crowd when stocks crash. They also have a psychological penchant for avoiding stocks that decline in value. This works to the advantage of an investor whose base instinct is frugality. No investor can be cost conscious without first developing an awareness of value, and one cannot form a notion of value without first applying due diligence to establish a basis for value. The investor who can rationally size up a company's prospects and be ready to pounce when the quote is right possesses an insurmountable competitive advantage over investors who follow what Buffett calls "the institutional imperative" (the tendency of professional investors to follow each other's lead).

History supports the concept of buying low, whether you are buying high-growth technology stocks, low-P/E industrial stocks, or simply putting your money in an index fund and letting it compound. Suppose, for example, you had invested $5,000 a year into the Dow Jones Industrials stocks at the beginning of each year starting in 1970. By the end of 1999, your $5,000 yearly investments would have grown to around $1,117,000, or a compounded annualized gain of about 9 percent a year. If you had chosen to invest your $5,000 at the market's yearly high, you would have had roughly the same amount. That's because the market has a tendency to record its high of the year around December 31.

However, if you had decided to invest $5,000 at the market's yearly low, you would have had just under $1.5 million, or 34 percent more money, by the end of 1999. This relationship held for various time periods over the past 50 years. Investing money when the market was hitting a yearly low point automatically led to more wealth later on. The results can be seen in Table 4.1.

As you can see, it was possible to enhance your returns beyond what the Dow Industrials index provided simply by being cost conscious. It didn't seem to matter what time period was chosen; buying

TABLE 4.1   The value of buying low: What $5,000 yearly investments in the market become.

Start Date	Yearly High*	Yearly Low†	Difference
1990	$116,567	$161,857	38.9%
1985	$251,020	$365,173	45.5%
1980	$507,648	$712,758	40.4%
1975	$814,268	$1,119,331	37.5%
1970	$1,117,563	$1,494,738	33.7%
1965	$1,413,305	$1,858,216	31.5%
1960	$1,794,009	$2,350,262	31.0%
1955	$2,315,573	$3,096,563	33.7%
1950	$3,303,152	$4,433,716	34.2%

*Assuming one invested at the market's yearly highs.
†Assuming one invested at the market's yearly lows.

at the yearly low consistently increased a portfolio's terminal wealth between 30 and 45 percent. This is a statistically significant difference that shouldn't be overlooked. Of course, no one ever knows when the market has hit its yearly high or low. Only in retrospect can we make such judgments. But the facts seem pretty clear that it's better to buy during a falling market than during a rising one. You didn't have to hit the exact bottom of the market each year to enjoy gains far in excess of someone who bought near the highs. Interestingly, these results were obtained across the spectrum of market conditions. Whether in a bullish or bearish mood, the market tends to provide enough intra-year volatility to give investors a chance to reap abnormal gains. These chances should be exploited to the fullest.

STEP 2: KEEP IT CONCENTRATED

It's rare these days to find an investor who is completely satisfied with his or her own portfolio. Some lament that they have made poor investment choices during the bull market and failed to keep pace with indexes. Many investors have criticized themselves for following a fad that went bust. Probably the most common problem I've encountered has to do with diversification. Few investors have developed any sort of strategy for blending and balancing stocks within their portfolios. At its worst manifestation, some investors have hoarded stocks like vases and own shares in dozens of companies. Some own more than a dozen mutual funds, several of which may hold the same types of stocks. They take diversification to the extreme to feel safe.

However, diversification is the bane of high returns. A tiny percentage of professional investors have been able to cobble a market-beating track record over long periods by owning dozens of stocks. Among those who did, only a handful—such as Peter Lynch—could attribute their success to diligence and elegant stock-picking. The rest are usually living off a few stocks that luckily delivered tremendous returns and kept the entire portfolio ahead of the market for years. A fund manager who obtains an 80 percent 1-year return can live off that one period for several more years. Even if his performance lags in subsequent years, the 80 percent one-time return is usually enough to keep the portfolio above the Dow Industrials or S&P 500 for several years.

Great value-oriented investors such as Warren Buffett and Philip Fisher have no use for diversification. They are keenly aware that diversification poses no long-term benefit to a portfolio and drags down potential returns. "Diversification is a protection against ignorance," Buffett told investors at the 1996 annual meeting. The more stocks one owns, the more difficult it is to keep track of one's winners and losers and to keep a pulse on the financial performance of so many companies. Moreover, it gets exceedingly difficult to boost yearly returns above expectations. Once you own 30 or more stocks, boosting returns is as difficult as spinning around a Carnival cruise ship in Miami harbor.

The percentage of investors who own 25 or more different stocks is appalling. It is not this number of 25 or more which itself is appalling. Rather, it is that in the great majority of instances only a small percentage of such holdings is in attractive stocks about which the investor has a high degree of knowledge. Investors have been so oversold on diversification that fear of having too many eggs in one basket has caused them to put far too little into companies they thoroughly know and far too much in others about which they know nothing at all. It never seems to occur to them that buying a company without having sufficient knowledge of it may be even more dangerous than having inadequate diversification.[2]

A properly diversified portfolio, in academic parlance, is one that eliminates "nonsystematic" risk, that is, the risk that a single stock can cause material disruptions to returns. By combining 20 to 30 or more stocks in a portfolio, you could eliminate the risk that one stock imploded and caused your entire portfolio to suffer. For every stock that unexpectedly declined, you could expect one to rise and offset the loss. Being well diversified has never protected the investor from losses. Even the largest, best-run mutual funds lose money when the market falls. A large portfolio merely *reduces the probability of loss*. You are always a hostage to "systematic" risk, that is, the risk of an unforeseen event causing the entire stock market to drop. The best you can do, academic research has shown, is to spread your money into different instruments such as bonds and foreign stocks to insulate yourself from a stock market meltdown.

Value investors such as Buffett ignore blanket statements about risk and return and don't measure risk by share-price movements as academics do. To Buffett, investors take on risk when they fail to be diligent, that is, when they pay more for a company than it later proves to be worth. Reduce the uncertainty surrounding owning a business, and you don't have to worry much about aberrant share-price fluctuations causing paper losses. "I put heavy weight on certainty," Buffett said in 1994. "If you do that, the whole idea of a risk factor doesn't make any sense to me. You don't [invest] where you take a significant risk. But it's not risky to buy securities at a fraction of what they're worth."[3] A well-rounded portfolio of 8 to 12 companies bought at reduced prices and offering strong growth potential should lead to superior returns.

Money manager and Buffett biographer Robert Hagstrom Jr. made this point clear in 1999 by showing that diversification necessarily leads to mediocrity. Hagstrom asked a computer to randomly assemble 12,000 portfolios of different sizes taken from stocks that posted revenues and earnings between 1979 and 1986. Hagstrom divided the stocks into four groups; 3,000 random portfolios holding 250 stocks, 3,000 portfolios holding 100 stocks, 3,000 portfolios holding 50 stocks; and 3,000 portfolios holding just 15 stocks. Then he plotted the annual rate of return of each of these distinct 12,000 portfolios over 10-year and 18-year time periods. By choosing longer time periods, Hagstrom was able to capture a full economic cycle and the market's shifting preference for styles (large caps versus small caps, growth stocks versus value stocks, etc.). His research quantified what many of the master investors already suspected.

To improve your chances of beating the market, you must keep your portfolio small.

The data showed that randomly selected portfolios tended to post returns that fell slightly below returns of the S&P 500 of the same period, which is to be expected. Because the S&P 500 contains nearly all of the best performing stocks of the 1980s and 1990s, it follows that a portfolio randomly selected from *all* stocks should exhibit somewhat lower performance. However, Hagstrom found significant differences in the ranges of performance when comparing portfolios by size. Specifically, portfolios with the largest number of stocks tended to post returns that barely deviated from the mean return of all similarly sized portfolios. The smallest portfolios, in contrast, offered the highest deviation of average returns. An investor stood a better chance of woefully underperforming the market with a portfolio of 15 stocks. However, the investor also stood the same higher probability of greatly outperforming the S&P 500.

During the 10-year period ending in 1996, the S&P 500 provided investors a 15.23 percent annual return. Returns of the random portfolios in Hagstrom's study were similar, between 13.75 and 13.91 percent, no matter their size, but the portfolios displayed wildly different ranges of performance. Among the 3,000 smallest portfolios, those with 15 stocks, returns ranged from 4.41 percent a year to 26.59 percent, with the majority of them falling between 11 and 16 percent. Fifty-stock portfolios provided returns between 8.62 and 19.17 percent, with most returns falling between 12.3 and 15.4 percent. As portfolio sizes grew, the range of returns narrowed considerably. The data indicated that size minimizes deviation but acts as both floor and ceiling to performance (Tables 4.2 and 4.3). "I submit this as convincing evidence," Hagstrom wrote, "that the probabilities go up as the size of the portfolio goes down. With a 15-stock portfolio, you have a 1-in-4 chance of outperforming the market. With a 250-stock portfolio, your chances are 1 in 50."[4]

Of course, it isn't enough just to keep a portfolio small. Holding 15 stocks, as Hagstrom's data suggested, gives you a much greater chance of beating the market. It also gives you an equally high chance of

TABLE 4.2   Ten-year holding period ending 1996.

	Portfolio Size				
	15 Stocks	50 Stocks	100 Stocks	250 Stocks	S&P 500
Average return	13.75%	13.87%	13.86%	13.91%	**15.23%**
Standard range*	11.0–16.5%	12.3–15.4%	12.8–15.0%	13.3–14.6%	
Lowest return	4.41%	8.62%	10.02%	11.47%	
Highest return	26.59%	19.17%	18.32%	16.00%	

Standard range shows the range of returns for approximately two-thirds of the portfolios.
Source: Robert Hagstrom, Jr., The Warren Buffett Portfolio, New York, John Wiley & Sons, 1999.

falling behind. For portfolio concentration to work, it must be premised on intelligent stock-picking. Buffett has often said that investors should try to focus on buying as few stocks as possible during their lifetimes. For those who aren't confident enough to hold a small number of stocks, Buffett suggests they put their money in an index fund. The advantages of funds, Buffett notes, are that they minimize taxes and transaction costs and regularly keep pace with the indexes they attempt to mimic. In addition, as Hagstrom showed, most actively managed funds will likely lag behind the market over time because they hold too many stocks and can't familiarize themselves enough with any of them.

Buffett, exhibiting his characteristic aplomb, probably said it better in 1991: "If you have a harem of 40 women, you never get to know any of them very well."[5]

TABLE 4.3   Eighteen-year holding period ending 1996.

	Portfolio Size				
	15 Stocks	50 Stocks	100 Stocks	250 Stocks	S&P 500
Average return	17.34%	17.47%	17.57%	17.61%	**16.32%**
Standard range*	15.1–19.6%	16.2–18.7%	16.7–18.5%	17.1–18.1%	
Lowest return	8.77%	13.56%	14.71%	16.04%	
Highest return	25.04%	21.80%	20.65%	19.20%	

Standard range shows the range of returns for approximately two-thirds of the portfolios.
Source: Robert Hagstrom, Jr., The Warren Buffett Portfolio, New York, John Wiley & Sons, 1999.

STEP 3: STAY MINDFUL OF COSTS

Investors frequently ask how to enhance their portfolios' returns. The answer: start by being cost conscious. Most investors unwittingly throw away a small fortune over their stock-picking careers paying too much for trades, trading too frequently, and making poor choices. When compounded over time, the money you burn on these activities can add up to several hundred thousand dollars, if not $1 million or more.

Lower your commissions.   Before commissions were deregulated in 1975, most investors regularly paid their favorite broker several hundred dollars per trade. Over time, this undesirable gratuity compounded into tens of thousands of dollars for high–net worth investors—money that was no longer compounding for them. Remember, every dollar you invest (or don't invest) has an opportunity cost. Assume that you typically pay your broker $5,000 a year in commissions. Over a 20-year period, you will be giving your broker $100,000 (and making him very happy, to be sure), but, because of compounding, the money you paid in commissions actually could have been turned into $300,000 or more if left in your account.

Let's assume that, instead of paying a broker $5,000 a year, you paid him or her five *percent* on a $100,000 portfolio that grows 10 percent a year. In this case, you will hand $320,000 over to the broker over a 20-year period. Had you kept that money and paid zero commissions, the $320,000 would have grown to $706,000. Obviously, an investor can't eliminate commissions entirely, but you can come awfully close these days. Using deep discount brokers such as Brown & Co. (which charges as little as $5 per trade for up to 5,000 shares), you can save yourself a couple hundred thousand dollars over the long term. Let's say that you make 20 trades a year at Brown & Co. on a $100,000 portfolio that grows at 10 percent. After 20 years, you have given the broker just $2,000, the future value of which was just $6,400.

Reinvest all dividends.   One of the most amazing track records in investing belonged to John Neff, who piloted the Winsdor Fund for 31 years before retiring in December 1995. Neff was a "value investor;" that is, he waited until stock prices dropped sharply before buying and emphasized dividend-paying stocks to maximize his returns.

Over that great 31-year period, Neff beat the S&P 500 21 times and sported an annual compounded return of 13.9 percent versus 10.6 percent for the index. A $10,000 investment with Neff in 1964 turned into $565,200 by the end of 1995. By comparison, a $10,000 investment in the S&P 500 index returned $227,200. Astonishingly, dividends accounted for about 40 percent of the yearly gains investors received from owning the fund during Neff's tenure. Neff realized, rightly, that if he could find stocks sporting dividend yields of 4 to 5 percent, then half his work was done. After all, if you want your stocks to provide 10 percent average annual gains and if 5 percent comes from dividends, you need only a 5 percent rise in the share price to attain your goal.

That was Neff's great discovery. The share price of the Windsor fund merely doubled over those 31 years, from $7.75 to $15.55. The net asset value hardly budged through the years because Windsor Fund derived such a high percentage of its gains from stock dividends, which the fund returned to investors each year. The power of compounding did the rest. Had individuals reinvested all the dividends Neff's fund returned to them each year, their $7.75 initial investment would have turned into $437.59. Dividends reinvested from the fund's first year of existence compounded over the next 30 years. Second-year dividends compounded for 29 years, and so on, adding layer upon layer of gains for investors.

5

UNDERSTANDING
OPPORTUNITY COSTS

ATHEMATICS LIES AT THE HEART of virtually every endeavor in which Warren Buffett engages, so much so that he often quips about his incessant fascination with numbers. He once joked that he spent 6 percent of his net worth buying his wife Susie an engagement ring, thus depriving himself of immeasurable millions in future gains. He muses that drinking several Cherry Cokes a day has been a "lifesaver" because it supplies him with tens of thousands of calories that prevents him from starving. He once justified his poor, high-fat diet by noting that he would need to consume 25 million calories before his death just to avoid starving. "Why not get on with it," he said."[1] Buffett exercises extreme caution when donating to charities, and he requires foundations to quantify that they are making good use of the money received. He has conditioned giving favors and money to his children on their losing weight by a specified date. Buffett prefers to speak to crowds of high school or university students rather than to elderly investors because he thinks that a higher percentage of the students will actually listen and heed his advice.

Mathematics also shows us that virtually anyone can evolve into a millionaire through patient, diligent investing. An individual who socks away a few thousand dollars every year starting at the age of 21 can easily amass $1 million by retirement. The power of time and the power of compounding ensure that any individual who can save money consistently can attain a decent degree of wealth by the age of 65 or 70. If that same individual can manage to save an extra few thousand dollars more each year, the pile of assets attained at retirement would be much larger. If that individual manages to earn a few extra percentage points of gain each year, either through good stock-picking or wise account management, the amount of money earned at the end is many times greater.

Most individuals these days are astute enough to understand the power of time and understand the need to fund their own retirement rather than to rely on government programs whose long-term viability doesn't seem guaranteed anymore. However, compounding works two ways. An investment that compounds at, say, 20 percent annual rates, will swell into a tremendous amount after 30 years. Conversely, a missed opportunity that could have compounded at 20 percent a year has the opposite effect on your portfolio. A poorly chosen stock that rises just 5 percent a year ultimately costs you tens of thousands of dollars in lost opportunities. Money that is misspent today and not invested can have the same injurious effect on your future net worth.

At any given moment, you have tens of thousands of investment opportunities worldwide from which to choose. You may decide to put your available cash into shares of Intel or into a home remodeling project. You may decide to spend $50 at a restaurant, or on a new pair of slacks, or on a new golf putter. You may be faced with the choice of buying a new automobile or funding a college account for a child. No matter how you choose, every possible use of your money must bring a return—tangible or intangible—or else you should not spend the money. When making the choice of buying, say, shares of Intel or new carpeting, you must think about the *opportunity costs* of the money spent.

The goal of every business is to maximize the total return on investment. Every dollar spent by an enterprise on a capital project must generate the highest possible return. Thus, every project must represent the best use of cash possible because the enterprise can, and should, sink its money into any project that offers a higher return. As an investor, you must also look at all spending decisions as opportunities—won or lost. Every dollar spent on a single item is a dollar unavailable for other items. That dollar must provide a suitable return—measured against what you could have earned on that dollar somewhere else.

We look at our investments similarly. Because the market tempts us with thousands of potential investments each day, we tend to screen our stock choices until we find those that meet our risk and return characteristics. Likewise, we've learned to benchmark our investments by comparing their performance against the S&P 500 index or some other proxy. If your portfolio rose just 8 percent in a year in which the S&P 500 index rose 20 percent, the opportunity cost on your money was great—you lost the chance at an extra 12 percent a year because the investments you chose did poorly.

It was once joked that if Bill Gates, the founder of Microsoft and the world's richest man, saw a $100 bill on a sidewalk, he would ignore it and keep walking. When you're worth $85 billion or so, as Gates was toward the end of 1999, it's not worth your time to bend over and put a C-note in your pocket. Gates would burn up more than $100 of his time in doing so, which would make the activity economically unprofitable. From his perspective, what's the point in giving up more than $100 in time in order to acquire $100?

Warren Buffett wouldn't see it that way. To him, a $100 bill lying on a sidewalk should not be valued on its present-day worth or on the present-day efforts needed to accumulate it, but on the future value of the greenback. Suppose, for example, that Buffett could compound $100 at 25 percent annual rates. In 10 years, his $100 discovery would be worth $931. After 30 years, it would be worth $80,779, unadjusted for inflation. Knowing this, even Gates might consider breaking his stride and bending over for a few seconds. Indeed, Buffett once was seen picking up a penny on an elevator on his way to the office and remarked to the stunned witnesses, "the beginning of the next billion."[2]

To understand Buffett's frugal convictions, one must view them from the point of view of mathematics and by using the types of calculation just shown. To Buffett, every dollar not accumulated now or spent needlessly could have productively been turned into numerous dollars later. Thus, everything you buy or do not buy has the potential to greatly increase or decrease your net worth, depending on the rate of return you can obtain on investments. This principle applies whether you spend money on a poorly chosen investment or on an unnecessary personal expense or luxury item.

CAN I INTEREST YOU IN A $20 MILLION AUTOMOBILE?

Knowing that he can compound money at 20 percent annual rates or more, an investor such as Buffett is more apt to be a net *saver* rather than a net *consumer* of goods. Buffett knows that every dollar spent on superfluous items can cost him tens of thousands of dollars in money later on. Every dollar unwisely spent on a stock can have the same effect. Similarly, every dollar spent on an overpriced stock can cut his rate-of-return potential, which has the effect of seriously eroding the terminal value of Buffett's portfolio.

Say, for example, you had the ability and the eagerness to buy either a $50,000 BMW or a $25,000 Toyota Camry. Which would you choose? An economist would argue that you should choose the vehicle that provides the most utility, but there's more to it than that. Emotional, irrational criteria may cause you to favor one vehicle over the other. The BMW certainly offers more status and perhaps more driving pleasure, two benefits that are hard to quantify in dollar terms. The Camry, in contrast, may offer more practicality and better gas mileage, benefits that are easier to quantify.

To an investor, the difference between a $25,000 Camry and a $50,000 BMW lies in the *opportunity costs*, that is, the money you forego to choose one automobile over the other. If you choose the BMW, you will spend $25,000 more up front. If you could have compounded $25,000 at 15 percent a year for 30 years, you actually gave up $1,655,294. That how much less you would have in you bank account in 30 years. Suddenly, that BMW looks terribly expensive, doesn't it? Compounding $25,000 at 20 percent results in an opportunity cost of $5,934,408. If you can compound the money at 25 percent annual rates, you give up $20,194,839 to buy the BMW.

As you can see, the mathematics of consumption yields potent results. Table 5.1 shows how much money you potentially give up when making routine purchases at stores or restaurants. Every time you attend a movie rather than rent the same film for $3, you potentially give up more than $17,000 in net worth later on (that assumes

TABLE 5.1   What you give up over 30 years making routine purchases.

	Your Expected Investment Returns		
	15%	20%	25%
Buy a $50,000 car rather than a $25,000 car	$1,655,294	$5,934,408	$20,194,839
Spend $10,000 on stock that provides zero returns	$662,117	$2,373,763	$8,077,936
Vacation at Disney World (family of four)	$166,529	$593,441	$2,019,484
Smoke two packs of cigarettes a day	$128,120	$459,323	$1,563,081
Eat out two times a month more often	$19,864	$246,871	$840,105
Pay $20 a week more buying brand-label groceries	$68,860	$246,871	$840,105
Pay $1,000 more for an in-season vacation	$66,212	$237,376	$807,794
Buy a $1,000 suit instead of a $250 suit	$49,659	$178,032	$605,845
Lose $50 a month gambling on a riverboat	$39,727	$142,426	$484,676
Drive 30 miles to work for 1 year (gasoline costs)	$47,275	$169,487	$576,765
Buy $5 in lottery tickets every week for 1 year	$17,215	$61,718	$210,026
Pay $20 a month more for heating you home	$15,891	$56,970	$193,870
A day at the ballpark (family of four)	$8,608	$30,859	$105,013
Get a haircut every month instead of every 2 months	$3,973	$14,243	$48,468
Buy a $25 bottle of wine	$1,655	$5,934	$20,191
Watch a movie in a theater rather than rent it	$1,457	$5,222	$17,771

you can compound the money at 25 percent rates). If you can save $20 a month on your heating bill, the long-term savings—again, depending on your reinvestment returns—can amount to almost $194,000. The simple act of buying a few state lottery tickets every month can leave you more than $200,000 poorer in 30 years. A trip to Disney

World for you and your family can ultimately cost you $2 million at retirement.

BUFFETT THE RATIONAL SAVER

No one advises you to give up pleasures, hobbies, or a fun day at the ballpark for the sake of amassing a greater pile of wealth, but great investors such as Buffett remain cognizant of the true costs of their activities. If you can compound money at great rates, as Buffett can, it behooves you to become a saver rather than a consumer. If you don't really need that $50,000 BMW and can get by on a $25,000 Camry, a Cadillac, or a Lincoln, you'll be several million dollars ahead later on as a result. Incidentally, as of this writing, Buffett was driving the same Lincoln Town Car he has owned for several years. The book value of the vehicle likely was below $15,000.

Seen in the context of opportunity costs, Buffett's frugal habits are perfectly consistent. Because he can compound money at very high rates, Buffett takes great care in seeing that no money in his household is wasted, although he can afford to buy anything he desires. If Buffett had lived a more extravagant lifestyle and spent some of his capital gains along the way he would have several billion dollars less today because of the power of compounding. For example, when Buffett closed his investment partnership in 1969, he had amassed a reported $25 million. If instead of reinvesting all the money, Buffett had bought a $5 million mansion in Omaha and stuffed it with $1 million in furniture and amenities, he would have cost himself $5 billion in wealth by 1999.

Buffett has to make such choices because of his high opportunity costs. In contrast, a household that has no opportunity costs, that is, it doesn't invest or derives no returns from investments, may be just as well off making the types of purchases listed in Table 5.1. A household with zero opportunity costs can be a net consumer with no detrimental impact to its long-term fortune, but, to Buffett, money saved is money compounded. He has been known buy 50 12-packs of Coca-Cola at once from the grocery store to get a volume discount.[3] Each year, the money he saves buying cases of pop will ultimately increase his net worth by thousands of dollars.

6

C H A P T E R

MAXIMIZING GAINS
WITH A BUY-AND-HOLD
STRATEGY

BOUT 15 YEARS AGO, I visited a local carnival
with a friend who lost about $200 playing a dice
game. Watching him continue to plunk down $5
on each roll in the hopes of winning cash prizes
of between $25 and $200, in retrospect, seemed
pathetic.

The odds were stacked heavily against him, although he
never realized it. To win money, he had to roll eight dice
simultaneously and produce a sum near 45, or an average of
5.6 per die. The laws of probability dictated that the majority of my friend's rolls would yield a total of between 24 and
32—scores that, coincidentally, cost him $5 and forced him
to roll again.

The enthusiasm with which my friend embraced the
game and his subsequent dejection reminds me of the market-timing and day-trading phenomena, which have become
two of the great shams of the bull market. More than enough
anecdotal evidence has surfaced the past few years to show
that, contrary to investor-held fantasies spurred by more

than a dozen best-selling books, short-term trading can't work consistently and that most people who engage in the activity lose money. This evidence hasn't stopped countless investors from actively trading their portfolios in the hopes of quicker gains. In the early 1990s, investors held the averaged stock nearly 2 years before they sold it. By 1999, they were holding stocks for little more than 1 year.

Buffett detests rapid trading. To him, it is a money-wasting activity that usually leads to inferior returns for investors. Further, it causes wide disparities in pricing that may prompt management to take unnatural or irrational actions to stem investors' biases. "Consistently rational prices are produced by rational owners," he wrote in a special letter to shareholders in 1988. On a more holistic level, stock trading serves as a giant economic siphon that pulls money away from productive use and puts it into the pockets of the financial industry.

Buffett once suggested, only half jokingly, that the United States should adopt a 100 percent capital gains tax on the profits of stocks held less than 1 year. "Most of our large positions are going to be held for many years, and the scorecard on our investment decisions will be provided by business results over that period, and not by prices on any given day," he told the *Omaha World-Herald* more than two decades ago. "Just as it would be foolish to focus unduly on short-term prospects when acquiring an entire company, we think it equally unsound to become mesmerized by the prospective near-term earnings when purchasing small pieces of a company."[1]

Certainly, many investors who casually buy and sell stocks online a few times a week may believe they are on the road to success, but their success is due only to the extraordinary persistence of the bull market, not to their own acumen. Since early 1998, the number of individual investors who flip stocks as fast as hamburgers has grown to number in the tens of thousands. Lured by the fabulous success of Internet stocks and by the advent of online trading, many have concluded that it's a breeze to amass a small fortune by hitting a few keystrokes each day.

Market analyst and investment manager Charles Ellis, in a now-famous formula published in 1975, virtually proved the dictum that the more often you trade, the *worse* your returns. The biggest factors causing weak returns, Ellis discovered, were commissions. The more you trade, the higher the commissions paid relative to your portfolio. As such, if you wished to beat the market, each trade must beat the market by several percentage points for you to keep pace. For example, if you wanted to beat the market by, say, five percentage points a year, and you expected the market to rise 10 percent, you would need a 15 percent return on your average investment, that is, if you traded in a vacuum. But since commissions and dealer spreads can average more than 2 percent of the value of each trade, your average return would need to be much higher, perhaps 18 percent. And, if you held the average stock less than 1 year—a turnover rate in excess of 100 percent— your average return would have to be still higher. Investors with turnover rates in excess of 200 percent, Ellis concluded, could not hope to beat the market unless each trade, on average, beat an index by several percentage points.

In 1998, finance professors Terrance Odean and Brad Barber, then of the University of California, Davis, confirmed that frequent trading leads to inferior returns. Odean and Barber dissected the trading activity of 78,000 households over a 6-year period ending in December 1996. Interestingly, they discovered that the average investor picked stocks that kept pace with the S&P 500. During the 6-year period, the average household earned 17.7 percent a year, which was slightly ahead of the market's 6-year return of 17.1 percent. However, the net return— subtracting commissions and bid-ask spreads—was 15.6 percent a year, fully 1.5 percentage points behind the market. Yearly returns fell as trading activity picked up.

Odean and Barber found that the 20 percent of households that traded the most, as measured by portfolio turnover, earned an average yearly *net* return of just 10.0 percent. Households trading the least obtained an average *net* return of 17.5 percent. In other words, investors were their own worst enemies. If they would have left their portfolios alone, they could have garnered yearly returns that would have been the envy of most mutual fund managers. Alas, in their pursuit of better gains, they committed countless unforced errors. The difference between a 10 percent yearly return and a 17 percent return is astounding when you compound results over a decade or two.

The study's conclusion was that the cost and frequency of trading explained nearly all of the poor performance of households during that 5-year period. The research led to the conclusion that investors engage in excessive trading due to psychological factors, namely "overconfidence." Investors seemed to attribute success mostly to their own stock-picking abilities, not to the bull market. They increasingly believed they could dart in and out of stocks by perfectly timing tops and bottoms and repurchase their favorite issues at a later date and still make a profit. But, as Ellis had shown two decades earlier, they unwittingly became their own anchor.

Buffett manifests confidence quite differently. Comparing Buffett with the investors Odean and Barber studied is like comparing a habitual lottery player to one who shuns the game. The addict buys lottery tickets incessantly believing "this will be my lucky week" or because he believes he has invented the right "system" for picking numbers. The non-player refuses to buy tickets because he has enough self-confidence he knows he can make more money elsewhere. He won't spend $5 a week on a ticket that offers a one-in-seven million chance of winning $10 million. He knows better ways to earn $10 million that don't involve gambling.

Buffett, in fact, is so confident in his stock-picking ability that he is wont to continue holding an investment perpetually. Rather than lull himself into believing he can win by continually darting in and out of the market, Buffett believes he can earn and retain more money picking a few choice companies and letting them grow over time. "All you do is buy shares in a great business for less than the business is intrinsically worth, with managers of the highest integrity and ability. Then you hold those shares forever," he told a *Forbes* reporter in 1990.

To make the point, Buffett's portfolio is concentrated in a small number of companies he has owned for years. He began accumulating stock in *The Washington Post* in the mid-1970s until he owned 1,869,000 shares. In 1985, he sold about 10 percent of his holdings but has kept the remaining 1,727,765 to this day. He continues to hold all 96,000,000 million shares of Gillette bought in 1989. He originally bought a preferred stock that converted into 12,000,000 shares; there have been three splits since. He vows never to sell his 200,000,000 shares of Coca-Cola despite the recent slump in revenues and earnings.

Buffett began studying and buying shares of GEICO (Government Employees Insurance) at the age of 21. He reportedly made a nearly 50 percent gain on his first GEICO investment in a single year. Later, when Wall Street believed GEICO was on the verge of bankruptcy, Buffett began accumulating large stakes in the insurer. By 1983, he owned 6.8 million shares, which turned into more than 34 million shares—51 percent of the company—by virtue of a 5-for-1 split. In August 1995, he announced he would buy the remaining 49 percent of GEICO and bring the company under Berkshire's umbrella.

Such patience has paid off. His $45 million investment in GEICO in the 1970s became worth $2.4 billion (a 54-fold increase in 20 years) when Buffett announced he was buying the rest of the company. He has held shares in *The Washington Post* for 27 years, over which time his $10.6 million investment grew to $930 million by the end of 1999, an 86-fold increase. During a period in which Wall Street's brokerages alternately told investors numerous times to buy and sell *The Washington Post*, Buffett held on for the maximum gain. Buffett has not paid a dime of capital gains taxes on *The Washington Post* since he sold a portion of his position in 1984.

Few investors can brag of attaining an 8,600 percent return on one investment because so few will hold a stock long enough to maximize the stock's potential. Even though the past few years has provided several stocks that surged 8,000 percent within a few years, such as Dell Computer, Qualcomm, or America Online, it's doubtful that many investors reaped the full gain. These stocks rallied so prodigiously *because* investors flipped them so rapidly. Turnover caused most of the gains. The majority of investors tripped themselves up playing the market's short-term lottery.

HOLDING PERIOD DETERMINES LIKELIHOOD OF GAIN

A September 16, 1999 article in *Barron's* noted the improbability of any short-term oriented investor beating the market. "If you make $125 on a trade and then shell out a $50 commission, you net just $75," the article said. "But if you lose $125, you're really down $175, once the commission is added in." The magazine determined that a trader who tries to scalp eighth-point gains, as many day traders do, needs to rack up three winning trades for each loser. That is, their success rate of picking winners must be 75 percent just to break even.

This seems impossible on paper. Short-term, the market is almost perfectly random and unpredictable. Just like a roulette wheel that poses an equal chance of showing red or black, there is a near-equal probability that the next trade on a stock will be up or down an eighth of a point. Over time, anyone playing this timing game will have a 50–50 chance of making money.

Factor in commissions and the odds turn against you drastically. Let's say you had a $100,000 portfolio and during a year's time made 100 purchases, half of which returned $500 and half of which lost $500. At year's end you have no net gains. However, if each trade cost you $50 (on both the buy and sell side), your portfolio has actually lost $10,000. You can't break even until 60 percent of your trades are winners. To earn 10 percent on your money, 70 percent of your trades must be winners. To earn 20 percent on your money, 80 percent of your trades must be winners.

Is it possible to make money 70 percent or 80 percent of the time? Yes, but not by short-term trading. Figures 6.1 to 6.4 show the stock-price performance of each of the S&P 500 stocks from 1989 through 1999. I assumed a pattern of random investing (that is, you randomly picked one of the S&P 500 stocks on each day over that 10-year period). The charts show the "probability of gains," or the chances you had of picking a stock that made money for you over a stated time period. For this study, I selected 1-month, 3-month, 1-year, and 5-year holdings periods.

The data strongly confirmed what one would expect: the longer one's holding period, the more chances an investor had of making

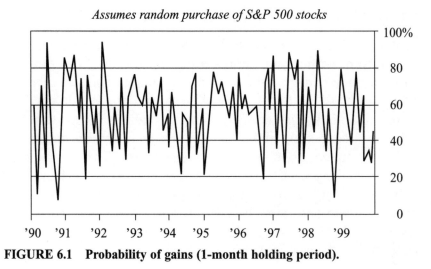

Assumes random purchase of S&P 500 stocks

FIGURE 6.1   Probability of gains (1-month holding period).

Assumes random purchase of S&P 500 stocks

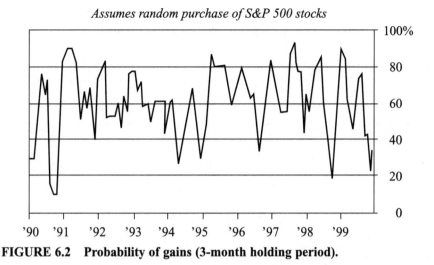

FIGURE 6.2   Probability of gains (3-month holding period).

money, regardless of how good that person was at picking stocks! For example, you stood a more than 80 percent chance of making money buying an S&P 500 stock during any period between 1989 and 1994 if you decided to hold the investment for 5 years. During some periods, your chances were in excess of 90 percent. What this means is that, on any given day you chose to buy an S&P 500 stock (for this study it didn't matter which day or which stock), your odds of pick-

Assumes random purchase of S&P 500 stocks

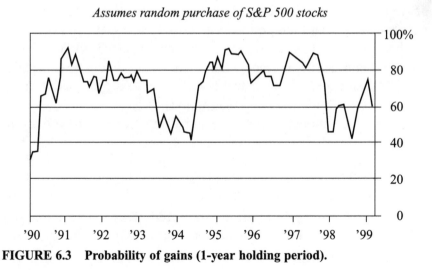

FIGURE 6.3   Probability of gains (1-year holding period).

Assumes random purchase of S&P 500 stocks

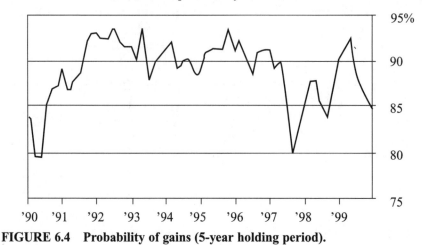

FIGURE 6.4   Probability of gains (5-year holding period).

ing a winner were at least 8 to 1 and sometimes 9 to 1 in your favor.

Certainly, the strength of the bull market helped increase your odds of gains. Your success rate will always be helped by a market that rises several consecutive years. However, as the figures show, your holding period was still predominantly successful.

If you held stocks just 1 year, your odds of making money, in general, were still excellent, but were more random. You ran increased risks of picking losers depending on when you made the investment. A 5-year holding period generally led to success rates close to 90 percent no matter what time period you chose to invest. In contrast, a 1-year holding period led to average success rates closer to 70 percent. During certain market periods, your chances of picking a winner fell below 50 percent if you held the stock just 1 year (you had a better chance of losing money during that period).

Returns were more random and significantly reduced as your holding period shortened. The average success rate for an investor with a 3-month holding period was just under 60 percent. Recall from these examples that, if success rates are 60 percent or below, your portfolio can lose money due to transactions costs. Note, too, from Figure 6.1, that the number of losing periods increased. There were numerous times when you had a better chance of picking a *money-losing* than a winning stock S&P 500 stock.

For example, if you had purchased an S&P 500 stock during the summers of 1998 or 1999 (never mind which stock on the index you selected), your chances of picking a winner were less than 20 percent. At least four of five S&P 500 stocks fell in the subsequent 3 months.

As holding periods decrease, the incidence of randomness increases. Table 6.1 for 1-month holding periods is most telling. Returns were highly variable and, for the most part, unpredictable. There were 30-day periods in which more than 80 percent of S&P stocks rose in price. If you were lucky enough to recognize those periods of market strength, you made great trading gains. Conversely, there were times when the overwhelmingly majority of stocks fell within the month. Your stock-picking ability wouldn't have mattered in such times—you would have lost money like everyone else.

In fact, during the 10-year period studied, the average success rate for a 1-month holding period was just slightly above 50 percent. Those odds may make you a winner in Las Vegas, but not on Wall Street, because if just half of your short-term trades were profitable, you would likely lose all your money over time because of dealer spreads and commissions. Your destiny would be no better than that of a roulette player's, who could

TABLE 6.1   Odds of picking a money-making S&P 500 stock.

Buying Period	Holding Period		
	1 Month	3 Months	1 Year
August 1998	8.9%	46.1%	63.0%
February 1998	89.3%	87.3%	58.8%
March 1997	24.1%	74.4%	83.8%
November 1996	86.4%	76.9%	88.4%
July 1996	19.1%	61.4%	81.1%
February 1995	78.1%	81.0%	90.1%
March 1994	20.5%	35.9%	56.6%
November 1992	76.1%	77.0%	75.5%
December 1991	93.2%	83.4%	85.1%
November 1991	25.4%	75.3%	72.9%
August 1990	5.6%	10.9%	71.9%
November 1989	60.2%	31.9%	29.3%

nearly break even perpetually were it not for the existence of 0 and 00 on the wheel. Those two wild-card numbers serve, just as a brokerage commission do, to siphon money from you slowly.

Given these types of statistics, it's no wonder the day-trading phenomenon seems to be losing its luster. Publicized cases of success aside, the real world of mathematics eventually catches up to all those who are consumed by the temptation of gains. People are learning all over again that dice are fun to play with but that you'll never profit from rolling them over and over.

THE PUNISHING COST TO SOCIETY OF TURNOVER

In the aggregate, rapid trading hurts the performance of individual portfolios. It can also act as an economic drag because it causes money to be misallocated and siphoned out of the entire financial system. Money that could be put to better use to raise productivity and corporate earnings gets wasted on commissions and cost related to frivolous trading.

Textbooks say you should buy shares of a company in order to share in the entity's earnings. If you own 200 shares of Merck and the company delivers $3.50 per share in earnings, you have a claim on $700 of the company's earnings (200 × $3.50). Of course, you can't walk into Merck's corporate headquarters and demand $700. If you're smart, you'll let Merck reinvest the money it earned on your behalf and turn $700 into, potentially, $7,000. Over time, the stock price will track the growth in earnings and may also deliver a 10-fold increase for you.

But what happens when the money you pay for your share of the earnings exceeds the actual earnings? This has been happening with alarming regularity. Investors have been flipping stocks so rapidly these days that they are paying more in commissions and dealer spreads to acquire their favorite stocks than these companies generate as profits. Buffett find this activity utterly illogical. "Bear in mind—this is a critical fact often ignored—that investors as a whole cannot get anything out of their businesses except what the businesses earn," Buffett told a private group of business leaders in 1999.

Table 6.2 shows just how costly short-term trading has been in the aggregate. In numerous cases, the cumulative transaction costs being paid to buy and sell certain stocks is exceeding the total gains all these investors could hope to reap. Consider the following examples.

TABLE 6.2   Turnover ratios for select S&P 500 stocks as of February 2000.

Company Name	Shares (mil.)	Annualized Volume	Turnover Ratio	Transaction Costs ($mil.)	Estimated Income ($mil.)
Yahoo!	398.0	4301.8	10.8	$796	$155
Rite Aid	258.9	1178.0	4.6	$218	$65
Peoplesoft	268.5	1033.9	3.9	$191	$62
Seagram Ltd.	432.6	278.9	0.6	$52	$17
Comcast	751.9	1261.7	1.7	$233	$83
Bethlehem Steel	131.5	315.4	2.4	$58	$24
America Online	2201.8	9763.2	4.4	$1,806	$771
Homestake Mining	228.0	420.0	1.8	$78	$34
Cabletron Systems	172.2	663.0	3.9	$123	$62
Network Appliance	145.7	535.3	3.7	$99	$60
Qualcomm	646.4	5607.5	8.7	$1,037	$679
Parametric Technology	268.1	1054.6	3.9	$195	$131
Xilinx	312.5	1713.6	5.5	$317	$228
Citrix Systems	171.8	1054.3	6.1	$195	$146
Novell	326.6	1474.5	4.5	$273	$242
KLA-Tencor	174.9	1067.9	6.1	$198	$194
Oracle	2862.3	8141.0	2.8	$1,506	$1,631
Seagate Technology	228.7	601.0	2.6	$111	$121
Rowan Co.	83.2	252.8	3.0	$47	$53
3Com	357.6	2132.5	6.0	$395	$451
Transocean Sedco	100.6	420.1	4.2	$78	$89
Baker-Hughes	327.1	581.7	1.8	$108	$131
Mattel	286.1	851.5	3.0	$158	$197
Quintiles Transnational	78.0	470.4	6.0	$87	$112
Clear Channel Comm.	263.6	362.1	1.4	$67	$87
SUN Microsystems	1554.7	5362.5	3.4	$992	$1,415
ADC Telecommunications	300.3	1003.4	3.3	$186	$270
Compuware	367.9	1525.2	4.1	$282	$453
Andrew	82.2	219.6	2.7	$41	$67
Dell Computer	2543.0	7431.6	2.9	$1,375	$2,289

continued on next page

TABLE 6.2   continued

Company Name	Shares (mil.)	Annualized Volume	Turnover Ratio	Transaction Costs ($mil.)	Estimated Income ($mil.)
LSI Logic	282.8	1065.3	3.8	$197	$328
Bed Bath & Beyond	139.4	381.9	2.7	$71	$121
Newmont Mining	167.2	414.5	2.5	$77	$139
BMC Software	236.6	1182.4	5.0	$219	$412
Mirage Resorts	190.0	486.2	2.6	$90	$171
Alza	87.3	385.6	4.4	$71	$137
Conexant Systems	392.8	939.8	2.4	$174	$338
Biogen	147.1	724.2	4.9	$134	$271
National Semiconductor	169.1	600.8	3.6	$111	$237
Adaptec	105.5	500.3	4.7	$93	$199
Paychex	246.3	448.3	1.8	$83	$180
Compaq Computer	1698.0	4476.9	2.6	$828	$1,834

By February 2000, the shares of Yahoo! were turning over at a rate of 10.8 times per year (that is, the average share was trading hands about every 33 days). At the time, Yahoo! had 398 million shares outstanding and yearly trading volume was running at a pace of 4.3 billion shares. For argument's sake, let's say that investors buying and selling Yahoo! pay a dealer spread of $1/8$ point ($0.125 per share) plus a commission rate of, say, $0.06 per share. The total transactions costs associated with trading 4.3 billion shares of Yahoo! would be $796 *million*. That's how much investors were paying in commissions and spreads to acquire Yahoo! within a year's time. However, the annualized net income of Yahoo! was just $155 million. In other words, investors were willing to pay more than $5 in commissions for the right to own a claim on every $1 the company was earning.

By early 2000, investors were holding the average share of PeopleSoft for about 92 days. Assuming $0.06 a share in commissions and $1/8$-point dealer spreads, the total cost of acquiring and selling PeopleSoft would total $191 million over a year's time. However, the company was estimated to earn about $62 million over that same period. Investors were also on track to pay the brokerage industry more than $1.8 billion a year to flip shares of America Online, whose earnings, on an annualized basis, were just $771 million. Trading was so rampant in several other stocks—Qualcomm, Oracle, and Dell Computer, among them—that investors were willing to fork over more than $1 billion a year for a piece of these companies' earnings (see Table 6.2).

In 1999, the average share of Apple Computer traded hands more than seven times, so that the average holding period was just about 50 days. More than 1.3 billion shares of Apple traded in 1999, although the company only had 175 million shares outstanding. Shareholders and institutions paid upward of $450 million in commissions and dealer spreads by flipping their Apple shares. The company's projected net income for the year was only $385 million.

The numbers are even more telling for Internet stocks, where investors are cumulatively paying hundreds of millions of dollars in commissions to acquire a piece of an unprofitable company. The only hope they have of recouping their transaction costs is if people keep piling on after them and bid the stock up. There is never any assurance of that happening, however, especially when holding periods run only a few months.

> If you and I were trading pieces of our business…we could escape transactional costs because there would be no brokers around to take a bite out of every trade we made. But in the real world investors have a habit of wanting to change chairs, or of at least getting advice as to whether they should, and that costs money—big money. The expenses they bear—I call them frictional costs—are for a wide range of items. There's the market maker's spread, and commissions, and sales loads, and 12b-1 fees, and management fees, and custodial fees, and wrap fees, and even subscriptions to financial publications. And don't brush these expenses off as irrelevancies. If you were evaluating a piece of investment real estate, would you not deduct management costs in figuring your return? Yes, of course—and in exactly the same way, stock market investors who are figuring their returns must face up to the frictional costs they bear.
>
> And what do they come to? My estimate is that investors in American stocks pay out well over $100 billion a year—say, $130 billion—to move around on those chairs or to buy advice as to whether they should! Perhaps $100 billion of that relates to the Fortune 500. In other words, investors are dissipating almost a third of everything that the Fortune 500 is earning for them— that $334 billion in 1998—by handing it over to various types of chair-changing and chair-advisory "helpers." And when that handoff is completed, the

investors who own the 500 are reaping less than a $250 billion return on their $10 trillion investment. In my view, that's slim pickings.

It also looks like a horrendous cost. I heard once about a cartoon in which a news commentator says, "There was no trading on the New York Stock Exchange today. Everyone was happy with what they owned." Well, if that were really the case, investors would every year keep around $130 billion in their pockets.[2]

This turnover, as much as it is coveted and encouraged by companies, actually creates no economic value for investors but simply provides a vast feeding trough for the brokerage industry. There is no doubt that looking at turnover this way might prompt some academic debate. After all, if an investor holds any of the stocks mentioned above for a period of years, the profits earned by the company will far exceed the cost of admission. The fact is that investors aren't holding these stocks very long any more. If current trends hold, more than 300 of the S&P 500 stocks will turn over, on average, at least once in 2000. Investors aren't holding most stocks long enough to enjoy even one year of profits.

What if this trend occurred year after year? The actual economic benefit to society of owning stocks would be negative, Buffett hints. More money would be siphoned out of the system in trading costs than companies would inject back in through profits. The cost of owning a claim on $1 of earnings would be far more than $1. The only value actually created would be the paper gains that can be whisked away by a poor market. To say that the recklessness of individuals is fully to blame would be wrong. Mutual funds and other institutions, who probably account for 60 to 75 percent of daily market volume, are prime culprits. Their short-term-oriented, "finger-on-the-trigger" trading habits are causing a huge leakage that would serve investors better if stocks were held longer and the money remained in shareholder's pockets.

Companies also are to blame for encouraging this turnover. Executives tease the financial industry by providing earnings guidance that encourages brokerages and funds to make quarterly bets on the direction of stocks. Likewise, they enthusiastically split their stock, which throws more shares into the trading den and adds to turnover and transactions costs. Buffett would have none of this. The turnover rate for Berkshire Hathaway's shares is among the lowest in the United States. It's not unusual to find shareholders who have held their

Berkshire stock 20 years or more. Buffett himself has occasionally donated small amounts of stock but has not sold a single share of Berkshire in the open market since he began accumulating positions in the 1960s. Buffett has chosen not to split Berkshire's stock either, believing that a lower share price would merely encourage more rapid trading and give excuses to the brokerage industry to encourage timing bets. As a result, Buffett has minimized economic leakage. Berkshire investors retain a higher proportion of the company's yearly earnings than perhaps any other shareholder group.

To date, few CEOs other than Buffett seem at all worried about rapid stock turnover, although, frankly, they should be. As Buffett has pointed out on many occasions, a preacher shouldn't judge his success by weekly turnover in the pews, but by longevity of the congregation. "Our goal is to have our shareholder–partners profit from the achievements of the business rather than from the foolish behavior of their co-owners," Buffett says.[3] Valuation is a function of corporate success, not of turnover. Keep your earnings rising at 15 percent annual rates, and the stock will continue to rise over time, whether 1,000 shares or 10 million trade every day. "I would really like the idea that nobody wanted to leave their seats so that there wouldn't be a seat available for anybody else," Buffett says.[4]

AVOIDING THE CHAIN
LINK OF ERRORS

CONOMIC ANALYST AND AUTHOR Peter Bernstein, in his distinguished 1996 book *Against the Gods— The Remarkable Story of Risk,* reminds us that numbers play an imperious role in every important endeavor in which mankind partakes. Simple events such as taking a shower in the morning, brewing a cup of coffee, or turning on the furnace were impossible to perform until man devised uniform standards of weights and measures and spent centuries testing and validating laws of physics.

Absent that type of mathematical certainty, we would live at the whims of fate. We could not measure, predict, or adapt to the weather, for example, without first understanding how to quantify its patterns. We could not prepare our favorite dinners without knowing proportions. We could not place bets on a horse without first creating some slide rule for distinguishing the performance of fillies. Likewise, we could not price a bar of soap, an automobile, a house, an insurance policy, and a share of Microsoft stock without first being able to quantify their economic costs and benefits. "Without numbers, there are no odds and no probabilities," Bernstein wrote. "Without odds and probabilities, the only way to deal with risk is to appeal to the gods and the fates. Without numbers, risk is wholly a matter of gut."[1]

The game of investment, in its bare-bones essence, is a game of probabilities. An investor needs to quantify risks, make mental calculations of potential return, stir up those assumptions in a pot, and produce a stock-picking strategy that works the majority of the time. Unwittingly, many professional investors trip themselves up by creating complex stock-picking systems that rely on dozens of variables. They may, for example, study a stock's price movements over a 5-year or 10-year period and track nuances in trading volume and daily volatility. Or they may attempt to dissect the U.S. economy in every detail, seeking relationships between variables that may help them predict an outcome. Tens of thousands of investors rely on computers to sort through mountains of data on profit margins, sales growth, or inventory buildups. Others find solace in "competitive analysis." They try to compare one company's price history, profit margins, P/E ratios, or sales growth with the entire industry's in an attempt to find the next great winners from among dozens of similarly priced stocks.

We can't fault investors for wanting to quantify their suspicions. A key element of risk management is to reduce as much uncertainty from an equation as possible. For example, if an analysis of data shows that a company's sales tend to rise by 5 percent every time interest rates drop 0.25 percent, then you have removed some uncertainty from forecasting. Armed with such information, you stand a better chance of predicting the future course of sales and earnings than an investor who lacks those data.

Too much analysis, however, inevitably leads to trouble. There comes a point at which stock-picking systems break down and prove futile because they are too complicated. Warren Buffett is keenly aware of the limitations of data and shuns most artifices routinely used by professional investors today. There is no computer in his Omaha office, nor does he profess to operate one very well. Buffett has told interviewers that he doesn't use a calculator and has no need to check stock quotes during the day. In fact, Berkshire Hathaway Vice-Chairman Charlie Munger once acknowledged that he never saw Buffett perform rigorous calculations on any prospective stock purchase.

Buffett hasn't hurt himself by shunning basic tools. His lack of resources has probably served him better than if he had operated

Bloomberg terminals, Quotrons, or statistical software packages. Buffett knows all too well the mathematical trappings of complex systems. Faced with the opportunity of performing detailed analysis of information to help him compete with the world's money managers, he prefers to keep it simple. So should you.

THE CHAIN RULE—WHAT AN ASSEMBLY LINE HAS IN COMMON WITH STOCK PICKING

Let's say you bought a machine for your factory that had five working parts, and each part had a 5 percent chance of failing over an 8-hour shift. Assume, too, that each part relied on the other parts (that is, a breakdown in one movable part caused the next one to fail as well). What is the expected failure rate of your machine over an 8-hour period? Is it 5 percent—the failure rate of every part? Not even close. Believe it or not, failure will occur almost 23 percent of the time. The machine would likely break down about once every 4$^{1}/_{2}$ shifts.

That rate seems improbably high considering that all five parts operate smoothly 95 of every 100 shifts. The higher failure rate occurs because the components' failure rate are linked. The success and failure rates are multiplied with each other. In this case, the whole is worse than the sum of the parts.

Success rate for a system = (success rate of part 1) $\times$ (success rate of part 2) $\times$ (success rate of part 3), etc.

For a system with five parts, each with a 95 percent success rate, the expected failure rate would be:

$$0.95 \times 0.95 \times 0.95 \times 0.95 \times 0.95 =$$
$$0.774 \text{ (success rate of 77.4\%)}$$

$$\text{Failure rate} = 1 - \text{success rate}$$

$$= 1 - 0.774$$

$$= 0.226 \text{ or } 22.6\%$$

This mathematical principle is very important to design engineers and plant managers who oversee production lines or who develop new products. Their goals are to create a nearly flawless operating system from multiple components. Those goals can be attained two ways. They must either engineer parts so precisely that each part's failure rate is infinitesimally small or create backup systems that keep the process working if one part fails. Today's personal computers, for example, operate smoothly (despite having thousands of microscopic components) because each part has an insignificantly low failure rate. In contrast, jet airliners fail so rarely because they are designed with dozens of backup systems that maintain the entity should key components fail. Spacecraft such as the Space Shuttle rely on both features. They contain advanced circuitry and telemetry components that have extremely low failure rates. Space shuttles are also equipped with dozens of backup systems in case of failure.

This principle of linked errors has very important meaning for investors. Because we rely on "systems" when we pick stocks—technical chart patterns, earnings forecasts, or discounted cash flow models, for example—we subject ourselves to the same mathematical problems that confront design engineers. First, we can overcomplicate things and, as a result, unwittingly become our own worst enemies. A stock-picking system behaves no differently from an auto assembly line. The more "components" you add to your investing model—that is, the more complicated you make your stock-picking "system"—the more often it will fail, pure and simple. Second, because the probability of errors multiplies as fast as you add more layers of detail to your analysis, you must learn to avoid relying on models that use numerous variables, especially models based on future forecasts. "Extra care in thinking is not all good but also introduces extra error," Charles Munger, once said. "Most good things have undesired 'side effects,' and thinking is no exception."[2]

Let's say that you were trying to predict how Microsoft's stock might perform over the next year. It's a daunting task, even for experienced analysts and market strategists. Here are the variables you would want to consider.

1. *Microsoft's sales over the next 12 months:* To calculate this, you must try to predict the level of software sales worldwide (all brands) and then try to predict Microsoft's market share. To calculate worldwide software sales, you might have to estimate the growth rate of national economies over the next year and predict

corporate demand for PCs and networks. This necessitates that you take into account changes in interest rates worldwide in addition to currency fluctuations. Then you must estimate the average price Microsoft will charge for its software (assuming you can guess the mix of products it will sell) and how Microsoft will report the revenues on an accounting basis.

2. *Microsoft's operating profit margins*: To derive this, you must estimate Microsoft's inventory costs, its mix of fixed and variable costs over the next 12 months, and the level of administrative expense it plans to carry on its books.

3. *Microsoft's nonoperating expenses*: You would have to calculate how much interest it will have to pay on its debt, if any. Also, you would need to determine how much interest income Microsoft could expect from its cash and bond holdings.

4. *The number of shares outstanding*: You will need to calculate shares outstanding to estimate earnings per share. To derive this figure, you'll need to estimate how many additional shares Microsoft might float to pay for acquisitions or grant to employees for profit-sharing plans. Further, you'll need to calculate how many outstanding stock options might be exercised during the year.

As much labor as this requires, you're only half way there. You must next predict how the stock market will behave over the next year. Will there be a bear market or a bull market? Will technology stocks decline or soar? If they are to soar, why? What P/E ratio will investors be willing to pay for Microsoft's stock over the next year? Will it be higher or lower than the industry average? Higher or lower than its own historical average? Why?

Such a rigorous dialogue might seem futile to a lay investor, but this roughly describes the methods used by brokerage analysts to predict quarterly earnings, stock-price movements, and larger market trends. No wonder their predictions are wrong nearly all of the time. By relying on so many variables to predict stock-price performance (sales, market share, interest rates, currency rates, operating costs, shares outstanding, options, earnings per share, and the public's prevailing mood over stocks), analysts unwittingly expose themselves to the chain link of errors. As their models grow more complicated and detailed, the rate of failure increases.

Let's suppose that each of these assumptions about sales, profit margins, market share, interest rates, shares outstanding, and so forth, bore a 20 percent chance of being wrong (an 80 percent success rate). The analysts' final prediction about Microsoft's stock price would bear such a high failure rate that it would be practically worthless to rely on it. If the analysts used, say, eight variables to predict Microsoft's stock price, the prediction would bear a success rate of 16.7 percent (that is, an 83.3 percent chance of being wrong). Because each variable was used to help predict other variables in the equation, the failure rates become linked and multiplied with each other, rendering the model useless.

This is the chief reason value investors such as Warren Buffett have little use for market forecasts or extravagant stock-picking systems. Complicated systems can be fraught with high failure rates as outlined in the Microsoft example. As investing tools, they come close to being worthless or, at the very least, unwieldy and impractical. When researching a company to buy, your goal is to minimize your chances of failure, not increase your failings. The investor who labors to predict Microsoft's near-term earnings and share-price performance might just as well try to predict next month's weather patterns in Indonesia. There would be the same chances of success. What began as a logical study of events would necessarily degenerate into a sequence of predictions, premised on each other, whose conclusions might bear no direct cause-and-effect relationship. One faulty forecast would beget another and another. In the end, the investor might not be any better off than if she had randomly selected Microsoft's fate out of a hat.

HITTING FOR A
HIGH AVERAGE

I
F YOU ARE AT LEAST 50 YEARS OLD, you probably have
vivid memories of Ted Williams, one of the greatest
hitters in baseball history. His impact on the game, both
as a player and as an inspiration to generations of hitters who followed, continues to this day. Williams combined power (521 lifetime home runs) with patience (he
received more walks than any batsman in his day) and control (a .344 lifetime average) as no player had ever done
before. He had the intelligence of a lead-off hitter and the
brawn of a power hitter; the patience of a bench warmer, and
the bat control of a singles hitter.

His contribution to the game was to reduce hitting to a
mathematical exercise. Fittingly, his greatest legacy was a
thesis on batting, *The Science of Hitting*, a book that attracted Warren Buffett's attention. Williams' basic thesis was that
the strike zone could be carved into 77 mini-zones that pitted the abilities of the hitter against the pitcher. Williams
knew, for example, that a high and inside strike pitted his
weakness against the pitcher's strength. If he consistently
swung at those pitches, his batting average would suffer. A
low and outside pitch produced the same results—a success
rate far below Williams' lifetime batting average. However,

if Williams received a pitch in his optimum strength zone, he put all his muscle into it, knowing that he could consistently produce a higher batting average. In constructing a template for success, Williams outlined a pattern of patience. He realized that it was often better to take a pitch on the fringe of the strike zone rather than swing for a low average. A called strike was better than making an out.

Buffett extends the same reasoning to stock picking. The stock market is like a major league pitcher who fires thousands of pitches a day, with each pitch representing a certain stock at a certain price. As the batter you must decide which of the thousands of pitches to swing at and which you will let whiz by. What distinguishes you from a baseball player, however, is that you don't have to swing—ever. The game of investing doesn't force you to take the bat off your shoulder and swing, unlike the batter in the stadium. No one will call you out; as Buffett says:

> In investments, there's no such thing as a called strike. You can stand there at the plate and the pitcher can throw the ball right down the middle, and if it's General Motors at $47 and you don't know enough to decide on General Motors at $47, you let it go right on by and no one's going to call a strike. The only way you can have a strike is to swing and miss.

Professional money managers must swing at pitches whether or not they wish to. The pressures to perform force them to switch in and out of stocks hundreds of times each year as information changes. They must worry about beating the S&P 500, beating their peers, successfully predicting quarterly earnings for 100 to 200 companies, and dressing up their portfolios for their marketing staffs. You needn't. You have the luxury of letting thousands of pitches pass you by before you call a broker—or use the Internet—and buy 100 shares of an attractive stock. You can study 1,000 stocks a month and pick only one if you like. You can walk away from Charles Schwab's stock until the price falls to a level at which you're comfortable buying. Or you can switch gears and look at any of the other 10,000 stocks trading that day.

The stock market doesn't compel you to act, although it may dearly tempt you. You'll never risk any cash by walking away from an investment you don't fully understand whose price isn't attractive enough, and you'll improve your batting average in the process. Once you discover a stock to your liking, one the market has offered up at a ridiculously low price, swing for the fences. Buffett notes that great opportunities—the ones that get you a .900 batting average or better— truly are rare. You may find two dozen such opportunities over a 20- year period. The number of good opportunities, those offering attractive enough batting averages, might be closer to 100. Poor opportunities number in the hundreds each day.

I depict Buffett's baseball analogy in Figure 8.1, which resembles a strike zone. In the same way that Ted Williams carved up home plate into high-average and low-average zones, you should consider creating a schematic that assesses your investing batting average. In this case, the goal is to swing only at pitches offering the highest probability of success. Your success rate will be a function of two chief factors,

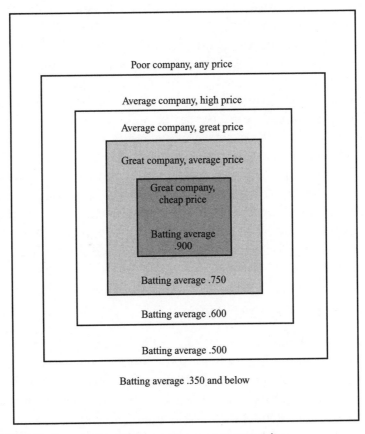

FIGURE 8.1   Investor's strike zone (your success rate).

the quality of the company and whether or not the stock is attractively priced. Generally speaking, the higher the price paid or the lower the quality of company chosen, the lower your chances of success. Statistics show that your holding period will also have an impact on your batting average. When you are trying to time the market for a short period, at best you'll have a 50 percent chance of picking a winning stock (and that's only if the stock is attractively priced). Because day-to-day fluctuations in stocks tend to be random and unpredictable, it follows that you'll have a 50–50 chance of picking a winner if you intend to hold a stock only a short time. Factor in taxes, commissions, and dealer spreads and your chances of success (that is, making money) decrease dramatically.

You should avoid situations where your chances of success are even at best. Instead concentrate on investments where you have high confidence in earning a profit. Just as Ted Williams looked for pitches in his .400 zone, you need to look for stocks offering a better than, say, 75 percent chance of success (a batting average of .750). How do you find such opportunities? As I'll show in subsequent chapters, success in the market is linked mostly to the price you pay. Buy a growth stock at an attractively low price with the intention of holding the stock indefinitely and your chances of making money are excellent. In fact, during the 1990s, investors generally had a greater than 80 percent chance of making money if they were willing to hold their stocks for more than a few years. Success rates dropped quickly for investors who weren't willing to hold their stocks as long. Likewise, batting averages dropped as prices rose. Paying 15 times earnings for a good company produced a high batting average in the 1990s. Paying 30 times earnings for the same company reduced the batting average significantly.

A 30-YEAR PLATE APPEARANCE

Just how long should an investor keep the bat on his or her shoulder while waiting for that right pitch? To be frank, you have the luxury of waiting indefinitely, Buffett says. If the stock never reaches the right price, don't swing. In fact, you really don't have to swing. You can take a pass on any stock and look at 10,000 other companies if you wish and invest in any of those, but make sure that those pitches are delivered at the right price. Buffett has studied nearly every large U.S. company over the past 40 years, some of them many times, and feels comfortable waiting for each of them to reach the right price. He has likely made mental notes of the maximum price he will pay for each one and can wait patiently—sometimes for years—before he swings the bat.

Buffett's patience serves as a great check and balance to his portfolio. It affords him time to conduct due diligence and prevents him from acting emotionally. By setting his price and rate-of-return targets years in advance, Buffett systemizes his stock-picking, making sure never to commit the types of "unforced errors" that plague most investors (see Part 4 on how Buffett avoids losses).

Recall that in 1998 he bought 129 million ounces of silver at prices at about $5 an ounce. When asked why he made such an unconventional investment, Buffett remarked that he had studied the silver market for more than 30 years and that the price of silver finally seemed attractive to him. Indeed, after adjusting for inflation, silver had just hit a 650-year bottom when Buffett made his play. Silver traded near its cheapest price since the 100 Years War between England and France. Talk about a long plate appearance! Buffett had his eye on Coca-Cola's stock for years before he finally began building positions in the late 1980s. One can only guess how long he had studied Capital Cities/ABC or Walt Disney before he took the plunge. Buffett had owned both stocks before and sold them but kept an eye on the companies for years (he watched Disney for three decades) before he was satisfied with the price again.

PUT YOUR FAVORITE STOCKS IN INVENTORY

Buffett, like many other great investors, tends to be very discriminating—he avoids the temptation of buying a stock that seems alluring at the moment. Any stock can potentially be a value if the price is right, but Buffett doesn't allow himself to be fooled into buying stocks just because they are undervalued.

Eventually, each of the 10,000 or so U.S.-listed stocks, including the Qualcomms and Oracles of the world, will trade at an undervalued price, but only a small fraction of the 10,000 companies offer compelling long-term growth prospects. Most have poor fundamentals or an erratic growth history and should be shunned. Many others will provide periodic trading gains and then languish when the investment community tires of their story and seeks short-term profits elsewhere. As you hone your stock-picking over time, you will eventually whittle down your short list of buy candidates to a few dozen. Then, you can zero in on this list and purchase them, one at a time, as their prices fall to favorable levels.

You should avoided the temptation of buying stocks simply because you have cash on hand, Buffett believes. More often than not, a heavy wallet invites mistakes. At the beginning of 1999, Buffett was holding more than $35 billion in cash and bonds in Berkshire Hathaway's investment portfolio. He was content to hold this great sum of money, which was equal to the total yearly output of dozens of smaller countries, indefinitely until he found suitably priced companies to purchase. In contrast, most investors feel a psychological need to put their loose change to work almost immediately. Rather than patiently wait for their favorite stocks to decline, they purchase shares of lower quality companies without spending time to study their fundamental properties.

Buffett avoids this trap by identifying all the stocks he wishes to own over next several years and buys them one at a time, but only when they fall to an attractive price. If the stocks do not fall to his desired price immediately, he takes no action. He knows that the odds favor a decline in price sooner or later. In the interim, he will devote his attention to other desirable companies whose prices may already have fallen to appealing levels.

To help you practice the taking-strike method, you should keep a list of your prospective stock picks. The list should include the maximum price you would willingly pay for the company today. Post this list (use the one presented in Table 8.1 as a template) in a convenient place and check it periodically.

The obvious advantage to warehousing stocks is that it forces you to be vigilant. Before buying, you must determine a reasonable value of the company, which means studying the enterprise. Putting some time into the valuation process will greatly decrease your chances of buying prematurely. Buying companies in this manner also allows you to build the portfolio you really want and prevents you from adding undesirable stocks simply because you have idle money. In addition, the method harnesses your impatience and—most important—ensures top performance because you will not overpay for any company.

TABLE 8.1 Buy points

Name	Price	Will Buy at	Comments
American Express	$135	$100	Not cheap enough
Amgen	$65	$45	Too expensive
Cisco Systems	$130	<$60	Too much downside risk
Federal Express	$33	<$40	Can buy now!
General Electric	$135	$135	Can buy now!
Intel	$115	$70	Too much price volatility
Nike	$39	$45	Can't pass up
Nucor	$45	<$50	Buy
Procter & Gamble	$65	<$85	Prepare to buy
SUN Microsystems	$95	$65	Too overvalued
Walt Disney	$38	$25	Worried about earnings

You should update your checklist periodically to make sure your target prices are reasonable. If a company's growth prospects dwindle, the original buying price you set may be too high. Conversely, if the company's fundamentals improve, the stock may not retreat to your buying level again. In such cases, you must reappraise the company to determine whether it is truly worth a higher share price.

The point is, when you don't have to invest, don't feel you *should* invest. Once you attain confidence in your own stock picking, you'll naturally make fewer and fewer buy-and-sell decisions. Being a successful investor gives you the same luxury as having a 20-game lead over the second place team in September. You can rest the bat on your shoulder and take strikes indefinitely because it won't change the outcome of the season.

One can see why Buffett embraces the "taking strikes" concept. Mathematically, it limits errors and improves the odds of profiting. Buffett is keenly aware that investing is an exercise in probabilities. If you bat .600 in the market—that is, you choose winners 60 percent of the time—you'll do reasonably well with your portfolio. Increase your odds to 75 percent and you'll do exceptionally well. Boost your chances even further—to 80 percent or more—and you'll enjoy astounding returns over time. Nothing increases your odds better than latching onto a good growth stock at a reasonable price.

Taking strikes also builds patience and temperance. Patience builds diligence and reasoning. Diligence ultimately provides strong results. While waiting for the right pitch, you force yourself to study companies carefully before buying. Instead of impulsively spending $5,000 on America Online at an uncomfortable price, you can spend time researching the company, reading financial statements, and learning about its industry, its valuation, and business model. You should not buy until you are completely comfortable with the price of America Online's stock and sufficiently knowledgeable about the company. The same holds for any company, be it Microsoft, an electric utility, John Deere, or a $1 biotechnology stock.

PART

ANALYZING COMPANIES LIKE BUFFETT

9

VALUING A BUSINESS

SSUME YOU OWN AN ARCADE in a small town and wish to sell it. To help determine the sale price, you apply several standards of value to calculate the arcade's true worth. The arcade takes in $100,000 a year in revenues. "I will consider any offer," you tell your friends. "But, I'm really at a loss in determining what the business is worth."

At first glance, you might conclude that the arcade should sell for $50,000, or one-half of the yearly revenues. By your best estimation, $50,000 is the *liquidation value* of the arcade, the amount of money the building, fixtures, vending machines, and electronic games would fetch if sold by auction. You would have to dismiss your conclusions, however, because they did not take into account the profit-making potential of the machines. A new owner would be willing to pay more than $50,000.

Next, you briefly consider selling the business for $30,000—the *replacement cost* of all the vending machines and games. "I would accept that price if the machines didn't generate revenues and earnings," you tell yourself. "But they do, and I'll need to be compensated for the machines' earnings power."

On second thought, you consider selling the arcade for $90,000, which happens to be the net worth, or *book value*, of the arcade (the assets of the business minus the short-term and long-term liabilities). This figure is considerably more than the $50,000 liquidation value. Intuitively, however, you come to realize that book value does not adequately represent the arcade's value. If the arcade generates high returns on assets and equity, then the business is worth far more than equity alone.

After further thought, you consider selling the arcade for $65,000—the *historical cost* of the arcade when you bought it 6 years before, but is that realistic? A $65,000 price tag assumes that the value of the business has not risen even a dollar in six years. "Why, my profitability has doubled since I bought it," you remind yourself. "That fact alone should make the business more valuable than what I paid for it."

After several more hours of thought, you come up with a sales price of $100,000—or one times the revenues. That seems reasonable, considering that a similar arcade in a neighboring city just sold for one times the yearly revenues. On paper, this seems like the best solution, but it, too, contains a flawed assumption. You assumed that *fair market value* is the proper way of appraising the arcade business. You must take into account the possibility that the price for the other arcade may have been arbitrary. One man's opinion about a business is not necessarily everyone's opinion.

As you study the deal more carefully, you begin to include more and more relevant variables into the sale price. "Perhaps I should ask for $600,000, or six times the arcade's yearly revenues," you tell yourself. After all, each vending machine and electronic game had 6 more years of useful life, over which time the business would generate $600,000 in revenues for the new owner. Ultimately, you talk yourself out of that, too. A buyer would be foolish to pay $600,000. The $100,000 the business generates in revenues will be worth less and less each year. If the new owner can get a 15 percent return on his investments, the present value of next years' revenues will be only $86,956. By the sixth year, the present value of $100,000 in revenues will be only $49,718.

Bewildered, you ask your neighbor, an accountant, for advice. "I think it's worth $215,000," she tells you.

"How did you derive that figure," you ask.

I projected that your machines will earn $100,000 in revenues in the first year and that revenues would grow 4 percent a year. Then I subtracted all the costs associated with operating the business—salaries, taxes, depreciation, raw materials, supplies, utilities, rent, maintenance, insurance, and debt. I figured these costs would also rise at 4 percent a year. I figured your business would earn an average of $35,000 a year after taxes over the next decade. After the tenth year, I assumed that after-tax profits would grow at 8 percent rates because your games will be fully depreciated by then and you will be able to milk them for extra cash flow.

Then I analyzed the variability of earnings and cash flow you have experienced the past 6 years. Because you have had some yearly fluctuations in performance, I have deemed your business to be more risky than other similar investments I have looked at. An investor will likely require a 15 percent yearly return to compensate them for the extra risk they take on. To get a 15 percent yearly return, I have determined that a buyer cannot pay more than $215,000. That is the *intrinsic value* of your arcade. Take it or leave it.

At this point, you are beside yourself and ready to deal.

How much is a business really worth? As the example above shows, the answer depends on how one frames the question. One buyer may be willing to pay $50,000 for a business, and another might be willing to spend $250,000. On Wall Street, the same subjectivity prevails. One buyer may be willing to pay $50 for a share of stock, and another might be willing to spend $150 for a share of the same company. Obviously, both investors can't be right, although both will probably insist they are. It's this subjective interplay of price and value that makes investing as much an art as a science. Even the most seasoned analysts and fund managers on Wall Street can differ widely in how to value, say, McDonald's, Microsoft, or Duke Energy. Some won't dare touch Microsoft at $100 a share; others would think nothing of paying $150. Many wouldn't touch a money-losing Internet company with a 10-*mile* pole; others gleefully place price targets of $200 per share on the same company.

Theoretically, disputes over value should be slight. If all investors relied on the same facts and looked at those facts objectively, their analyses should produce roughly similar values. Like the arcade, every asset possesses an inherent intrinsic value that reflects both the long-term earnings power of the enterprise and the risks of holding the investment over time. Intrinsic value is dynamic—a firm's value changes with fluctuations in interest rates, the U.S. dollar, corporate earnings and sales, debt levels, and the economy, to name just a few factors. But at any given point in time, an investor ought to be able to reasonably value a business given the information at hand.

Whether or not your assessment of value proves correct will be based on the assumptions you used. But by taking into account all the pertinent factors, as the arcade owner's neighbor did, you can quickly determine whether a stock you wish to buy is worth the price. That's your main goal when buying—to narrow the dartboard of choices and reduce the chances of making an error. Don't expect to pinpoint a company's value to the penny. At best, you might be able to calculate a company's value to within 20 percent of the firm's underlying value, but if you can come within 20 percent, you will have considerably narrowed your chances of making a wrong decision, namely overpaying for the target stock.

For centuries, valuing businesses for sale was completely subjective. Not until the twentieth century could buyers amass enough data on a company and its industry to construct a reasonable estimate of value. Even then, they often lacked the analytical tools to make a sincere judgment. Forecasting methods weren't perfected until the early part of the 1900s. In 1938, John Burr Williams postulated that a company is worth no less and no more than what owners can take out of it in earnings. You can determine what a company is worth by calculating what it can earn over its *eternal* lifetime and adjusting earnings for inflation and the time value of money. If you estimate that Intel will earn $175 billion over its expected life, after adjusting for inflation and your risk tolerance, then you should be willing to pay up to $175 billion to acquire the whole company.

If Intel had 1.75 billion shares outstanding, each share must reflect the appraised value of the whole and should sell for no more than $100. Similarly, if you reasonably estimate that Wells Fargo Bank can earn $50 billion in net income over its life, you should be willing to pay $50 billion to acquire all of its shares—no more and no less. That's Wells Fargo's *intrinsic* value—the fair price for a share of the company's forward earnings. If Wells Fargo had 400 million shares outstanding, then the intrinsic value of each share would be $125. That's the most an investor should want to pay for a piece of Wells Fargo.

"To appraise the investment value, it is necessary to estimate the future payments," Williams wrote. "The annuity of payments, adjusted for changes in the value of money itself, may then be discounted at the pure interest rate demanded by the investor."[1] To Williams, four concepts are vital to appraising a company:

1. You must see yourself as an owner of the business and appraise a public company as you would a private enterprise.
2. You must estimate the company's future earnings potential.
3. You must determine whether future earnings will be erratic or a steady "annuity."
4. You must adjust the value of future earnings by the time value of your money.

Why did Williams base his valuation model on earnings rather than on share price? Earnings are tangible. An owner can stuff the earnings into his pocket at the end of each year and reinvest them any way he sees fit. A stock's share price, in contrast, doesn't reflect a company's worth (although many academics would disagree). Stock prices reflect investors' shifting perceptions of worth. The market's perceptions can be greatly distorted by fear, greed, misinformation, panic, or unusual supply-and-demand disruptions at the stock exchange. Indeed, there is no guarantee that a stock will ever rise after you buy it. It may fall despite years of record sales and earnings. Similarly, stocks can rise dramatically even though a company's sales and earnings are in decline.

Over the long term, a stock should rise at about the rate the business rises in value. Over the short term, anything is possible. An investor must appraise a publicly traded company the same way a buyer of the arcade would, by the profits it can put in the owner's pocket. If you bought the arcade described earlier, you would base the purchase price on how much the business earns after taxes, or how much excess cash flow it can generate each year. Certainly, you would not base the purchase price on the Dow Jones Industrial Average. You wouldn't say to the seller, "the Dow fell 4 percent this week, so I must reduce our negotiated price by $10,000." The seller would laugh at you. Nor would you expect the seller the raise his asking price by $10,000 if the Dow Industrials rose significantly. The public's perception of economic value has no bearing on the price of the arcade. Movements in stock prices don't cause the intrinsic value of a business to fluctuate. They are the *effect* of what people perceive to be changes in intrinsic value. It's a mistake investors make every day in the market.

Seeing a stock as an ownership interest is the first step toward valuing the enterprise. Benjamin Graham taught Buffett to see stock quotes in this context. Rather than accept the market's latest quote, Graham wrote in 1934, you must ask yourself whether the value being attached to the company's stock is a proper one.

> It is an almost unbelievable fact that Wall Street never asks, "How much is the business selling for?" Yet this should be the first question in considering a stock purchase. If a business man were offered a 5% interest in some concern for $10,000, his first mental process would be to multiply the asked price of 20 and thus establish a proposed value of $200,000 for the entire undertaking. The rest of his calculation would turn about the question whether the business was a "good buy" at $200,000.[2]

Graham's approach rests on a simple supposition: You, as an investor, own the earnings. Your judgments of value must rest, first and foremost, on what the business can return to you in the form of year-ly net income, not on what the market says the shares are worth. The market price merely gives you a point of reference that allows you to determine whether the company is undervalued, correctly valued, or not worth its present price.

ESTIMATING EARNINGS

In determining what to pay for a stock, Warren Buffett first must place some sort of value on the firm. Without taking this first deliberate step, no investor, even Buffett, could determine whether the price paid was too high or too low. Lacking that information, neither Buffett nor you could determine whether or not the stock can deliver a good return because returns are linked inextricably to price, and price must be linked to value.

Recall that a firm's intrinsic value is simply the sum total of its future expected earnings, with each year's earnings "discounted" by the time value of money. Admittedly, this is the most difficult aspect to valuing a business. The best analysts on Wall Street, operating off million-dollar research budgets, have completely misjudged companies and entire industries on occasion. This is one reason why Warren Buffett loves companies that exhibit certainty. He can avoid the trap of trying to forecast the unknown, or clearing 7-foot hurdles, as he calls it. "Charlie [Munger] and I have not learned how to solve difficult business problems. What we have learned is to avoid them," he says. "To the extent that we have been successful, it is because we concentrated on identifying one-foot hurdles that we could step over rather than because we acquired any ability to clear seven-footers."[3]

Companies such as American Express, Wells Fargo, Gillette, and Coca-Cola have exhibited such steady earnings growth over long periods that Buffett can make quick, rational assumptions about their futures. Stability is an important determinant in valuing an enterprise. The more unstable a company's record, the more unstable will be its future. It follows that the company will bear higher risk and not be worth as much as a company exhibiting consistency. Unfortunately, 99 percent of the world's companies lack the consistency of an American Express. Lacking a stable track record from which to extrapolate, investors are often forced to make spurious assumptions about the future.

Where Buffett differs from other business analysts is that he assumes, correctly, that standards of valuation are universal. He is not swayed by new-era preachings that claim that technology businesses deserve to be treated differently, or more leniently, because of their novelty. All businesses must be judged ultimately by how they can convert sales to earnings and the annual rate at which they can increase earnings. An Internet company can be, and should be, valued by using the same yardsticks as a railroad, an electric utility, a software developer, a filmmaker, or a retailer. All of these enterprises are worth no more and no less than the present value of their expected earnings. If they are not expected to earn money sometime in the future, Buffett says, they have no value. "So valued, all businesses, from manufacturers of buggy whips to operators of cellular telephones, become economic equals."[4]

> Intelligent investing is not complex, though that is far from saying that it is easy. What an investor needs is the ability to correctly evaluate selected businesses. Note the word "selected": You don't have to be an expert on every company, or even many. You only have to be able to evaluate companies within your circle of competence. The size of that circle is not very important; knowing it boundaries, however, is vital.

Your goal as an investor should simply be to purchase, at a rational price, a part interest in an easily-understandable business whose earnings are virtually certain to be materially higher five, ten and twenty years from now. Over time, you will find only a few companies that meet these standards—so when you see one that qualifies, you should buy a meaningful amount of stock. You must also resist the temptation to stray from your guidelines: if you aren't willing to own a stock for ten years, don't even think about owning it for ten minutes.[5]

When estimating future earnings, investors should look first to the past. Research has shown that a company's growth record is, in most cases, the most reliable predictor of its future course. That notion holds whether you are studying a steadily growing company such as Merck or a highly leveraged cyclical mining company such as Inco. A company that has attained annual earnings growth of 15 percent in the past 25 years is not likely to post future results that deviate far from that level. That it could attain such a growth streak through recessions, wars, high interest-rate environments, and market crashes is testament to the company's ability to sustain itself going forward.

Unfortunately, a small fraction of the thousands of public companies have attained this degree of consistency. They include, among others, Abbott Laboratories, Merck & Co., Philip Morris, McDonald's, Coca-Cola, Genuine Parts, Emerson Electric, Automatic Data Processing, and Walgreen. If you were to plot these companies' yearly earnings back to the mid-1960s, you would find a nearly consistent trend—earnings growing at steady rates during both strong and weak economies. Companies able to post this level of consistency over long periods have a high probability of doing the same in the future. Not surprisingly, these types of companies also exhibit steady growth in yearly sales.

Mistakes come when investors attempt to extrapolate beyond a company's true growth rate and assume a company can suddenly depart from its past. A company that generated 10 percent yearly growth for the past 50 years won't suddenly generate 14 percent growth. In reality, you should expect the opposite: Sooner or later, the company's growth rate will ultimately slow as it becomes more difficult to locate new markets and find incremental sales. Nevertheless, you can feel confident that a steady, past growth rate can be duplicated. For example, consider a company that has attained earnings growth between 12 and 14 percent in each of the past 10 years. You can reasonably assume the company will attain the mean growth rate (13 percent) over the next 10 years. Thus, you can arrive at an intrinsic value rather quickly, because you can estimate the key component—future earnings—with a high level of confidence as shown in Table 9.1.

Notice that over the 20-year period, our hypothetical company experienced a more than 11-fold increase in its per-share earnings. If investors assigned the same P/E ratio to the stock in 2009 as in 1989, the stock will also rise more than 11-fold. Given the company's early

TABLE 9.1   Steady growth company.

	EPS	Growth Rate
1989	$3.00	
1990	$3.39	13%
1991	$3.80	12%
1992	$4.33	14%
1993	$4.89	13%
1994	$5.48	12%
1995	$6.24	14%
1996	$7.06	13%
1997	$7.90	12%
1998	$9.01	14%
1999	$10.18	13%
	Estimated Earnings	
2000	$11.50	
2001	$13.00	13%
2002	$14.69	13%
2003	$16.60	13%
2004	$18.76	13%
2005	$21.20	13%
2006	$23.95	13%
2007	$27.07	13%
2008	$30.59	13%
2009	$34.56	13%

consistency, chances are good that future earnings come close to your projections.

What about cyclical companies, whose earnings fluctuate with the business cycle? For the most part, Buffett avoids them, unless their stock is being mispriced in the marketplace and there exists some catalyst that helps ensure the shares rise in price. It's not that Buffett disavows cyclicals, for Berkshire Hathaway has owned a number of them in its portfolio through the years, including GATX, Exxon, Alcoa, Amerada Hess, Cleveland Cliffs Iron, General Dynamics, Handy & Harman, Kaiser Aluminum, and Woolworth, not to mention several banks. Buffett has generally purchased these companies as their industries were rebounding or after a bleak market period in which investors had pushed stock prices to historical lows.

The problem with cyclicals is that they display no long-term operating consistency. Alcoa may earn $6 per share when the economy peaks and less than $1 per share in a recession. Woolworth has shown an ability to go from the peak of prosperity to the abyss in a year's time. Because their operating histories are checkered, cyclical companies don't offer the predictability Buffett requires. That fact probably won't change any time soon. Unless mankind can rescind recessions or smooth out the roller-coaster trend of raw-materials prices, many companies are destined to post earnings that ebb and flow, with little long-term growth along the way. Stocks such as Sears Roebuck, Eastman Kodak, or General Motors are today posting per-share earnings that aren't much higher than those in the mid-1970s. Not coincidentally, their share prices have grown very little over the past quarter century.

Benjamin Graham taught Buffett to value cyclical companies based on their "average earnings," making sure never to pay a huge premium for any single year's earnings. By averaging a company's yearly earnings over, say, the past 7 to 10 years, you can also determine with reasonable accuracy average future earnings. Graham also suggested that an investor should never pay more than 16 times a company's average earnings. For example, a mining company such as Inco can post yearly earnings as high as $5 per share in strong economic times, but it can lose more than $1 per share in weaker times. Historically, Inco's annual earnings have averaged about $1 per share. Graham would have counseled investors not to pay more than $16 for a share of Inco, no matter the condition of the economy.

By averaging past earnings, you obtain a more realistic appraisal and avoid extrapolating unsustainable trends into the future. Too often, investors will chase a company such as Inco when it is earning $5 per share, forgetting that the odds favor a rapid decline in earnings at some point. Another advantage to using average earnings is that you do not have to forecast movements in the economy—the averaging method does that for you, as shown in Table 9.2.

TABLE 9.2   Average earnings.

	EPS
1990	$1.55
1991	$1.25
1992	–$0.40
1993	–$0.90
1994	$0.10
1995	$0.85
1996	$1.60
1997	$1.85
1998	$2.25
1999	$2.30
Average	$1.05
Estimated Earnings	
2000	$1.05
2001	$1.05
2002	$1.05
2003	$1.05
2004	$1.05
2005	$1.05
2006	$1.05
2007	$1.05
2008	$1.05
2009	$1.05

DISCOUNTING EARNINGS FOR RISK

The purpose of identifying and estimating earnings is to determine the level of *business risk* present. The more risky a company's earnings (that is, the more unpredictable they are), the less you should pay for the enterprise, holding other factors equal. A company's intrinsic value is inextricably linked to its operating consistency. A highly cyclical company with a history of fluctuating earnings does not appeal to Buffett as a long-term investment because it is so hard to value. Most analysts would have a difficult time trying to forecast earnings for the hypothetical company shown in Table 9.2. The company possesses far too much business risk.

The level of business risk is crucial to Buffett and to any appraiser because it ultimately determines the price you should be willing to pay for a stock. Once you determine a proper growth rate for the company's earnings, you must apply a *discounting factor* that compensates you for the time value of your money. For example, a certificate of deposit earns 5 percent a year, but, its real return, adjusted for inflation, is less. A 10-year AAA corporate bond may earn 6.5 percent, but when you adjust for inflation, default, and business risk, the real return is less. The same applies to common stocks, only in this case, the risk you bear is an *opportunity cost*, that is, what you gave up in returns elsewhere to buy this one stock.

To Buffett, valuing a company is no different than valuing a bond (a point raised in Chapter 15). When appraising a bond, you calculate each year's income stream, or "coupon," and discount each year's income by a rate that fully reflects all the risks and opportunity costs inherent in owning the instrument. The same applies to a business, except that the coupon is the company's yearly cash flow, or earnings. Because you, as a shareholder, have a claim on the company's earnings, just like a bond investor has a claim on the coupon, it follows that your valuation should be based on the stream of yearly coupons you expect from the company.

Opportunity costs represent what you could have earned on your money in a similar investment bearing the same risk. For example, say you had the opportunity to invest in a laundromat that offered a potential 15 percent yearly return, or you could buy shares of a railroad stock selling for $50. Both ventures carry equal risk. To determine the value of the railroad, you must estimate its future yearly earnings or cash flows and "discount" them by 15 percent each year. If the result yields a value greater than $50 per share, you should invest in the railroad. If you arrive at a value of less than $50 per share, the stock is overvalued and the laundromat offers the better investment.

To discount earnings, you divide each future year's earnings, or cash flow, by your chosen discount rate. For example, supposing the enterprise is expected to earn $10,000 a year over the next 5 years and the opportunity costs are 15 percent. Table 9.3 shows how you would discount the 5-year stream of earnings.

In the first year, you divided the $10,000 profit by 1.15 to reflect the 15 percent discount rate. The resulting figure, $8,696, shows what those profits really would be worth to you. In the second year, you have to discount $10,000 twice by a factor of 1.15. Thus, you divide $10,000 by the square of 1.15. In the third year, profits are divided by the cube of 1.15, and so on. As you can see, the value of $10,000 shrinks considerably over time as the discounting factor compounds. After 5 years, $10,000 in profits is worth only $4,972 in today's dollars, and the enterprise has generated a total of $33,522 in discounted profits for shareholders. This business has an intrinsic value of $33,522—the total amount that owners could expect to take out of the company.

The value of the enterprise is the sum total of all future discounted earnings. In the example presented in Table 9.3, we found the enterprise to be worth $33,522, assuming a 5-year operating life. If we assumed a 10-year life, the enterprise would be worth considerably more because the cumulative total of yearly profits would be greater.

TABLE 9.3   Discounting an enterprise's yearly income at a rate of 15 percent.

Year	Income	Divided By	Discounted Value
1	$10,000	1.15	$8,696
2	$10,000	$(1.15)^2$	$7,561
3	$10,000	$(1.15)^3$	$6,575
4	$10,000	$(1.15)^4$	$5,718
5	$10,000	$(1.15)^5$	$4,972
Total	**$50,000**		**$33,522**

Another way to look at the discount rate is to view it as a hurdle. It shows the most you should be willing to pay for a stock to get your expected return. Suppose you discount Microsoft's earnings at 15 percent a year and, by doing so, determine the stock to be worth $75 per share. In reality you have determined the risk-reward profile for Microsoft. For Microsoft to give you, at a minimum, a 15 percent yearly return, you cannot pay more than $75 for the stock. If you pay more than $75, you run the risk that it will return less than 15 percent. If you can obtain Microsoft for $50 per share, you have helped ensure a rate of return in excess of 15 percent.

What is the appropriate discount rate? Academics argue ceaselessly on this point. Valuation specialists have been known to apply discount rates as low as 3 percent to companies (which can yield a very high valuation) or as high as 25 percent to the same types of companies (which makes most stocks seem overvalued) depending on how they interpret their data. Because choosing a discount rate is the most critical step to valuation and the step most prone to errors in judgment, Buffett opts for the easiest solution. He discounts earnings at the same rate offered by long-term Treasury bonds, preferably 10-year instruments. This makes rational sense for three reasons:

1. Buffett views all stock investments in the context of bond yields. If he cannot obtain a potential rate of return on a stock that can beat a bond's yield, he will opt to buy bonds. Thus, his first-screen method of appraising a company is to set a hurdle rate that meets or exceeds that of government bond yields.

2. Buffett doesn't have to waste his efforts trying to determine an appropriate, unique discount rate for every stock he studies. Discount rates are dynamic and change constantly based on shifts in interest rates, earnings estimates, stock volatility, and the company's financial structure. An appraisal of, say, Sears Roebuck is relevant to the moment it is done. Two days later, it's possible that new information forces an analyst to change the discount rate and appraise the company differently. To avoid having to adapt his model constantly, Buffett keeps his appraisal parameters rather rigid.

3. Discount rates used by most money managers don't adequately define volatility, and these managers produce results that don't

accurately measure the company's standing. To derive a discount
rate, academics suggest that investors take into account the fluctuations of the company's stock as a proxy for risk. Higher
volatility translates into higher risk and requires you to use a
higher discount rate. Buffett defines risk differently. He focuses
on *business risk*, that is, the predictability of the company's yearly earnings coupons. A cyclical company such as DuPont with
highly variant yearly earnings bears much higher risk and
deserves a higher discount rate than a company such as
Walgreen, whose earnings have been growing at 12 to 14 percent
annual rates for years. If a company possesses no business risk,
that is, its yearly earnings are totally predictable, it is no more
risky in Buffett's eyes than a government bond and deserves the
same low discount rate. By focusing first on companies showing
little variation in their earnings growth rates, Buffett can justify
discounting earnings at Treasury bond rates. "Risk comes from
not knowing what you're doing," he says.

Buffett also differs measurably in how he applies the discount rate
calculation. Business analysts are taught to project a company's earnings out as far as possible, discounting each year's earnings along the
way. They then attach a "continuing value" that reflects the company's
assumed growth rate to eternity. Thus, a valuation for a company such
as McDonald's may resemble Table 9.4.

Buffett, from all accounts, doesn't rely on this formula. Instead,
he will use the company's growth rate and the discount rate to determine whether the stock is more or less attractive than a bond. In the
example shown in Table 9.4. Buffett will compare McDonald's 2000
per-share earnings ($2.50) as his point of comparison. To discount
those earnings into the future, Buffett divides $2.50 by the Treasury
bond rate—say, 6 percent—to obtain a discounted value of $40 ($2.50
/ 0.06 = $40). The $40 price becomes his hurdle rate. If McDonald's
earnings remained fixed at $2.50 per year perpetually, the company
becomes a proxy for a bond. Thus, if the stock trades for less than
$40, it offers a more attractive price than a bond because the earnings
yield (see Chapter 15) will be greater than a Treasury bond's 6-per-
cent yield. If McDonald's stock price were $50, the earnings yield
would be just 5 percent ($2.50 / $50 = 0.05), or less than the 6 per-

TABLE 9.4   Valuing McDonald's

EPS growth rate, first 10 years	12%
EPS growth rate, all years thereafter	5%
Discount rate	10%

	EPS	Divided By	Equals
2000	$2.50	1.1	$2.27
2001	$2.80	$(1.10)^2$	$2.31
2002	$3.14	$(1.10)^3$	$2.36
2003	$3.51	$(1.10)^4$	$2.40
2004	$3.93	$(1.10)^5$	$2.44
2005	$4.41	$(1.10)^6$	$2.49
2006	$4.93	$(1.10)^7$	$2.53
2007	$5.53	$(1.10)^8$	$2.58
2008	$6.19	$(1.10)^9$	$2.63
2009	$6.93	$(1.10)^{10}$	$2.67
First 10 years			**$24.68**
Plus continuing value $(\$7.76/0.05)/(1.10)^{10}$			**59.92**
Minus debt per share			$6.00
Equals intrinsic value			**$53.92**

cent coupon rate of the bond. Buffett would buy the bond rather than McDonald's stock.

McDonald's is not worth just $40 to Buffett; rather, $40 represents the bond-parity price, the level at which Buffett would be indifferent. Because there is a risk that McDonald's can't maintain its $2.50 per share in yearly earnings, Buffett may be inclined to buy the bond, whose coupon is fixed. The stock can be worth considerably more than $40 if McDonald's increases its yearly earnings. As future earnings rise, the yearly coupon yield rises relative to Buffett's original purchase price (explained in more detail in Chapter 15), making it more valuable to him over time. Thus, he will be willing to pay a premium to snare McDonald's rising coupons. In the example shown in Table 9.4, we assumed that McDonald's earnings would grow at 12 percent annual rate for 10 years. At those rates, McDonald's is a steal at $40 compared to a 6-percent bond because its future coupon keeps increasing, whereas the bond is fixed.

The chief paradox of valuation, especially for high-growth companies, is that it relies on the unreliable. To derive a value in the present tense, one must be able to predict the future or at least develop reasonable conclusions about a company's growth prospects. If you cannot predict how much money a company can earn 3 years, 5 years, or even 10 years down the road, your analysis will be fatally flawed. More than likely, you'll overestimate future growth and value the company too richly. Therein lies the problem, Buffett believes. Soaring valuations become self-fulfilling prophecies as investors come to believe that their favorite stocks can continue to accelerate their earnings or post a track record of growth that runs contrary to its own history. The only way to justify high earnings multiples in growth stocks is by assuming that these companies' future track records of performance will be rosy, perhaps even rosier than in the past.

However, the future is the least reliable determinant of value. To pay 100 times earnings for a stock such as Oracle, one must prove that it is worth 100 times its earnings. Oracle's past growth rate alone couldn't justify such a price. That leaves the investor the unenviable task of showing that Oracle's future earnings stream is worthy of a P/E of 100. Price-to-earnings ratios that high can be justified only if Oracle's sales and earnings grow at perhaps 30 to 40 percent a year for the next 10 to 15 years. What is the probability of that occurring? First, few companies in history have been able to grow at such outstanding rates for such a long period. Second, a company's future prospects are nebulous at best and almost impossible to predict with much certainty. Therefore, one must assign a low level of certainty to any predictions made about Oracle.

Indeed, as stock prices shot higher and higher in the late 1990s, analysts routinely avoided valuing companies in their research reports. They simply couldn't justify current prices with the types of analysis postulated by John Burr Williams and now taught in nearly every business school. Those who attempted to value high-growth companies were forced to assume that these companies could attain an ever-increasing market share and could post accelerating earnings growth. Most analysts resorted to nonsensical methods to justify their "buy" recommendations. If a company exceeded its quarterly earnings estimate, it was a worthy purchase, no matter how high the price. Likewise, high valuations were deemed practical if only because a competitor traded at a similar valuation. Some companies were touted simply for their "takeover premium," that is, what they *could* be worth *if* bought by another company.

To value a company based solely on the future necessarily forces you to make a series of assumptions that may prove terribly wrong. As Benjamin Graham put it:

> The more dependent the valuation becomes on anticipations of the future—and the less it is tied to a figure demonstrated by past performance—the more vulnerable it becomes to possible miscalculation and serious error. A large part of the value found for a high-multiplier growth stock is derived from future projects which differ markedly from past performance—except perhaps in the growth rate itself. Thus it may be said that security analysts today [Graham wrote this in 1973] find themselves compelled to become most mathematical and "scientific" in the very situations which lend themselves least auspiciously to exact treatment.[6]

Naturally, a company's intrinsic value is dynamic and constantly changes based on economic conditions, interest rates, debt levels, and changes in the marketplace. Intrinsic value changes from day to day for each company but rarely at the rate at which a company's stock price fluctuates. A stock can rise from $50 to $100 in a 3-month period even though the company's intrinsic value may adjust from $60 to $65. Likewise, a stock can fall from $20 to $5 at the same time that intrinsic value may rise from $5 to $6. Ultimately, price and value must walk in lockstep. Wide disparities between market price and company value cannot last indefinitely. If the market prices a stock at $100 even though the company is worth only $65, something must give—either intrinsic value accelerates or the stock plummets to $65 or less.

As Buffett sees it, intrinsic value is elusive—every asset possesses a true worth that can be discovered through rigorous analysis. Scrape away enough material from the surface and you can ferret out value, just as Michaelangelo extracted life forms he believed were already embedded in blocks of marble. But pinpointing intrinsic value is exceedingly difficult, excruciating, and ultimately subjective. If it were easy, Wall Street's top analysts would all be in agreement on the price America Online should sell for, but such consensus almost never occurs. For every analyst or fund manager who calls America Online a "bargain," you can find one, perhaps 10, analysts apt to sell their shares at the same price.

Benjamin Graham circumvented this dilemma by insisting on a "margin of safety." If you're not sure whether Wells Fargo is worth $80 a share or $100, give yourself a cushion. Wait until the price falls far below $80 before buying—just to be safe.

10

BOOK VALUE
Buffett's Favorite Yardstick of Growth

THE FIRST SENTENCE of Warren Buffett's yearly letters to Berkshire Hathaway shareholders speaks volumes about what really matters to the 69-year-old CEO and investment manager. In it, Buffett recites his track record for the year just ended, using the company's growth in the balance sheet as his yardstick:

> Our gain in net worth during 1998 was $25.9 billion, which increased the per-share book value of both our Class A and Class B stock by 48.3%. . . . Over the past 34 years (that is, since present management took over) per-share book value has grown from $19 to $37,801, a rate of 24.7% compounded annually.

Many CEOs begin their annual reports by applauding the company's growth in earnings or the fact that sales grew faster than the industry. Still others pat themselves on the back for effecting a large merger or taking steps to alter the company's financial structure. Some will even stoop to taking credit for a gargantuan leap in stock price the preceding year. Conversely, some will complain how an overseas recession or rising interest rates took a toll on profit margins and earnings. Buffett is one of the few who cites his balance sheet accomplishments and failures.

Buffett is keenly aware that book-value growth is probably the most important ingredient in rewarding shareholders over time. A company that can continually increase per-share book value at high rates necessarily must also increase earnings at high rates. Therefore, it follows that an increase in book value over time must lead to proportionate increases in intrinsic value and share price. "The percentage change in book value in any given year is likely to be reasonably close to that year's change in intrinsic value," he wrote to shareholders in 1996.[1]

Over long periods, in fact, there is a strong correlation between book-value growth and share-price growth. Companies such as U.S. Steel and General Motors have seen little tangible increase in per-share book value in the past 35 years. That's the chief reason their stocks have moved sideways for so long. General Motors' stock traded in 1999 for just $20 above its 1965 peak price. USX trades lower today than it did in the *1950s*! In contrast, Cisco Systems' per-share book value increased at 91 percent annual rates in the 1990s. Not coincidentally, Cisco's share price increased at 92 percent annual rates over the same period. Oracle's share price and book value grew at collaborative rates of 33 percent and 31 percent, respectively, during the 1990s. Many other companies—Clear Channel Communications, Adaptec, Compaq Computer, Countrywide Credit, Nike, Fannie Mae, and Novell—experienced nearly identical annualized increases in book value and share price in the 1990s. A number of higher-growth companies—Sun Microsystems, Solectron, Microsoft, Intel, Amgen, Harley-Davidson, Medtronic, Dell Computer, and EMC—experienced share-price growth far in excess of book-value growth (Figure 10.1).

The first to notice such a correlation was Edgar Lawrence Smith, whose 1924 book, *Common Stocks as Long-Term Investments,* has been a favorite of many famed money managers, including Buffett. Smith wrote that there is no better way to increase the value of a stock than to increase the value of the firm. Management could best accomplish this by continually increasing the company's retained earnings and book value. If management can take steps to successfully reinvest profits on shareholders' behalf, their efforts should be rewarded by an escalating share price.

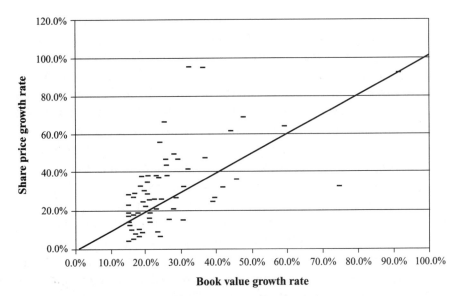

FIGURE 10.1   Book-value performance of high-growth S&P 500 companies between 1990 and 1999.

Smith's notion that value rises with retained earnings is central to Buffett's business judgment and analysis. As Buffett's annual report shows, he views growth in book value as the key to assessing whether management has successfully increased the firm's intrinsic value. To Buffett, short-term share-price movements are irrelevant in assessing managers' abilities. Theoretically, managements can do little to control the daily biases of the market. Momentum-oriented investors can become enthusiastic about a stock and cause it to double in price, a common occurrence in 1998 and 1999, regardless of the company's reported financial results. Conversely, these same investors can dump their shares and send the stock down 30 percent in a matter of hours, despite record earnings. In either situation, managers should not be held accountable—they should not take credit for the rally, and they should not try to react to the decline.

If shareholders act rationally and are not prone to sell in a panic or buy during a frenzy, stock-price movements should roughly approximate the growth in book value and intrinsic value. Historically, Berkshire Hathaway's stock has traded closer to the company's intrinsic value than perhaps 99 percent of U.S. listed companies. Buffett keeps speculative activities in the stock to a minimum by refusing to split the shares and by issuing annual reports that provide more than enough information for investors to value the company. Moreover, he spurns Wall Street's quarterly earnings game and won't comment on interim earnings or give guidance to analysts. "If we do that, we're on a different merry-go-round" that caters to short-term investors. "Shareholders choose us. We've never told anyone to buy or sell Berkshire."[2]

Lacking cooperation from management, analysts don't bother trying to predict Berkshire's earnings, which helps keep momentum-oriented institutions from wanting to dart in and out of the stock. Speculative rallies and panic-driven sell-offs are quite rare for Berkshire's stock, which is how Buffett wants it. "We do not want to maximize the price at which Berkshire shares trade. We wish instead for them to trade in a narrow range centered at intrinsic business value," he told shareholders in 1988. "Charlie and I are bothered as much by significant overvaluation as significant undervaluation. Both extremes will inevitably produce results for many shareholders that will differ sharply from Berkshire's business results."[3]

The relevant measure of performance, Buffett believes, is the company's growth in per-share book value. When assessing his own year-to-year performance as CEO, Buffett compares the growth of Berkshire Hathaway's book value during the year to the gains of the S&P 500 index (Table 10.1). If Berkshire's book value grows faster than the stock index, Buffett has done a better job than the index of delivering value to shareholders. And because book value is tangible, not fleeting like a stock price, it is the better barometer or performance. A stock can decline 30 percent in a month for little reason. A company's book value cannot, unless management takes drastic steps to restructure operations or has caused a huge accounting loss.

The scattergram in Figure 10.1 helps reinforce the interrelation between share price and book value. I compared the growth rate of per-share book value against the rate at which the stock climbed for the fastest growing S&P 500 companies in the 1990s. The trend line that runs through the diagram shows the expected result of the study. At any point on the trend line, the book value and stock price grew at the same rate. Companies above the line saw their stock rise faster than book value during the 1990s. Companies below the line saw their

TABLE 10.1 Per-share book-value growth of select S&P 500 companies for fiscal years 1989 to 1999.

	10-Year Growth Rate	1998–1999	1997–1998	1996–1997	1995–1996	1994–1995	1993–1994	1992–1993	1991–1992	1990–1991	1989–1990
Cisco Systems	90.8%	57.0%	60.0%	47.2%	71.5%	53.9%	71.4%	88.0%	82.9%	72.9%	543.0%
United Healthcare	74.3%	-7.5%	14.7%	13.7%	12.5%	159.9%	31.4%	87.0%	118.3%	77.8%	669.6%
Clear Channel Communications	59.0%	91.2%	166.7%	181.8%	24.9%	30.8%	176.3%	21.1%	613.5%	15.6%	-84.1%
Solectron	47.5%	105.0%	25.1%	20.3%	22.9%	35.05%	24.7%	103.2%	69.5%	25.7%	75.9%
Cabletron Systems	45.5%	-7.7%	-0.9%	28.5%	31.0%	38.5%	45.2%	40.9%	44.1%	96.8%	244.0%
Microsoft	43.7%	69.7%	55.7%	28.8%	29.5%	27.4%	33.2%	42.7%	55.9%	43.9%	57.0%
BMC Software	41.6%	53.3%	35.0%	42.0%	26.6%	24.7%	14.2%	55.0%	55.9%	39.7%	81.1%
Conseco	39.3%	-0.2%	20.1%	64.8%	96.8%	-38.5%	54.6%	41.3%	164.9%	35.7%	80.5%
Comcast Corp.	38.6%	186.6%	186.3%	75.2%	-155.8%	6.6%	-0.2%	339.9%	-986.8%	-178.6%	-112.9%
Comverse Technology	36.5%	-0.2%	21.1%	50.4%	10.6%	12.9%	134.1%	71.1%	25.3%	9.6%	124.3%
Dell Computer	36.0%	81.8%	28.1%	21.2%	56.4%	45.7%	-9.4%	30.8%	98.4%	36.4%	5.2%
EMC	32.1%	38.0%	39.2%	38.5%	35.8%	63.3%	118.6%	28.0%	12.2%	8.2%	-15.5%
Home Depot	31.7%	22.2%	17.3%	18.5%	37.7%	21.3%	20.6%	29.7%	107.6%	30.2%	31.2%
Office Depot	30.6%	-2.2%	14.2%	14.2%	34.5%	21.9%	37.8%	19.9%	48.7%	9.2%	157.4%
Oracle	30.6%	27.4%	25.4%	27.5%	48.3%	67.3%	39.3%	19.4%	23.0%	-14.4%	62.7%
Amgen	28.9%	21.5%	6.2%	23.9%	30.7%	10.3%	27.5%	70.1%	28.2%	74.8%	13.2%
Adaptec	28.2%	-5.6%	28.6%	27.8%	34.3%	26.4%	28.2%	57.5%	16.5%	15.0%	68.3%
Applied Materials	27.7%	33.6%	5.9%	21.8%	32.2%	73.2%	54.2%	22.9%	25.7%	690.0%	15.0%
Franklin Resources	27.7%	16.8%	23.2%	26.5%	21.6%	25.7%	30.0%	46.5%	28.6%	26.4%	33.3%
Viacom	26.4%	-5.9%	6.3%	11.9%	-0.2%	288.5%	21.0%	8.0%	69.6%	-0.2%	0.4%
Staples	25.8%	40.5%	22.6%	21.6%	41.7%	14.8%	11.7%	31.0%	71.8%	830.0%	7.2%
Intel	25.7%	8.5%	25.5%	41.2%	31.8%	25.1%	37.9%	20.1%	20.4%	30.2%	19.9%
Berkshire Hathaway	**29.0%**	**48.3%**	**34.1%**	**31.8%**	**43.1%**	**13.9%**	**14.3%**	**20.3%**	**39.6%**	**7.4%**	**44.4%**

stocks lag behind the change in book value. Each dash on the chart represents a fast-growing S&P 500 company, one whose book value grew at more than 15 percent annual rates during the decade.

By and large, the dashes seem to scatter around the trend line, indicating a rather close correlation between the two variables. Companies whose book value grew at, say, 20 percent annual rates experienced at least 20 percent annual increases in their stock prices. A few companies, such as Dell Computer, EMC, Microsoft, and Solectron (four of the highest dashes on the chart), experienced stock-price increases far in excess of the growth in book value. This means that shareholders were paying a premium for a manager's ability to increase the company's intrinsic value. Companies above the trend line were rewarded in the 1990s with a rising "price-to-book" ratio; that is, investors were willing to pay more than $1 for every $1 increase in shareholder's equity. The reason they were was that corporate returns on equity soared in the late 1990s to levels not seen since the late 1920s. Increased revenues, leaner cost structures, asset sales, restructurings, and stock buy-backs all fueled a significant jump in returns on equity; as a result, shareholders were willing to pay more for a $1 of equity than ever before.

Although Berkshire Hathaway's stock has fluctuated more closely around the company's true value, it has, nevertheless, been subject to periods of undervaluation and overvaluation. When Buffett took control of the company, book value was around $19 per share, more than Buffett believed the company was worth. Today, Buffett believes Berkshire is worth quite a bit more than its $37,987 per-share book value because of the strength of its core insurance businesses and its rock-solid balance sheet.

HOW TO GROW BOOK VALUE

Buffett's book-value scorecard clearly ranks him among the top CEOs of the twentieth century. Since he took control of Berkshire Hathaway in 1965, the company's per-share book value has grown from $19 to $37,987, a 24 percent compounded annual increase. No other public company attained such a growth record over that same period. How did Buffett do it? He owes much of the growth to the rising value of Berskhire's stock holdings, which are carried on its balance sheet at their current market value. By carefully selecting growth companies for Berkshire's portfolio and buying them at a sincere price, Buffett helped ensure the rapid growth in the company's intrinsic value and share price.

If the Coca-Cola stock Buffett holds rises $500 million in value, Berkshire's book value rises by $500 million as well. These days, it takes just a $2.50 per-share gain in Coca-Cola to add $500 million in value. A $500 million decline causes the opposite effect. Every $1 increase in Gillette's common stock causes a $96 million dollar increase in Berkshire's book value (Berkshire owns 96 million shares). The rise in Coke's stock since Buffett bought it in the 1980s has caused Berkshire's book value to rise by $10.3 billion, or nearly $6,800 per class-A share. Berkshire's holdings of *The Washington Post* have increased the company's book value by more than $900 million, or nearly $600 per share. The 20-year rally in GEICO's stock added $2.4 billion to Berkshire's book value and likely more since Berkshire took GEICO private in 1996.

Because few companies have the latitude, or the legal ability, to stuff their balance sheets with common stocks as Berkshire Hathaway has, they must increase book value the old-fashioned way, by expanding their profits, generating high returns on assets, and carefully acquiring companies that add economic value. When book value legitimately increases for these reasons, management increases intrinsic value and causes the stock price to rise. When earnings growth does not lead to growth in book value, something is amiss, as the following examples will show. Similarly, managers can take actions to raise book value in ways that don't lead to an increase in earnings and intrinsic value. When comparing a company's growth record, be mindful of the following facts.

A company can increase book value simply by issuing more shares. Internet companies have been notorious the past few years for issuing tens of millions of new shares to stave off bankruptcy. The money raised from these offerings has been used to pay bills and to expand their markets. Each new round of financing injects huge amounts of money into the balance sheet, giving the appearance that these companies have substantial net worth. In reality, many are still bleeding red ink because their business models are not profitable.

Companies can fabricate constantly higher book values by acquiring other companies.   Management consultant Peter Drucker once said "dealmaking is romantic (and) sexy. That's why you have deals that make no sense." It's entirely possible (in fact, likely these days) that an acquisition adds to book value immediately but detracts from a company's earnings progress and impedes its intrinsic value. Usually, this is the result of the acquiring company's paying too much for the target and not getting $1 in value for every $1 spent on the transaction. Unfortunately, the results of poorly arranged deals may not be evident for a few years, when management may be forced to take asset write-downs or sell the acquired entity at a loss. When the acquiring company's share price sells at a large premium to book value (as most do today), it can substantially increase book value by issuing shares to pay for the acquisition. Book value would increase even though no real intrinsic value is created at the outset.

Book value can be increased simply by letting profits sit in the bank, drawing interest.   If a company stuffs its yearly profits in a savings account paying 5 percent interest, its book value will continue to rise each year, holding other factors constant. Yet is management adding value by doing so? Interest income will certainly rise by larger dollar amounts each year due to compounding, and book value will grow each year (at decreasing rates), but return on equity will slowly fall until it reaches 5 percent, and intrinsic value will grow at slowing rates.

BOOK VALUE PAINTS A BETTER PICTURE THAN EARNINGS

Why does Buffett focus on book value as a yardstick of performance rather than on earnings or stock price? Buffett doesn't rely on stock-price movements because they are so fickle. He tells investors never to measure a CEO's performance based on how much the stock has gained from year to year. Over long periods, a stock will move in tandem with the company's performance. In the short term, there may be no correlation between the two.

Buffett dwells on book value because earnings are pliable; a CEO can manipulate them in dozens of ways that inflate a company's bottom line for several years. Using restructuring charges, asset sales, write-offs, employee layoffs, or "asset impairment" charges, U.S. corporations can generously, and legally, cook their books and give the impression they are functioning on all cylinders when, in fact, they could be throwing their profits down the drain. Take, for example, the giant telephone companies such as AT&T, BellSouth, Bell Atlantic, and SBC Communications. On paper, they posted gradually higher earnings almost every year during the 1990s. And investors, who were fixated on the bottom line, rewarded that performance with steadily rising stock prices. The three "Baby Bell" stocks, for example, quadrupled between 1986 and 1999.

But these gains were mostly hollow because they were manufactured by frequent asset write-offs, restructuring charges, and layoffs. Each time AT&T or BellSouth wrote off $1 billion for cost-cutting measures, they reduced their shareholders' equity by that same amount. AT&T took so many write-offs during the 1980s and early 1990s that the sum total of its accounting charges exceeded the earnings it reported. In other words, management created no real value.

If you had happened to be the sole owner of these companies, Buffett points out, you could not have kept the profits for yourself but would have had to reinvest the money every year just to maintain the business. "If you have owned 100 percent of a great many capital-intensive businesses during the decade, retained earnings that were credited fully and with painstaking precision to you under standard accounting methods would have resulted in minor to zero economic value,"[4] he says. The results of the Baby Bells' efforts can be seen in Table 10.2, which tracks the changes in earnings and book value for three companies over a 13-year period. It's immediately apparent that these enterprises did little to improve intrinsic value for shareholders. Bell Atlantic's per-share book value actually fell during that prolonged period, even though accounting earnings grew at 5.7 percent annual rates. BellSouth's book value grew at just 2 percent annual rates; SBC Communications' book value grew 1.7 percent a year. Nevertheless, their shares surged.

Understanding changes in book value is key to assessing whether a company is truly worth owning, in Buffett's view. The telephone companies, for example, have been unable to increase book value because their assets tend to depreciate rapidly, one of the reasons they take accounting charges. The equipment on which they spend billions of dollars soon wears out and becomes technologically obsolete. Telephone companies historically spend the bulk of their yearly net income replac-

TABLE 10.2   Was real value created?

	Bell Atlantic		BellSouth		SBC Communications	
	Book Value Per Share	EPS	Book Value Per Share	EPS	Book Value Per Share	EPS
1986	$10.45	$1.46	$5.90	$0.85	$6.52	$0.86
1987	$11.03	$1.56	$6.22	$0.87	$6.82	$0.87
1988	$11.64	$1.66	$6.38	$0.88	$7.08	$0.88
1989	$10.89	$1.67	$6.80	$0.87	$6.96	$0.91
1990	$11.36	$1.69	$6.63	$0.85	$7.15	$0.92
1991	$9.89	$1.71	$6.75	$0.78	$7.38	$0.96
1992	$9.00	$1.62	$6.99	$0.85	$7.76	$1.09
1993	$9.43	$1.70	$6.80	$0.90	$6.34	$1.20
1994	$6.97	$1.77	$7.24	$1.05	$6.86	$1.37
1995	$7.63	$1.94	$5.95	$1.12	$5.13	$1.55
1996	$8.48	$1.98	$6.68	$1.27	$5.70	$1.73
1997	$8.24	$2.48	$7.64	$1.41	$5.38	$1.84
1998	$8.39	$2.72	$8.26	$1.65	$6.52	$2.08
1999	$9.80	$3.00	$7.60	$2.00	$8.10	$2.15
Growth rate	**–0.5%**	**5.7%**	**2.0%**	**6.8%**	**1.7%**	**7.3%**

Source: ValueLine Investment Survey.

ing switches, networks, and other infrastructure rather than reinvesting the money to foster growth. Newer technologies emerge to replace the old and, in the process, render some employees useless. Occasionally, telephone companies must depreciate the value of equipment and facilities and announce layoffs. This is their way of acknowledging that the equipment they have bought with shareholders' money is not holding its value. Not surprisingly, Buffett has shunned phone stocks.

THOSE DISGRACEFUL ACCOUNTING CHARGES

Buffett is highly suspicious of accounting charges because they clear the deck of problems in one fell swoop and bury evidence of mismanagement that may persist for years longer. In his 1998 annual report to shareholders, Buffett labeled the growing use of accounting charges and write-offs a "disgrace" and accused CEOs of exploiting accounting rules to distort performance and prop their share price.

> A significant and growing number of otherwise high-grade managers…have come to the view that it's okay to manipulate earnings to satisfy what they believe are Wall Street's desires. Indeed, many CEOs think this kind of manipulation is not only okay, but actually their duty. These managers start with the assumption, all too common, that their job at all times is to encourage the highest stock price possible (a premise with which we adamantly disagree). To pump the price, they strive, admirably, for operational excellence. But when operations don't produce the result hoped for, these CEOs resort to unadmirable accounting stratagems that either manufacture the desired "earnings" or set the stage for them in the future.[5]

As an example, let's say that Boeing takes a $1 billion quarterly charge to cover cost-cutting moves it plans to take over the next several quarters. In subsequent periods, Boeing holds a "reserve" that is used up as it actually incurs $1 billion in costs. This mechanism allows Boeing to make some of its overhead costs invisible to the income statement, thereby lifting per-unit profits.

As Buffett noted in his annual report, this is like a golfer who shoots 90, yet records an artificially high score of 140, and creates a "bad-swing reserve" to take 50 strokes off subsequent rounds. Although the golfer's real scores might be 90, 115, 72, 80, 77, and 106, which reveals an erratic duffer, to be sure, he instead uses his reserve to records rounds of 140, 80, 80, 80, 80, and 80. The tournament's judges ignore the 140, because it did not really occur, and award a trophy for the player's low scores and consistency.

A company that takes a "big-bath" accounting charge is, in effect, doing the same. In the example above, Boeing can artificially inflate pre-tax earnings by $1 billion in subsequent years by lumping all those costs into the current year. Wall Street will applaud Boeing for cutting costs, ignore the destruction of book value that is occurring, and reward Boeing's future performance with a higher share price than it really deserves. Of course, none of the earnings scores that follow are realistic—the one "big-bath" quarter at Boeing was not as bleak as it seemed and the following periods were "juiced" by accounting gimmickry. Without pause, the bad swings were erased from the scorecard.

Dozens of companies such as Motorola, Boeing, Nike, and several large banks significantly dressed up their 1999 earnings by taking billions of dollars of charges in previous quarters. S&P 500 companies took "nonrecurring" charges equal to between 20 and 25 percent of their reported earnings in 1998. This was the highest level of accounting manipulation since 1991 to 1992, when many large companies were forced to take huge charges to write off the future costs of providing retirement benefits. Thus, for every $1 in per-share earnings these companies reported on their bottom line, upward of 25 cents may have been "cooked." In contrast, charges against earnings accounted for much less than 10 percent of reported earnings for most of the 1990s.

Motorola, in taking a nearly $2 billion charge in 1998, wiped out 13 percent of the book value it had built up for shareholders over several decades. Wall Street rewarded the behavior by pushing up Motorola's stock 200 percent over the next 15 months. "Unfortunately, CEOs who use variations for these scoring schemes in real life tend to become addicted to the games they're playing—after all, it's easier to fiddle with the scorecard than to spend hours on the practice tee—and never muster the will to give them up," Buffett says.[6]

Nonetheless, it's highly likely the bad swings will keep occurring. When a company takes a restructuring charge, management all but acknowledges that it mismanaged corporate assets or tolerated a bloated cost structure, neither of which should be rewarded. Suffice it to say, investors should scrutinize accounting charges very carefully. Given that nearly every major industrial company announces at least one charge per year, it's becoming nearly impossible to judge accurately their bottom lines. Upward of 40 percent of quarterly earnings statements are manipulated and cannot be taken at face value because of previous charges, mergers (another major source of dubious accounting, says Buffett), and asset sales.

Investors' tolerance of charges in the past few years seems to say a lot about our need for quick fixes. Market strategists adamantly defend today's stock prices on the presumption that corporate earnings can continue to grow strongly. However, if the earnings are false to begin with, this must eventually catch up to the bottom line, causing stock prices to land in the rough. "Berkshire Hathaway has kept entirely clear of these practices," Buffett says. "If we are to disappoint you, we would rather it be with our earnings than with our accounting."[7]

UNDERSTANDING
RETURN ON EQUITY

HE 1990S TRULY were an extraordinary period, for investors and corporate America alike. Not only were stock investors amply rewarded with gains averaging nearly 20 percent a year, but corporations displayed their best internal performance of the century. The two results, of course, went hand in hand. Had corporations not been so profitable and efficient, investors would not have been so willing to pay high premiums for their earnings. It's also doubtful that the stock market would have rallied by even a fraction of the amount it did.

Indeed, some of the weakest market periods during the twentieth century coincided with slowdowns in corporate earnings growth and dwindling returns on equity. Low returns on equity have tended to produce low stock valuations, and vice versa. As the decade closed it was apparent that U.S. corporations deserved valuations above historical norms simply because they generated returns on investors' capital far in excess of levels seen throughout the twentieth century.

The high returns on shareholders' equity (ROE) posted by the nation's largest companies in the 1990s were a major factor in the strong showing by the stock market. Those gains were made possible by some spectacular achievements: continued improved earnings, better internal productivity, a reduction of overhead costs, and strong top-line sales gains, to name just a few. The tools companies used to produce these results—restructurings, layoffs, share buybacks, and management's success in utilizing assets—fueled one of the most impressive improvements in ROE in history.

Returns on equity for the S&P 500 companies averaged between 10 and 15 percent for most of the twentieth century but rose sharply in the 1990s. By the end of the decade, corporate returns on equity jumped above 20 percent. That's a phenomenal rate considering that the 20-percent level was an *average* of 500 companies. Many technology companies consistently posted ROEs in excess of 30 percent in the 1990s, as did many consumer products companies such as Coca-Cola and Philip Morris and pharmaceutical companies such as Warner-Lambert, Abbott Laboratories, and Merck. Because companies produced such elevated returns on their shareholder's equity (or book value), investors were willing to bid their stocks to huge premiums to book value. Whereas stocks tended to trade for between one and two times shareholders' equity throughout most of the century, they traded, on average, for more than six times shareholders' equity by late 1999.

But even before 1999, Buffett began questioning whether corporations could continue to generate returns on equity in excess of 20 percent. If they couldn't, he said, stocks could not be worth as much as six times equity. History favored Buffett's assessment. American companies turned less charitable in the 1990s toward issuing dividends and retained an increasing share of their yearly earnings. In addition, the U.S. economy seemed capable of sustaining growth rates of just 3 to 4 percent each year. Under those conditions, it would be nearly impossible for corporations to continue generating 20 percent ROEs indefinitely. It would take yearly earnings growth in excess of 20 percent a year to produce 20 percent ROEs—an impossibility unless the economy were growing at rates far in excess of 10 percent a year.

Returns on equity play an important role in analyzing companies and putting stock prices and valuation levels in proper context. Most investors tend to concentrate on a company's past and projected earnings growth. Even top analysts tend to fixate on bottom-line growth as a yardstick for success. However, a company's ability to produce high returns on owners' capital is equally as crucial to long-term growth. In some respects, ROE may be a more important gauge of performance because companies can resort to any number of mechanisms to distort their accounting earnings. Warren Buffett expressed this sentiment more than 20 years ago:

> The primary test of managerial economic performance is the achievement of a high earnings rate on equity capital employed (without undue leverage, accounting gimmickry, etc.) and not the achievement of consistent gains in earnings per share. In our view, many businesses would be better understood by their shareholder owners, as well as the general public, if management and financial analysts modified the primary emphasis they place upon earnings per share, and upon yearly changes in that figure.[1]

CALCULATING RETURN ON EQUITY

Return on equity is the ratio of yearly profits to the average equity needed to produce those profits:

$$ROE = \frac{\text{net income}}{(\text{ending equity} + \text{beginning equity}) / 2}$$

If a company earned $10 million, started the year with $20 million in shareholders' equity, and finished with $30 million, its ROE would be roughly 40 percent.

$$ROE = \frac{\$10 \text{ million}}{(\$20 \text{ million} + \$30 \text{ million}) / 2}$$

$$= 0.40 \text{ or } 40\%$$

In this case, management obtained a 40 percent return on the resources shareholders provided them to generate profits. Shareholders' equity—assets minus liabilities—represents the investors' stake in the net assets of the company. It is the total of the capital contributed to the company and the company's earnings to date on that capital, minus a few extraordinary items. When a company posts a high ROE, it is efficiently using the assets shareholders have provided. It follows that the company is increasing its shareholders' equity at rapid rates, which should lead to equally rapid increases in stock price.

Buffett believes that companies that can generate and *sustain* high ROEs should be coveted because they are relatively rare. They should be purchased when their stocks trade at attractive levels relative to their earnings growth and ROEs because it is extremely difficult for companies to maintain high ROEs as they increase in size. In fact, many of the largest, most prosperous U.S. companies—General Electric, Microsoft, Wal-Mart, and Cisco Systems, among them—have displayed steadily decreasing ROEs over the years by virtue of their size. These companies found it easy to earn enough profits to record a 30 percent ROE when shareholders' equity was only $1 billion. Today, it's excruciatingly difficult for them to maintain 30 percent ROEs when equity is, say, $10 billion or $20 billion. In general, for a company to maintain a constant ROE, it needs to exhibit earnings growth in excess of ROE. That is, it takes more than 25 percent earnings growth to maintain a 25 percent ROE. This applies for companies that don't pay dividends (dividends reduce shareholders' equity and make it easier to post high ROEs). If management wishes to maintain a company's ROE at 25 percent, it must find ways to create more than $1 in shareholders' equity for every $1 of net income produced. Table 11.1 shows that Microsoft would have to

TABLE 11.1   ROE projections for Microsoft.

	Beginning Equity	Net Income	Ending Equity	ROE	Net Increased Growth
2000	$8,000	$2,825	$10,825	30.0%	
2001	$10,825	$3,825	$14,650	30.0%	35.4%
2002	$14,650	$5,179	$19,829	30.0%	35.4%
2003	$19,829	$7,012	$26,841	30.0%	35.4%
2004	$26,841	$9,491	$36,332	30.0%	35.4%
2005	$36,332	$12,847	$49,179	30.0%	35.4%
2006	$49,179	$17,390	$66,569	30.0%	35.4%
2007	$66,569	$23,540	$90,109	30.0%	35.4%
2008	$90,109	$31,865	$121,974	30.0%	35.4%
2009	$121,974	$43,130	$165,104	30.0%	35.4%
2010	$165,104	$58,380	$223,484	30.0%	35.4%

post average yearly earnings growth of 35.4 percent to maintain a 30 percent yearly ROE (Microsoft's average ROE during the 1990s). Beginning with $8 billion in shareholder's equity, Microsoft would have to increase equity to $223 billion by 2010 to attain those growth rates.

The key to understanding ROEs, Buffett notes, is to make sure that management maximizes use of the extra resources given it. Any company can continue to produce ever-larger earnings every year simply by depositing its income in the bank and letting it draw interest. If Microsoft shut down operations and reinvested yearly net income at 5 percent rates, earnings would continue growing, but ROE would plummet; as shown in Table 11.2.

By doing nothing, Microsoft's management could deliver 5 percent earnings growth for investors and brag of "record earnings" each year, but management would fail in its obligation to use corporate assets wisely. By 2010, Microsoft's ROE would fall to 10 percent. ROE would continue to fall for another 70 years until it reached 5 percent and parity with earnings growth. Indeed, when net income does not grow as fast as equity, management has not maximized use of the extra resources given it.

TABLE 11.2   Decreased ROE projections for Microsoft.

	Beginning Equity	Net Income	Ending Equity	ROE	Net Increased Growth
2000	$8,000	$2,825	$10,825	30.0%	
2001	$10,825	$2,966	$13,791	24.1%	5.0%
2002	$13,791	$3,115	$16,906	20.3%	5.0%
2003	$16,906	$3,270	$20,176	17.6%	5.0%
2004	$20,176	$3,434	$23,610	15.7%	5.0%
2005	$23,610	$3,605	$27,215	14.2%	5.0%
2006	$27,215	$3,786	$31,001	13.0%	5.0%
2007	$31,001	$3,975	$34,976	12.0%	5.0%
2008	$34,976	$4,174	$39,150	11.3%	5.0%
2009	$39,150	$4,383	$43,533	10.6%	5.0%
2010	$43,533	$4,602	$48,134	10.0%	5.0%

Most companies define "record earnings" as a new high in earnings per share. Since businesses customarily add from year to year to their equity share, we find nothing particularly noteworthy in a management performance combining, say, a 10 percent increase in equity capital and a 5 percent increase in earnings per share. After all, even a totally dormant savings account will produce steadily rising interest earnings each year because of compounding.[2]

Focusing on companies producing high ROEs, Buffett says, is a formula for success, because, as shown above, high ROEs must necessarily lead to strong earnings growth, a steady increase in shareholders' equity, a steady increase in the company's intrinsic value, and a steady increase in stock price. If Microsoft maintained a 30 percent ROE and the company never paid a dividend, its net income and shareholders' equity would rise at 35.4 percent annual rates. We also could expect the stock to rise at 35.4 percent annual rates over long periods. If the stock rose at the same rate that shareholders' equity increased, the stock would persistently trade at the same *price-to-book value ratio.*

Table 11.3 lists yearly ROE for 23 of the best-performing technology companies in the 1990s. These companies all boasted consistently high ROEs. Not surprisingly, their stocks rose at rates that greatly exceeded the market. If they could continue to maintain current ROEs, their stocks would more than likely outpace the general market in the coming years. Using the Microsoft example, you can try to project each of the 23 companies' beginning and ending equity and net income growth for the next 10 years and estimate how fast their stocks might rise. Several of the companies have displayed highly consistent ROEs, including First Data, Micros Systems, and Microsoft. An investor could project their future ROEs with a higher degree of confidence.

When evaluating two nearly identical companies, the one producing higher ROEs will almost always provide better returns for you over time. Five other points are worth considering when evaluating ROEs.

High returns on equity attained with little or no debt are better than similar returns attained with high debt.   The more debt added to the balance sheet, the lower the company's shareholders' equity when holding other factors constant because debt is subtracted from assets to calculate equity. Companies employing debt wisely can greatly improve ROE figures because net income is compared against a rela-

TABLE 11.3 Yearly returns on equity—technology stocks.

| | | | | | | | | | | | | ROE | |
	1989	1990	1991	1992	1993	1994	1995	1996	1997	1998	1999 (est.)	Average	Predictability
Semiconductor industry													
Altera	23.1%	21.9%	21.9%	12.1%	17.4%	9.2%	34.0%	29.5%	28.2%	17.5%	17.0%	21.1%	
Dallas Semiconductor	13.4%	14.2%	13.0%	13.7%	15.5%	15.3%	15.6%	14.1%	18.4%	13.4%	14.5%	14.6%	High
Intel	17.4%	18.1%	18.0%	19.8%	30.4%	27.7%	28.8%	30.6%	36.0%	26.4%	25.0%	25.3%	
Linear Technology	15.3%	16.4%	18.9%	20.3%	22.4%	25.4%	27.5%	30.4%	22.8%	23.9%	21.4%	22.2%	High
Maxim Integrated Products	19.2%	20.1%	19.8%	18.9%	17.8%	18.5%	21.8%	37.9%	29.4%	28.2%	22.3%	23.1%	High
Xilinx	26.8%	19.1%	19.6%	22.1%	23.9%	24.9%	32.8%	23.2%	23.0%	15.0%	20.0%	22.8%	High
Hardware													
American Power Conversion	39.9%	36.6%	35.7%	36.6%	36.8%	33.6%	24.0%	23.6%	23.3%	22.8%	23.0%	30.5%	
Cisco Systems	56.0%	20.1%	33.9%	34.4%	36.2%	37.1%	34.8%	32.4%	33.0%	26.4%	22.0%	33.3%	
Dell Computer	6.4%	24.3%	18.6%	27.5%	NMF	22.9%	28.0%	48.9%	73.0%	62.9%	56.5%	36.9%	
EMC Corp.	NMF	8.2%	10.4%	18.2%	30.3%	34.4%	32.0%	23.6%	22.7%	23.9%	23.0%	22.7%	
Micros Systems	11.8%	16.3%	17.1%	17.1%	19.2%	21.8%	21.7%	21.4%	22.8%	21.9%	22.9%	19.5%	High
Sun Microsystems	9.2%	12.0%	15.7%	11.7%	10.2%	12.0%	16.8%	23.2%	26.8%	25.8%	24.0%	17.0%	
Software													
Adobe Systems	57.3%	37.2%	28.2%	21.1%	19.5%	18.5%	19.4%	21.7%	26.1%	23.2%	37.0%	28.1%	
Autodesk	29.1%	26.0%	21.6%	18.5%	20.9%	22.6%	25.6%	18.4%	23.9%	22.3%	7.5%	21.5%	
BMC Software	35.3%	31.2%	32.5%	29.3%	33.9%	33.7%	33.5%	31.3%	30.6%	29.4%	27.5%	31.7%	High
BARRA		20.7%	17.9%	18.9%	14.8%	14.7%	22.0%	30.3%	25.2%	19.2%	22.0%	20.6%	High
Computer Associates	15.9%	14.6%	16.5%	23.3%	32.3%	37.1%	50.7%	64.1%	48.0%	47.7%	34.0%	34.9%	High
First Data Corp.			20.8%	17.8%	18.1%	20.5%	14.5%	17.2%	18.9%	18.6%	20.0%	18.5%	High
Microsoft	30.3%	30.4%	34.3%	32.3%	29.4%	27.2%	27.2%	31.5%	32.0%	28.8%	26.8%	30.0%	High
Oracle	35.5%	30.3%	NMF	14.1%	29.6%	38.3%	36.4%	34.0%	35.7%	32.3%	34.9%	32.1%	
Parametric Technology	29.6%	19.5%	24.6%	26.8%	29.2%	27.6%	26.6%	30.9%	34.0%	60.4%	34.4%	31.2%	
Sunguard Data Systems	14.7%	14.6%	13.2%	13.6%	11.3%	12.0%	12.2%	14.7%	15.5%	16.9%	17.0%	14.2%	High
Symantec	31.3%	33.3%	24.7%	NMF	13.4%	25.6%	NMF	19.8%	26.8%	24.7%	25.0%	25.0%	

Source: ValueLine Investment Survey.

141

tively small equity base. But higher debt is rarely desirable, particularly for a company with very cyclical earnings. Most of the technology companies listed in Table 11.3 attained their high ROEs with little or no long-term debt. Their balance sheets are strikingly clean—they are devoid of hard physical assets. Their only liabilities tend to be short-term bills that need paying.

High ROEs differ across industries.   Drug and consumer-products companies tend to possess higher than average debt levels and will tend to record higher ROEs. They can bear higher levels of debt because their sales are much more consistent and predictable than those of a cyclical manufacturer. Thus, they can safely use debt to expand rather than worry about having to meet interest payments during an economic slowdown. We can attribute the high ROEs of companies such as Philip Morris, PepsiCo, or Coca-Cola to the fact that debt typically equals 50 percent or more of equity.

Stock buybacks can result in high ROEs.   Companies can significantly manipulate ROEs through share buy backs and the granting of stock and options to employees. In the 1990s, dozens of top-notch companies bought back stock with the stated intention of improving earnings per share and ROEs. Schering-Plough, the pharmaceutical company, posted unusually high ROEs, in excess of 50 percent, during the late 1990s because it repurchased more than 150 million shares. Had Schering-Plough not been repurchasing stock, ROEs would have been between 20 and 30 percent.

ROEs follow the business cycle and ebb and flow with yearly increases in earnings.   If you see a cyclical company, such as J.C. Penney or Modine Manufacturing, posting high ROEs, beware. Those rates likely cannot be maintained and are probably the byproduct of a strong economy. Don't make the mistake of projecting future ROEs based on rates attained during economic peaks.

Beware of artificially inflated ROEs.   Companies can significantly manipulate ROEs with restructuring charges, assets sales, or one-time gains. Any event that decreases the company's assets, such as a restructuring charge or the sale of a division, also decreases the dollar value of shareholders' equity but gives an artificial boost to ROE. Companies that post high ROEs without relying on one-time gimmicks are truly rewarding shareholders.

USE ROE TO PREDICT FUTURE PERFORMANCE

There is some correlation between the trend of a company's ROE and the trend of future earnings, a point Warren Buffett has made on numerous occasions. If yearly ROEs are climbing, earnings also should be rising. If the ROE trend is steady, chances are that the earnings trend will likewise be steady and much more predictable. By focusing on ROE, an investor can more confidently make assumptions about future earnings. If you can estimate a company's future ROEs, then you can estimate the growth in shareholders' equity from one year to the next. And if you can estimate the growth in shareholders' equity, you can reasonably forecast the level of earnings needed to produce each year's ending equity. Using the Microsoft example, we were able to project a 30 percent yearly ROE through 2010. That allowed us to estimate Microsoft's year-end equity, which allowed us to calculate the net income needed to produce those figures. Using some simple calculations, we showed that Microsoft's earnings would grow at 35.4 percent annual rates.

Such assumptions rely, of course, on whether Microsoft can continue to produce 30 percent yearly ROEs. If the company's ROE falls short, you cannot expect 35.4 percent earnings growth. No company the size of Microsoft can continue to grow at 30 percent rates forever, a factor you must take into consideration when evaluating today's less-established technology companies. Table 11.3 listed companies that reported consistently high ROEs throughout the 1990s. The vast majority of technology companies, however, did not display that level of consistency. Even some of the companies on the list, including Oracle, Symantec, and Altera, experienced steep downturns in ROE for a year or so when their industries temporarily slumped.

Warren Buffett's portfolio of consumer-products and consumer cyclical stocks shows his preference for high, consistent ROEs. Coca-Cola and Gillette, for example, have steadily posted yearly ROEs between 30 and 50 percent, an astonishing record for companies that have existed for decades. Nearly all the other public companies in which Buffett owns large stakes boast average yearly ROEs of 15 percent or better. By virtue of their high internal returns and lower than average capital needs, these companies have managed to generate high returns on shareholders' money year after year and post earnings growth of between 10 and 20 percent. Table 11.4 presents the performance of several of Buffett's largest stock holdings during the 1990s.

TABLE 11.4 Yearly returns on equity—Warren Buffett's largest holdings.

	1989	1900	1991	1992	1993	1994	1995	1996	1997	1998	1999*	Average
Coca-Cola	34.2%	35.9%	36.6%	48.4%	47.7%	48.8%	55.4%	56.7%	56.5%	42.0%	39.0%	**45.6%**
American Express	20.3%	15.3%	14.3%	8.7%	13.4%	21.5%	19.0%	22.3%	20.8%	22.7%	21.5%	**18.2%**
Gillette	42.5%	42.5%	36.9%	34.3%	40.0%	34.6%	32.8%	27.4%	29.5%	31.4%	30.5%	**34.8%**
Freddie Mac	22.8%	19.4%	21.6%	17.4%	17.7%	19.0%	18.6%	18.5%	18.5%	15.7%	16.5%	**18.7%**
Wells Fargo	18.5%	17.1%	15.4%	16.9%	18.3%	20.8%	18.0%	19.0%	19.2%	14.0%	16.0%	**17.6%**
Walt Disney	23.1%	23.6%	16.4%	17.4%	17.7%	20.2%	20.2%	9.5%	10.9%	9.6%	7.0%	**16.0%**
Washington Post	21.0%	19.3%	12.8%	12.9%	12.9%	15.1%	16.1%	16.5%	19.8%	13.9%	13.5%	**15.8%**
General Dynamics	13.8%	NM	11.8%	7.2%	17.6%	16.9%	15.8%	15.8%	16.5%	16.4%	14.0%	**14.6%**

Estimated at the time of this writing.

145

BUFFETT'S MAGIC "15 PERCENT RULE"

ARREN BUFFETT KNOWS that when a company delivers consistent earnings growth of, say, 10 percent a year, one can also expect consistent share-price growth. In fact, for many companies, there is a nearly one-to-one correlation between long-term growth of earnings and growth in stock price. Companies that have increased earnings by 12 percent a year over long periods have likely seen their share price grow at annual rates close to 12 percent. "Put together a portfolio of companies whose aggregate earnings march upward over the years, and so also will the portfolio's market value," Buffett said in 1996.[1]

Whether you get exactly 12 percent or more or less than 12 percent depends on two factors: the ability of the company to maintain its consistency and the price you are willing to pay for that consistency. If the public grossly overprices a company's earnings stream, the rate of return you can expect will likely not exceed the growth in earnings. Consider what happened to Procter & Gamble in the 1970s. The stock traded for more than 50 times earnings before peaking in late 1972, although earnings were marching upward at only 12 percent annual rates. Procter & Gamble's stock fell steadily during the next several years despite the fact that earnings tripled. In essence, Procter & Gamble's P/E ratio contracted. By the early 1980s, Wall Street had hung such a low price tag on Procter & Gamble's earnings that its rate-of-return potential was unbelievably alluring. Procter & Gamble continued to produce stellar earnings during both bear and bull markets of the 1970s and 1980s, but the rate of return depended significantly on the price paid relative to earnings.

Before Buffett buys shares of a company, he makes sure the stock is capable of returning at least 15 percent a year for him over a long period. Fifteen percent is the minimum return Buffett requires to compensate him for inflation, the inevitable taxes from the sale of the investment, and the risk that taxes and inflation will rise in the ensuing years. For example, if a stock you bought delivers a 10 percent annual return, you'll likely lose 2 to 4 percent to inflation. You may lose 31 percent, possibly more, of your gains to federal taxes. In addition, you need a return well in excess of long-term Treasury bonds to compensate you for the extra risk you take on by owning stocks rather than bonds.

There's no disputing that getting 15 percent a year is *possible if you buy the right companies at the right prices*. Conversely, it's possible to buy into great businesses and get inferior returns because you chose the wrong price. It's possible, too, to enjoy extraordinary returns from good and poor businesses when buying at the right price. Most investors don't realize that price and returns are linked: The higher the price, the lower the rate of return potential, and vice versa. It's that simple. By late 1999, the rapid rise in stocks had severely diminished the long-term rate-of-return potential of many great companies.

To determine whether a stock can get him 15 percent, Buffett tries to estimate where a stock might trade in 10 years, based on its earnings growth rate and average P/E ratio, and compares it to today's price. If the future price, plus expected dividends, doesn't equate to a 15 percent annual return, Buffett is inclined to forget it.

For simplicity's sake, assume you had the opportunity to buy Hewlett-Packard at $120 per share (roughly its April 2000 price). Let's assume further that you want a minimum 15 percent long-term return on your money. In 10 years, Hewlett-Packard must trade for roughly $494 per share to get you a 15 percent annual return. The trick is to determine whether Hewlett-Packard can deliver a 15 percent return given the price ($120) you decided to pay. To make this calculation, you'll need to assemble a few variables:

*   *The current earnings of Hewlett-Packard.* As of this writing, the company's trailing 12-month earnings were $3.33 per share.
*   *The growth rate of Hewlett-Packard's earnings.* You can estimate future growth rates by applying past growth rates (which can be obtained from annual reports) or you can use the consensus growth-rate estimates of analysts, which are published on several financial websites, including Yahoo! (http://finance.yahoo.com).
*   *The average P/E ratio at which Hewlett-Packard's stock has traded.* It's important that you don't assume that current P/E ratios will endure over time. You must factor in high and low P/Es experienced during boom times and bust periods and during bull and bear markets. Because you can't predict the market's condition in 10 years, it's best to take an average P/E over long periods. Investors can obtain average P/Es from data in the *ValueLine Investment Survey.*
*   *The company's dividend payout ratio.* Dividends will be added to your total return over the 10-year period, so you must estimate how much a company such as Hewlett-Packard may pay in dividends in the future. If Hewlett-Packard has a history of returning 25 percent of its yearly earnings as dividends (you can calculate this average from *ValueLine*) then expect that 25 percent of the next decade's earnings will be returned to you.

RATE-OF-RETURN EXAMPLES

Hewlett-Packard.   Once you have this data, you can quickly calculate the rate-of-return potential for nearly any stock. The first example is Hewlett-Packard (Table 12.1), which traded at $120 in April 2000. Earnings were $3.33 per share and analysts were expecting earnings to increase at 15.2 percent annual rates. I assumed a 25 percent dividend payout ratio. If Hewlett-Packard can meet earnings estimates, 2009 earnings would be $13.71 per share. Multiplying $13.71 by Hewlett-Packard's average P/E ratio (17.7) yields a possible price of $242.63 per share. Add in the likely dividends of $19.66, and you have a possible total return of $262.29.

TABLE 12.1   Hewlett-Packard

Price	$120	Growth rate	15.2%
EPS	$3.33	Average P/E	17.7
P/E	36	Dividend payout	25%

Year	EPS
2000	$3.84
2001	$4.42
2002	$5.09
2003	$5.86
2004	$6.76
2005	$7.78
2006	$8.97
2007	$10.33
2008	$11.90
2009	$13.71
Total	**$81.98**

Price you need in 10 years to get 15%		$485.47
Expected 2010 price	$13.71 × 17.7 =	$242.63
plus expected dividends		$19.66
Total return		$262.29
Expected 10-year rate of return		**8.2%**
Highest price you can pay to get a 15% return		$64.83

At first blush, you might revel in getting $262.29 in 10 years, but, on an annualized basis, that translates into only an 8.1 percent return on your $120 investment. Because you were aiming for a 15 percent annual return, you must pass over Hewlett-Packard's stock. The only way Hewlett-Packard can give you a 15 percent return is if the stock price, plus dividends, can reach $485.47 in 10 years. There is, of course, one other way to meet your 15 percent annual hurdle rate— wait for Hewlett-Packard's stock to fall in price before buying. If your calculations project the 2009 price to be just $263.12, then the stock needs to trade for $64.83 today to meet your rate-of-return requirements. This will require a nearly 46 percent decline in price.

Intel.   Intel in the spring of 2000 rallied to more than 60 times earnings in the face of a strong growth phase for the semiconductor industry. As of this writing, Intel reached $135, or 64 times trailing earnings of $2.11 per share. Analysts expected Intel's earnings to increase at 19.3 percent annual rates going forward. Right away, that should make you suspicious (Table 12.2). The stock was trading at a P/E multiple of more than three times Intel's presumed growth rate. In addition, the P/E was three times that of Intel's historical average P/E (as obtained from *ValueLine*). Projecting out Intel's performance yields earnings of $12.32 in 2009. Multiplying $12.32 by the average P/E of 19 results in a projected stock price of roughly $234 in 10 years. Add in $3.79 in dividends and your total expected return would be about $238.

TABLE 12.2   Intel

Price	$135	Growth rate	19.3%
EPS	$2.11	Average P/E	19
P/E	$64	Dividend payout	6%

Year	EPS
2000	$2.52
2001	$3.00
2002	$3.58
2003	$4.27
2004	$5.10
2005	$6.08
2006	$7.26
2007	$8.66
2008	$10.33
2009	$12.32
Total	**$63.12**

Price you need in 10 years to get 15%		$546.15
Expected 2010 Price	$12.32 × 19 =	$234.12
plus expected dividends		$3.79
Total return		$237.91
Expected 10-year rate of return		**5.8%**
Highest price you can pay to get a 15% return		$58.81

Based on your $135 investment, Intel, assuming normal market conditions in 2009, would provide only a 5.8 percent annual total return, far below the 15 percent target rate you set. It's easy to see why Intel was potentially such a poor investment: You paid a price far in excess of the company's earnings and growth rate. To get a 15 percent return on $135, Intel must trade for about $546 in 10 years (before including $4 in dividends). That price is possible only if the market continues to grossly overvalue Intel's stock. As an alternative, you would wait for a decline in price before buying. Assuming Intel will give you a $238 return in 2009, today's price would have to be $58.81 to give you a 15 percent annual return. In other words, the stock would have to fall 56 percent before it met your target growth rate.

Coca-Cola.   Wonder why Coca-Cola's stock has treaded water for nearly 3 years now? In a word, it was so grossly overvalued relative to its expected earnings that it was doomed to provide negative returns from its 1998 peak. Table 12.3 summarizes Coke's rate-of-return potential with Buffett's 15 percent method. When Coke peaked at $89 in 1998, it traded for 68 times trailing earnings of 1.30 per share. At the time, analysts believed that Coca-Cola's earnings would increase at 14.5 percent annual rates. Based on *ValueLine* figures, Coca-Cola's stock has traded at an historical average P/E of 22. For this exercise, I presumed a 40 percent dividend payout ratio.

The numbers were compelling, but not for a buyer at $89. The stock would need to trade for almost $337 in 10 years (not counting dividends) to yield a 15 percent annual total return. Based on historical figures, however, Coke could be expected to reach just $110.77 by that time. Add in $11.80 in presumed dividends and Coke's total return would be only $122.57, a 3.3 percent annual return. For Coke to meet the 15 percent target, Coke would have needed to trade for $30, not for $89 as it did in mid-1998. It's no wonder Buffett did not add to his stake in Coca-Cola as it was plummeting in 1999 and early 2000. Based on his own criteria, the stock had not yet fallen enough to offer Buffett a suitable return. Any new money plowed into Coke at prices exceeding $29 might have generated an inferior rate of return.

Abbott Laboratories.   To the extent that Hewlett-Packard, Intel, and Coca-Cola were representative of market valuations in 1999 and early

TABLE 12.3   Coca-Cola

Price	$89	Growth rate	14.5%
EPS	$1.30	Average P/E	22
P/E	68	Dividend payout	40%

Year	EPS
2000	$1.49
2001	$1.70
2002	$1.95
2003	$2.23
2004	$2.56
2005	$2.93
2006	$3.35
2007	$3.84
2008	$4.40
2009	$5.03
Total	**$30.79**

Price you need in 10 years to get 15%		$360.05
Expected 2010 price	$5.03 × 22 =	$110.77
plus expected dividends		$11.80
Total return		$122.57
Expected 10-year rate of return		**3.3%**
Highest price you can pay to get a 15% return		$30.30

2000, there were few companies that could meet Buffett's 15 percent hurdle rate. The most high-flying stocks of the day—Intel, Dell Computer, EMC, Global Crossing, Cisco Systems, and Oracle, among them—offered such poor risk-and-reward potential that new investors could only get their gains off the backs of others. Chiefly, they had to depend on a continued harried market and high-velocity turnover to keep raising the prices of their favorite stocks and validate their purchases.

However, whereas a number of large-cap companies soared in price, others were falling to price levels that made them attractive for the first time in three to four years. When Abbott Laboratories fell to $29 in early 2000, it offered appealing potential. First, the P/E fell to

TABLE 12.4   Abbott Laboratories

Price	$29	Growth rate	12.3%
EPS	$1.67	Average P/E	18.2
P/E	17	Dividend payout	40%

Year	EPS
2000	$1.88
2001	$2.11
2002	$2.37
2003	$2.66
2004	$2.98
2005	$3.35
2006	$3.76
2007	$4.22
2008	$4.74
2009	$5.33
Total	**$33.39**

Price you need in 10 years to get 15%		$117.32
Expected 2010 price	$5.33 × 18.2 =	$96.96
plus expected dividends		$13.36
Total return		$110.32
Expected 10-year rate of return		**14.3%**
Highest price you can pay to get a 15% return		$27.27

about 17, below Abbott's historical average, and just 1.4 times its growth rate. Since the late 1950s, Abbott had posted one of the most remarkably consistent growth records of any large U.S. company, with a nearly impeccable record of posting yearly earnings gains of 12 to 15 percent. At the time, analysts were projecting a 12.3 percent growth rate for Abbott going forward. Dividends typically constitute 40 percent or more of Abbott earnings.

The rate-of-return picture is presented in Table 12.4. A buyer at $29 needed the stock to rise to $117 in 10 years to get a 15 percent return. The model predicted a return (price plus dividends) of nearly $110. Because Abbott traded near its historical average P/E, it needed merely to maintain its current growth rate to deliver total returns close to 15 percent. Using this model, Abbott still fell a little short of the 15 percent hurdle, but it came close enough to warrant investigation.

By applying Buffett's simple calculations, you would logically avoid most of today's popular stocks until they fell further in price. It's probably no coincidence that Buffett has not been a eager buyer of stocks over the past 18 months. As pointed out earlier, he hasn't even been willing to double up on Coca-Cola, Gillette, or Walt Disney during their recent falls from grace. He not only didn't buy more Disney, as it fell, he sold a portion, and perhaps all, of his holdings by the end of 1999.

This exercise hammers home an important point: *The price you pay determines your potential rate of return.* You will always get a higher rate of return buying General Electric at $80 rather than $120. When Coca-Cola peaked at around $89 in the middle of 1998, it traded for more than 60 times its yearly earnings. At the time, Coke was trumpeted by most brokerages and leading fund families as a can't-miss growth company. The trouble was, no one bothered to peg Coke's stock price to future performance. Even if Coke's sales didn't suffer, at a price of $89 the stock was destined, perhaps doomed, to provide negative returns to new investors.

When Walt Disney peaked in 1999 at $43, the expected rate of return over a 10-year period, using the models above, was just 0.5 percent a year. Given Disney's expected earnings, the stock would have to trade for $11 to secure a good chance of delivering 15 percent a year. If you wanted more than 15 percent, you would have had to buy below $11. Drug-store chain Walgreen offered the same abysmal return when it peaked in 1999 at around $45, or 48 times it earnings. By applying the formula, Walgreen would have had to fall to $12 before it offered a high probability of delivering a 15 percent long-term return. At $45, however, there was a distinct chance that Walgreen would deliver almost no gain over the next decade. Gillette would have had to fall another $16, to $22, before it cleared Buffett's hurdle rate. American Express would have to be cut in half.

The most predictable value destroyer among all the popular large-cap stocks was Charles Schwab, which, when it peaked at $52 (after splitting three-for-one), offered a nearly guaranteed negative return for new buyers. Given Schwab's presumed growth rates, an investor could not hope to get a long-term 15 percent return until the stock fell almost 80 percent, to around $11 after the split.

These figures are difficult to swallow but nonetheless telling. When you buy a stock that has already rallied several hundred percentage points in recent years, the rate-of-return potential going forward can be pathetically poor. Nevertheless, many investors assume that past results can be duplicated. They keep buying stocks such as Dell Computer or Qualcomm, thinking they can rise 60-fold again over the next 5 years. Nothing reduces the rate-of-return potential more than overpaying for a good company. As Peter Lynch once said, "it's a real tragedy when you buy a stock that's overpriced, the company is a big success, and still you don't make any money."

PUTTING GROWTH IN CONTEXT

WARREN BUFFETT WOULD BE the first to admit that no one, including himself, can accurately pinpoint the value on a company. Fifty different analysts, each studying the same data, could come up with 50 different valuations for an enterprise, even ones as predictable as Walgreen and Merck. Theoretically, their estimates should be reasonably close, but that rarely happens. A rigorous analysis of a company, for example, may involve more than 100 inputs and variables, many of which are based on the analyst's "hunch" or estimate. Changing one or two key assumptions, such as growth rate, market share, or interest rates, causes an abrupt change in value.

Buffett recognizes this inherent weakness in valuation and in its place, substitutes, a commonsense principle: "You'll know value when you see it." At the 1996 annual meeting he admitted that he rarely applies hard-core valuation techniques when researching stock ideas. "If [the value of the company] doesn't just scream out at you, it's too close."

Indeed, most investors have preconceived intuitive notions of value before they buy an asset. A home buyer, for example, may not be able to value exactly a 4,000 square-foot Georgian home in Beverly Hills, but at a price of $750,000, he knows it's a steal. Similarly, if American Airlines lowered the price of a round trip ticket from New York to Paris to $199, you'd recognize the value immediately. Likewise, you may be indifferent to Nike's stock at $50 per share, but you know that it's a bargain at $25.

Suffice it to say that by late 1999, Buffett could find few screaming values left. In his mind, Beverly Hills–like stocks were fully priced and offered sub-par rate-of-return potential.

Oftentimes, a little common sense will let you determine whether a stock is a screaming value or whether an outrageous price has robbed the stock of all future appeal. Chapters 11 and 12 discussed two methods for analyzing value. Both involved projecting future rates of return based on reasonable estimates of growth. In this chapter you can apply a quick Buffett-like analysis by dissecting the market's assumptions about a stock.

Textbooks tell us that a company cannot be worth more than what investors can take out of it in earnings. In other words, if a company is expected to earn a sum total of $10 billion in profits from here to eternity, after adjusting for inflation and risk, shareholders should be willing to pay $10 billion today to own all the stock. Thus, if Amazon.com's stock sells for $25 billion in the marketplace, as it did in early 2000, investors are betting that the *present value* of Amazon's future earnings will be $25 billion or more. If Amazon's earnings stream proves to be far greater than $25 billion, Amazon will be a screaming value. If Amazon can never earn $25 billion, its stock is grossly inflated.

The question to consider, then, is whether $25 billion is a reasonable number, or whether it grossly inflates the company's true potential. By using valuation templates found on the Internet, such as Stock Evaluator™, an intrinsic value calculator hosted by www.quicken.com, investors can quickly assess whether the market's current valuation of a stock is on target or off base. Stock Evaluator spits out a hypothetical value of a company based on growth rate assumptions users can plug in when they visit the site. It provides an effective tool for finding out the maximum you should be willing to pay for a company given the current level of interest rates, the company's past and future growth rates, and your rate-of-return criteria.

An investor can use intrinsic value tools such as Stock Evaluator in two ways. First, the real value of these tools is that they can provide a reasonable price range for buying. If data indicates a company is worth $50 per share, you should probably avoid the shares if they currently trade at $100. Conversely, if the stock trades for $25, extra investigation is warranted. Second, you can use Stock Evaluator to spot-check the market's current valuations, especially for popular technology stocks. Because it is difficult to estimate a company's future growth rate, Stock Evaluator allows you to take an indirect approach. You can start with the current stock price and determine the long-term growth rates necessary to justify that price. In other words, rather than question whether a stock is worth, say, $100 per share, try to determine what growth rate is necessary to make the company worth $100.

WELCOME TO THE UNITED STATES OF YAHOO! AND CISCO

In February 2000, I screened 200 of the largest U.S. companies to determine whether the market was correctly assessing these entities' future prospects. Using a discount rate of 15 percent, I asked Stock Evaluator's computer to determine what perpetual growth rate was needed to justify these companies' stock prices. The figures are presented in Table 13.1.

A few companies passed the test easily, indicating that they were worth at least the current value of their stock. Beleaguered tobacco maker Philip Morris, for example, would have to exhibit a meager 3 percent growth rate in earnings, perpetually, to justify its washed-out $21 share price. Philip Morris' earnings, by the way, had grown at 16 percent annual rates since the late-1950s. Therefore, the market was assuming that Philip Morris' historical growth rate would slow by more than 80 percent. The stock peaked at almost $57 in late 1998. In pushing the shares down to $21, the market was either correctly assessing Philip Morris' future or was selling shares in panic.

Abbott Laboratories, the pharmaceutical and medical-products company, would have to grow at 7 percent annual rates to justify its February 2000 price of $31. The stock slumped more than $20 at the end of 1999 over near-term concerns about its drug-development pipeline. Like Philip Morris, Abbott had exhibited 16 percent growth rates during

TABLE 13.1   Growth rates needed to support stock prices, February 2000.

	February 2000 Price	Growth Rate Needed to Justify Price	Yearly Sales ($mil)	2020 Sales ($mil)	2020 Sales as % of GDP
U.S. GDP		**3%**	**$8,900,000**	**$16,075,000**	
Yahoo!	360	63.0%	$589	$10,324,461	64%
Cisco Systems	124	39.0%	$12,154	$8,810,798	55%
Qualcomm	140	46.5%	$3,937	$8,164,280	51%
Wal-Mart	55	20.0%	$137,634	$5,276,557	33%
Motorola	155	29.0%	$30,931	$5,037,188	31%
JDS Uniphase	202	63.0%	$283	$4,960,649	31%
Amazon.com	75	48.5%	$1,639	$4,457,671	28%
General Electric	136	18.0%	$111,630	$3,057,884	19%
Sun Microsystems	83	29.5%	$11,726	$2,063,219	13%
Oracle	60	30.0%	$8,827	$1,677,568	10%
America Online	56	34.0%	$4,777	$1,664,375	10%
Walt Disney	38	22.0%	$23,402	$1,248,675	8%
Lucent Technologies	56	18.5%	$38,303	$1,141,826	7%
Microsoft	106	22.0%	$19,747	$1,053,653	7%
Dell Computer	38	21.5%	$18,243	$896,648	6%
Global Crossing	50	45.5%	$424	$766,700	5%
Intel	105	17.5%	$29,389	$739,507	5%
Charles Schwab	38	19.0%	$3,945	$127,934	1%
Qlogic	190	39.0%	$117	$84,817	1%
Polycom	65	22.5%	$200	$11,581	0%
CMGI	120	20.5%	$176	$7,333	0%
Hewlett-Packard	128	14.5%	$42,370	$635,577	4%
Procter & Gamble	94	14.0%	$38,125	$523,971	3%
Alcoa	38	10.5%	$16,323	$120,239	1%
Sears Roebuck	30	9.0%	$41,071	$230,179	1%
Abbott Laboratories	33	7.0%	$13,178	$50,995	0%
J.C. Penney	18	6.0%	$30,678	$98,389	1%
Mattel	11	5.0%	$4,782	$12,688	0%
Philip Morris	20	3.0%	$78,596	$141,953	1%

the 35 years leading up to 2000, more than twice the growth rate investors were estimating when they drove the stock to $31. Retailer J.C. Penney found itself in a similar pricing squeeze to begin the new millennium. Based on a price of $19 per share, the company would have to grow at modest 6 percent annual rates to justify its price. Since 1960, Penney's earnings had grown at compounded 9 percent rates.

But these stocks were the exception rather than the norm. Prices for many of Wall Street's favorite stocks assumed growth rates beyond belief. The most grossly overvalued stock was Yahoo!, the Internet portal that traded for $360 in February 2000. At the time, Yahoo! had about $600 million in sales and the company was beginning to report quarterly profits, but the market was valuing its stock at $90 billion, almost twice the market's appraisal of Philip Morris. Assuming a 15 percent discount rate, Yahoo! would have to increase its earnings at 63 percent yearly rates for the present value of earnings to equal $360 per share. That figure assumes that Yahoo! will maintain the same number of shares outstanding perpetually.

For argument's sake, assume that Yahoo! will increase sales at a 63 percent annual rate, a reasonable assumption because corporate earnings growth tends to track sales growth over long periods. By 2020, Yahoo's sales would be more than *$10.3 trillion*. Assuming the U.S. economy continued to grow at 3 percent rates, after inflation, Yahoo's 2020 sales would constitute 64 percent of the U.S. economy. If memories from biology class serve me right, not even paramecia multiply at that sustained rate.

Sounds far-fetched, doesn't it? But a buyer at $360 a share unwittingly placed his faith in Yahoo! attaining $10 trillion in sales some day. Any level short of $10 trillion guaranteed that the stock would eventually lose money if an investor held it long enough. After all, as Buffett has pointed out, a stock cannot be worth more than the earnings it will generate for investors.

At the height of folly, Berkshire Hathaway Vice-Chairman Charlie Munger once said, people will stretch their belief systems to justify virtually anything. "In self-appraisals of prospects and talents, it is the norm, as Demosthenes predicted, for people to be ridiculously overoptimistic," Munger told an assemblage of investment professionals in 1998. "For instance, a careful survey in Sweden showed that 90% of automobile drivers considered themselves above average. And people who are successfully selling something, as investment counselors do, make Swedish drivers sound like depressives. Virtually every investment expert's public assessment is that he is above average, no matter what is the evidence to the contrary."[1]

Cisco Systems emerged as the second most wildly appraised stock according to Stock Evaluator. To justify its $124 share price, Cisco's earnings would have to grow at 39 percent rates year after year. Many investors must have thought a 39 percent growth rate was feasible, despite the fact that no entity in world history has ever attained such a feat. Mathematics reaffirms that Cisco could not keep up the pace of growth. If Cisco's sales grew at 39 percent rates, for example, the company would boast $8.8 trillion in revenues by 2020. This would imply that Cisco's output would constitute 55 percent of the U.S. economy in 20 years. Combined, the sales of Cisco and Yahoo! would exceed total U.S. economic output by $3 trillion. Imagine an economy made up of just two companies!

Table 13.1 reaffirms that many of the most popular stocks of 1999 and 2000 traded at price levels that could never be justified by their present fundamentals. It also shows how investors had completely lost sight of reason in bidding up these stocks without regard to price and intrinsic value. To be sure, no one could be quite sure what a share of Cisco Systems was worth in early 2000. But in Buffett's eyes, the prices attached to these companies were senseless, no matter how fast they continued to grow.

Stock Evaluator showed that investors were presuming that Qualcomm, the telecommunications equipment company, would increase earnings at 46.5 percent annual rates when its stock traded at $140 in early 2000 (after adjusting for a four-for-one split). Interestingly, Qualcomm had lost about 30 percent of its value in the weeks before this chapter was completed, yet, even at a "reduced" price, Qualcomm was no bargain. Using the same projections made for Yahoo! and Cisco, we can see that the $140 price tag price implied $8.1 trillion in sales by 2020, fully 51 percent of the U.S. economy.

The price of Wal-Mart implied that the retailer would grow to be 33 percent of the economy by 2020. Motorola's hefty $155 price tag implied $5.0 trillion in sales by 2020. General Electric would have to attain almost $3.1 trillion in sales by 2020 to reconcile its $136 share price. America Online would be one-tenth the size of the economy, as would Oracle. Walt Disney would have to grow at 22 percent annual rates and constitute 8 percent of the economy. Amazon.com needed $4.5 trillion in sales to ensure that its $75 price in early 2000 was worth it.

Extended bull markets, you see, tend to obscure logic. Price and value become irrelevant and investors increasingly chase "momentum, " thinking that everything must continue to rally at rates beyond reason. Put these numbers in perspective. If the growth rates uncovered by Stock Evaluator were correct, the U.S. economy would one day consist of just a handful of companies, with Cisco, Yahoo!, and Qualcomm consuming the bulk of our economic output (keep in mind that a great deal of their sales come from overseas). Throw in Microsoft, Motorola, Oracle, and Intel for good measure, and there would be no need for any other employer to exist. We could all work for one of seven technology companies.

If you believed in such a rosy future, you were buying these stocks in early 2000. Buffett didn't and kept his money at bay. On this issue, Benjamin Graham articulated it best:

> This concept of an indefinitely favorable future is dangerous, even if it is true; because even if it is true you can easily overvalue the security, since you make it worth anything you want it to be worth. Beyond this, it is particularly dangerous too, because sometimes your ideas of the future turn out to be wrong. Then you have paid an awful lot for a future that isn't there. Your position then is pretty bad.

C H A P T E R

COVETING MOATS
The Quest for Stability

URING REGULAR VISITS to local McDonald's restaurants, I made it a point to read quota sheets the company posts on the back wall for its employees. The sheets totaled the number of orders placed for the day and itemized the number of orders that came from walk-in customers or from the drive-through line.

Over a year's time, I noticed that the numbers were remarkably consistent. With the exception of holidays or certain Sundays, roughly the same number of customers ate at these select franchises each and every day. Just as predictably, between 68 and 70 percent of each day's customers ordered their meals from the drive-through line. Consistency, you see, is the mother of capital gains.

Before its dining concept began losing its appeal in 1998, Cracker Barrel Old Country Store posted one of the more outstanding growth streaks in restaurant history. Earnings and sales grew at 15 to 20 percent rates for more than a decade, and the stock rallied in tandem with the growth in earnings. Consistency played a key part in Cracker Barrel's success. The average Cracker Barrel restaurant turned its table more than eight times a day, meaning that the average seat in each restaurant (there are usually 175 to 200 seats) was occupied by eight different people over a 24-hour period. No other restaurant turned its tables that often. As a result, the typical Cracker Barrel store could boast sales of between $3 million and $4 million a year—more than a McDonald's franchise attains. As a private investment, Cracker Barrel's stores were a gold mine. Because the company could seemingly count on eight table-turns a day, no matter the location of the restaurant, new Cracker Barrel locations could attain returns on an investment of 30 percent a year or more. That is, for every $1 million invested by Cracker Barrel building a new store, it could expect at least $300,000 in operating profits every year.

Warren Buffett craves consistency because consistency helps remove risk from a stock portfolio. Research has shown that a consistent track record of performance tends to result in consistent share-price growth. A company with a long track record of stable performance is much more likely to have a stable stock price than a company whose growth streak is pockmarked with sharp gains and losses. Inconsistent business performance is the bane of all investors. A company whose earnings growth fluctuates wildly over time, such as General Motors, Alcoa, Schlumberger, or Sears, will produce a trading pattern that resembles a roller coaster. During periods of rapid earnings growth, these stocks will ascend rapidly. Sooner or later, however, the company can no longer maintain its growth streak and investors flee in droves. What results is an up-and-down share price, where rallies of a year or two are followed by prolonged periods of decline.

These types of earnings fluctuations can sometimes produce no net results for investors over long periods. When Sears Roebuck's stock fell back to around $30 at the end of 1999, it traded for roughly where it did in 1972. By late 1999, General Motors traded about $15 above where it did in 1972. The decline in Schlumberger's stock in early 1999 brought the price back to the level it reached in 1980. Because these companies were never able to increase earnings consistently, their share prices bounced up and down in a large trading range for two decades or more. Along the way, they periodically fooled investors into thinking that consistent growth was at hand.

Buffett chooses companies with consistent track records so he can remove as much *stock-price risk* from investing as possible. He knows that if a company can deliver, say, 15 percent earnings growth year after year, the stock price will not show the level of intra-year gyrations common to most other stocks. Occasionally, these stocks will rally above the company's intrinsic value, in which case Buffett is likely to continue holding. On occasions when these stocks fall sharply in price, Buffett may go into the market and purchase more shares; in general, he will maintain his investment in the stock until it becomes apparent that the company's ascending legacy of earnings has been broken.

> The classic case is Coca-Cola, which went public in 1919....We have had depressions. We have had wars. Sugar prices have gone up and down. A million things have happened. How much more fruitful is it for us to think about whether the product is likely to sustain itself and its economics than to try to be questioning whether to jump in or out of the stock?[1]

Minimizing share-price fluctuations is crucial to great investors such as Buffett. Fluctuations cause most investors to rethink their strategy. Most investors are prone to fixate on share price as the true measure of a company's success but not on its income statements or balance sheet. To these investors, a rising price validates that the company is performing well. A declining price triggers the opposite reaction. The temptation is to sell a stock when it begins to decline or turn too volatile. Choosing stocks that won't exhibit much volatility removes the temptation to trade unnecessarily.

A proven track record is one important way to attain consistency. By focusing on companies with long and illustrious records of increasing net worth and value for shareholders, Buffett has managed to insulate his portfolio from broad fluctuations in value. The few occasions in recent years in which Buffett was susceptible to abnormal price fluctuations occurred when investors bid Buffett's stocks to unprecedented valuation levels. Coca-Cola traded at more than 60 times earnings at its 1998 peak, and Walt Disney and Gillette traded for more than 40 times earnings throughout 1998 and 1999. All three stocks, in retrospect, were destined (some say doomed) to give back a large portion of their previous gains and post inferior stock performance, but rarely has Buffett made the mistake of owning a company that simply did not perform to his, or the market's, expectations.

A company's track record can take a stock only so far, however. The second, equally important way to remove stock-price risk and avoid abnormal price fluctuations is to own companies whose *future* can be quantified and predicted with some degree of accuracy. Because stock prices reflect an enterprise's *forward* earnings more than past earnings, it's important for investors to fixate first on companies able to project and carry their consistency into the next decade and beyond.

Understandably, chasing posterity creates a conundrum for investors. Very little can be said of the future. The majority of U.S. companies and industries, in fact, will undergo major transformations over the next 10 to 15 years. Investors don't know, for example, how the economy will perform going forward, whether interest rates will rise or fall, or whether the U.S. dollar will catapult higher or collapse. Moreover, we cannot predict how the pace of technological and productivity change will alter the business climate. Today's popular industries may wither away within five years. The very technology stocks that Wall Street praises today as "no-brainers" may find their technological advantages overshadowed by new, yet unknown competition. The current pace of technological change and the pace of productivity improvements is outstripping investors' abilities to analyze that change. Investors who are not mindful of this sobering certainty will find themselves misled into poor choices.

> We think [new technology] is very beneficial from a societal standpoint. Our own emphasis is on trying to find businesses that are predictable in a general way as to where they'll be in 10 or 15 or 20 years. That means we look for businesses that in general aren't going to be susceptible to very much change. We view change as more of a threat investment-wise than an opportunity. That's quite contrary to the way most people are looking at equities right now. With a few exceptions, we do not get enthused about change as a way to make a lot of money. We're looking for the absence of change to protect ways that are already making a lot of money and allow them to make even more in the future.[2]

Older investors certainly can recall the mid-1980s, when the hottest technology stocks were hardware and software companies such as Coleco, Kaypro, Corona Computers, GRiD Systems, Mohawk Data Sciences, and Commodore. All were touted by the financial industry as sure-fire ways to play the almost-certain boom in personal computing. All fizzled faster than a bottle of warm diet root beer. At their peaks, they traded at P/E ratios in excess of 100.

By mid-1999, Warren Buffett came under intense criticism in the media for maintaining a stodgy posture and avoiding the high-flying Nasdaq stocks that had provided investors extraordinary gains the previous 2 years. His purposeful avoidance of technology stocks in particular was derided in financial magazines and on chatrooms. "When is he going to wake up and smell the roses?" one hedge fund manager told me over the phone. "He's got to get with the program because technology is the place to be." Internet chatrooms were equally harsh on Buffett's buying habits. "His days are over—he belongs in the previous century," said an anonymous posting on Yahoo!.

Buffett held his ground throughout, pointing out that, although technology was consuming an ever larger slice of the American economy, the group still seemed to lack the predictability that prudent investors require. If a company's future cannot be predicted, Buffett said, it cannot be valued. If a company cannot be valued, there is no indisputable way of ensuring a positive return on one's investment. A company whose future is totally unpredictable may be worth $200 per share, or just $2. No one will know until after the fact whether the stock's current price was on the mark or a grave error. "I'd probably take an Internet company and [ask students], 'How much is it worth?' And anybody that gave me an answer, I'd flunk," Buffett told shareholders in 1998.[3]

WHAT IS PREDICTABLE THESE DAYS?

As the millennium began, investors were bidding technology stocks to outlandish levels on the premise that their recent earnings growth rates could be duplicated indefinitely. In retrospect, investors might have used the passing of the century as their cue to pause and assess whether anything was as certain and stable as stock prices suggested.

WHAT IF...

1. Yahoo! and Amazon.com, two of the most widely held Internet stocks, never turn a significant profit? After all, they are just distributors of merchandise, and profit margins for distributors tend to be razor thin at best. Because Yahoo! and Amazon.com had yet to generate substantial profits by the year 2000, a prudent

investor could reasonably have concluded that these companies might never produce a significant profit for investors. At the very least, an investor should factor in the possibility of continued losses when valuing their shares.

2. The hardware that drives the Internet changes and replaces the technology offered by Cisco Systems? Would Cisco really be worth 140 times earnings, the price that new investors were forced to pay in early 2000?

3. A new form of microprocessor comes along and completely replaces the Pentium microchips that have made Intel the world's dominant chip supplier? As quickly as Intel established itself as the dominant components manufacturer, another rival technology could spring up and render the Pentium family moot.

4. A recession occurs again and causes the earnings of high-flying retailers such as Wal-Mart and Home Depot to plummet? By late 1999, prices of certain retailers had soared well beyond 40 times earnings, as if these companies were permanently insulated from economic weakness. Despite the fact that these companies were no less sensitive to the business cycle than in the past, investors wanted to believe that their peak growth rates were sustainable.

5. New technology renders the cable and wireless business obsolete? What will shares of Qualcomm, JDS Uniphase, Scientific-Atlanta, and others be worth then?

6. Personal computers become commodities, are given away for free by phone companies, and no longer house an operating system? What will become of the fortunes of Dell, Compaq, and Microsoft? Could they sustain a price of 70 times earnings, as they had in 1999?

Can these events occur? Maybe not, but you'd be silly to assume they couldn't, Buffett would say. History is littered with industries that were supplanted by an innovation that shook a complacent market. Even Bill Gates, Microsoft's founder and chairman, has acknowledged that the technology field has been changing so fast that virtually nothing is certain. Like a winding mountain road, the technology sector can derail any investor who chooses to think linearly. "I think the [earnings] multiples of technology stocks *should* be quite a bit lower than the multiples of stocks such as Coke and Gillette because we are subject to complete changes in the rules," Gates told business students at the University of Washington at Seattle in 1998.

As much as we would like to believe that Microsoft, Cisco Systems, Oracle, Northern Telecom, Lucent Technologies, and others will remain highly profitable for years to come, there exists some risk that they won't because of the quickening pace of innovation. The problem is we can't see that far into the future with technology, a point Buffett raises frequently. Oracle began 2000 priced at more than 110 times its earnings. That price could be justified only if Oracle's present growth rates continue for well more than a decade. As for Yahoo!, there really was no academic justification for the prodigious price at which it traded.

So, if the new paradigms on which today's stock prices are based eventually prove faulty, is there anything on which investors can truly rely? Yes, says Buffett. A number of companies have grown their core businesses for decades with few cyclical interruptions. Given the steadiness of their businesses, we can reasonably assume these companies will function similarly for the next several decades and continue to provide steady gains for investors. Coca-Cola has been in the same business, selling syrup, for more than 100 years. Its core strategy will likely never change. Close your eyes for a decade and you would awake to find Coke doing the same thing it's doing now—only its sales and profits would likely be much greater.

> Let's say you were going away for 10 years and you wanted to make one investment and you know everything you know now, and couldn't change it while you're gone. What would you think about? I (would want) certainty, where I knew the market was going to continue to grow, where I knew the leader was going to continue to be the leader— I mean worldwide—and where I knew that were would be big unit growth. I just don't know anything like Coke.[4]

One could say the same for Gillette, Anheuser Busch, Johnson & Johnson, Harley-Davidson, Tootsie Roll Industries, Wendy's International, Automatic Data Processing, Genuine Parts, Fannie Mae, William Wrigley, and Hershey. Granted, these companies lack the sex appeal of Qualcomm, Global Crossing, and JDS Uniphase, three of the hottest stocks in 1999, but they continue to deliver the goods for shareholders year in and year out. Fannie Mae has developed a wonderful business model that allows it to produce earnings growth between 12 and 17 percent year after year, no matter the direction of interest rates. Investors in Fannie Mae can look forward to consistent share-price increases as a result. Indeed, Fannie Mae was one of the least volatile large-cap stocks during the 1990s.

It is also doubtful that investors will witness any strategic changes at companies such as McDonald's. If the quota sheets at the restaurants are an indication, investors can count on consistent rates of return on their investment. Five years from now, odds are good that the same number of patrons will walk into a McDonald's restaurant every day and that a high percentage of them will use the drive-through window. In contrast, does any Internet stock currently offer even a fraction of the consistency and cash-generating potential McDonald's does? Will any in the future? If not, why have Internet stocks such as Yahoo! been priced in the market at twice the value of McDonald's? Can anyone say with any certainty what Cisco Systems or Sun Microsystems will look like in 15 years? Will they be in the same lines of business, or will their business models change radically?

If you can't envision these companies' futures, make sure you don't ever pay a price that anticipates that far ahead. Stock prices are supposed to reflect all the earnings a company can potentially generate for investors going forward, but if earnings cannot be predicted with much certainty, investors have assumed too much share-price risk. Companies trading at more than 100 times earnings today must be capable of generating 30 to 40 percent sales and earnings growth year after year—a mathematical impossibility.

Investors sometimes extend their faith to extremes. We hope that our best investments are immutable, that their hot growth streak can continue forever. The truth is that few—very few—companies ever enjoy such luxury. Even Microsoft's and Wal-Mart's growth rates have slowed considerably in recent years, as will the growth rates of today's highly touted technology stocks. Some will experience slowing growth much earlier than others.

Think back through the 1990s and you'll recall a lot of "sure-thing" trends that fizzled out because investors wrongly assumed the good times would last. Oil stocks were supposed to provide great returns because of constantly increasing demand for crude. Waste-hauling stocks were supposed to take advantage of a growing population and a critical shortage of landfill space. Microbrewers and golf-club manufacturers were supposed to be "wealth-effect" players. Medical-device stocks were supposed to rise indefinitely because of the growing worldwide need for health care. Health maintenance organization stocks were supposed to be a great way to make the shift into managed care.

Wasn't Boston Chicken supposed to be the dominant restaurant for families? Boston Chicken declared bankruptcy in 1999, just 18 months after the stock peaked at around $40 per share. Weren't PC components manufacturers Iomega and Western Digital supposed to have shared in the phenomenal growth of computers? Both were eaten alive by pricing pressures no one predicted. It's not easy, Buffett says, for businesses to grow unimpeded:

> There are people that are looking at what you're doing every day and trying to figure out a way to do it better, underprice you, bring out a better product or whatever it may be. A few companies make it. But here in the U.S., after all of these decades and decades and decades of wonderful economic development, we still only have about 400 companies that have hit the [profitability] level that would be required of a company with a market cap of $3 billion. And yet some companies are getting $3 billion of market cap virtually the day they come out. You want to think about the math of all this.[5]

The media like to poke fun at Buffett for missing the surge in technology stocks. Forgotten among their excoriations is the fact that Buffett never seems to put his money into losing stocks such as Boston Chicken either. He may have missed the ascent of Microsoft and Intel, but he also avoided countless other technology companies, such as Iomega and Western Digital, that spent their potential as quickly as a Fourth of July sparkler. Unfortunately, in the business world, sparklers greatly outnumber superstars. Blindly putting money into technology stocks is a sure-fire way to guarantee mediocre returns because few will attain the greatness of a Microsoft—just ask all the investors in computer stocks in the 1980s. If you had purchased equal amounts of stock of all the computer hardware companies that traded in the mid-1980s, you would have barely broken even as the century ended. The gains in Apple Computer, Compaq, and a few others barely offset the oftentimes horrific losses sustained by the rest.

Lacking any knowledge of the future, a mid-1980s investor had to pick and choose winners from a crowded field of "sure things," and most lost.

15

COMPARING STOCKS
TO BONDS

ONEY MANAGER AND AUTHOR Gerald Loeb once remarked that the worst way to combat inflation is to buy assets as a "supposed hedge" at an inflated price. If you haven't accurately priced in the risk of inflation or the possible loss of purchasing power, you can easily wind up with a great asset that generates negative returns. As an investor, you must strive for self-preservation. The investments you choose should, at the very least, compensate you for the natural depreciation of assets that occurs over time. In addition, investments should bear at least the same rate-of-return potential as similar assets of similar risk.

This concept is vital to accumulating wealth. If your assets cannot keep pace with inflation or the natural rate of depreciation of assets, your standard of living will drop. It is imperative that you pick a portfolio of assets that can appreciate in value faster than their natural depreciation rate. Indeed, the chief economic reason humans invest is to preserve their net worth from the effects of inflation.

It was long held that inflation aided investors because it gave companies the latitude to raise prices and report better profit margins, earnings, and returns on equity. Today, inflation is viewed as an antithetical force—it not only lowers the reported value of corporate earnings but also makes stocks less attractive than other instruments, namely bonds, that are theoretically priced for inflation. Consider this analogy Warren Buffett wrote for *Fortune* magazine in 1977:

> The arithmetic makes it plain that inflation is a far more devastating tax than anything that has been enacted by our legislature. The inflation tax has a fantastic ability to simply consume capital. It makes no difference to a widow with her savings in a 5 percent passbook account whether she pays 100 percent income tax on her interest income during a period of zero inflation, or pays no income taxes during years of 5 percent inflation. Either way, she is taxed in a manner that leaves her no real income whatsoever.[1]

Buffett views inflation as a mighty economic force that never can be eradicated. Inflation can lie dormant for years, as it did during the late 1990s, but it can never be tamed. As long as governments have the ability to infuse liquidity into an economy or to debase their own currencies, an investor must assume that politicians occasionally—acting in their own self-interests—will take fiscal steps that unwittingly lead to rising prices. "Like virginity, a stable price level seems capable of maintenance, but not of restoration," Buffett once quipped.[2]

The effects this can have on stock prices are potent. The last surge in inflation in this country, in 1994, caused stocks to slump in price for several months. By the end of 1994, after 11 months of sideways trading, many investors had thrown in the towel and had moved their money into bonds. Stocks that a year earlier sold for 20 times earnings were now priced at 8 and 9 times earnings.

Rising prices, coupled with Federal Reserve Board actions to raise interest rates, ultimately doomed the 1987 stock market, too. The proximate cause of the 1-day, 508-point plunge was an unexpectedly large trade deficit. Months before the crash, interest rates had begun rising, causing analysts to revise downward their valuations of common stocks. The prolonged bear market of the 1970s also had its roots in rising prices, which acted as an anchor to dozens of popular large-cap companies that had been bid up to prodigious multiples of their earnings.

When inflation rises over an extended period and bond yields rise, P/E ratios of stocks tend to drop. When inflation falls, bond yields fall and stocks rise. This correlative relationship between stocks, inflation, and bonds is sacrosanct and should never be ignored. Over long periods, stock and bond prices tend to react similarly to the same economic information. The true relation between stocks and bonds lies in their *coupons*, the amount of yearly returns you can expect to take out of each investment. Bond investors are intimately familiar with the notion of coupon. It is the amount the issuing entity (a corporation or government) pledges to pay each year as a percentage of the bond's par value. If a company issues a bond with a $1,000 par value and a coupon yield of 6.5 percent, the company has pledged to pay bond owners $65 a year (6.5 percent of $1,000) until the bond matures. No matter how many times or at what price the bond changes hands in subsequent years, the $65 yearly coupon remains fixed.

The yearly coupon payment never fluctuates, so a bond's value will be determined by three predominant factors: 1) the expected rate of inflation over the remaining life of the bond, 2) the prevailing yield on government bonds maturing at the same time, and 3) the *risk premium* bondholders demand based on their perceptions of the entity's financial stability. If bond investors expect inflation to reach 4 percent a year, they won't purchase a bond until it reaches a price that guarantees a yield to maturity of at least 4 percent. Otherwise they would lose purchasing power.

Common stocks offer their own form of coupon: the yearly earnings generated by the company. Whatever profits the company generates each year are legally owed to its stockholders. In most cases, however, the company retains profits and reinvests them to generate, you hope, higher earnings in the future. Thus, just as a bond possesses a yield to maturity, a stock has an *earnings yield*, according to Buffett, that allows you to compare it to bonds. As such, your goal in picking stocks is the same as that of a bond investor: to find an investment whose yearly returns, or coupons, more than compensate for inflation. Beyond that, you want to find stocks offering earnings yields that can beat risk-free government bond yields. This ensures that you can beat inflation and be adequately compensated for the risk of holding an instrument whose coupon is not assured. A bond pays you a set rate every year, whereas a company's earnings can fluctuate greatly from year to year.

If a 30-year Treasury bond yields 6 percent, a company earning a fixed profit of $1 per share each year needs to trade for $16.67 to yield the same 6 percent. Presuming the company possesses some risk, investors should theoretically wish to value the company at less than $16.67 per share, which creates a higher yield. At a price of $12, the $1 in earnings would represent an 8.33 percent yield. At $14, the earnings yield is 7.14 percent.

This direct relation between earnings, government bond yields, and stock price should hold in *perpetuity*, so long as the company can generate $1 per share on shareholders' behalf each year. If yields on government bonds rise, the yield on the stock should likewise rise— the stock must fall to keep the earnings yield at parity with bonds. If government bond yields fall, one would expect the stock to rise to keep the coupon yield in sync with bond yields.

STOCKS ARE BONDS WITH LESS PREDICTABLE COUPONS

Think of a stock as a bond substitute, Buffett says, a dynamic security that has the capability of providing you less or more income each year than it did the preceding year. Whereas a bond's yearly returns are known and can be plotted exactly to maturity, a company's returns can, at best, be guessed. If you must buy a stock, Buffett says, make sure that the company's earnings coupons:

1. can beat inflation
2. can beat government bond yields, which are priced to reflect inflation
3. can rise over time

The third point is perhaps the most important. You should strive to improve the rate of return on your original investment. You accomplish this by acquiring stock in companies whose earnings yields increase over time. *When earnings increase, the return on your original investment (the earnings yield) increases. The stock price will ultimately track the growth in coupon earnings.* For example, consider a company that earns $1 per share, trades at $20, and is growing at 25 percent annual rates. Table 15.1 shows how the coupon yields balloon.

By 2010, the company's earnings are providing a 46.6 percent return on the original investment, which is far in excess of inflation and the coupon returns of bonds. A 5 percent bond bought in 2000 would still return 5 percent in 2010. If interest rates never changed over that period,

TABLE 15.1   Coupon yields on $20.

Year	EPS	Coupon Return on $20 Price
2000	$1.00	5.0%
2001	1.25	6.3%
2002	1.56	7.8%
2003	1.95	9.8%
2004	2.44	12.2%
2005	3.05	15.3%
2009	3.81	19.1%
2007	4.77	23.9%
2008	5.96	29.8%
2009	7.45	37.3%
2010	9.31	46.6%

the price of the bond might stay fixed. The stock, however, is likely to surge in value. If the market continued valuing this company at 20 times earnings, a reasonable assumption, the shares would sell for $186.20 in 2010, an 831 percent return on the original $20 investment. The yearly earnings also would grow by 831 percent over the same period.

As impressive as this earnings stream seems, investors could enhance their returns further if one of two events occurred: 1) earnings growth accelerated above 25 percent or 2) the stock dropped below $20. Either scenario results in higher coupon returns over time. The company's long-term returns would beat inflation by a wide margin in the first year and, one would guess, all subsequent years. With such attractive returns possible, Buffett would gladly choose this stock over a bond, but this stock is not necessarily safe at any price. In fact, as the stock price rises, the coupon returns fall and become less attractive.

Let's suppose the stock traded at $40 instead of at $20. Yearly coupon returns would be one-half as rich as before. In fact, the stock would not offer bond-beating returns for, potentially, several years. If bond yields stood at 6 percent, this stock would not offer a coupon yield that handily beat bond returns until 2005. As an investor you would have to wait 5 years before the stock offered bond-beating results, as shown in Table 15.2.

TABLE 15.2   Coupon yields on $40.

Year	EPS	Coupon Return on $40 Price
2000	$1.00	2.5%
2001	1.25	3.1%
2002	1.56	3.9%
2003	1.95	4.9%
2004	2.44	6.1%
2005	3.05	7.6%
2009	3.81	9.5%
2007	4.77	11.9%
2008	5.96	14.9%
2009	7.45	18.6%
2010	9.31	23.3%

Also keep in mind that this rate-of-return scenario hinges on the company's ability to increase earnings at 25 percent annual rates. If the company cannot sustain a high growth rate, you must temper the rate-of-return assumptions. Moreover, interest rates could rise to 7 percent and suddenly decrease the attractiveness of the company's earnings record. You could easily overpay for this company's coupon stream and experience inferior, perhaps negative, stock-price returns. In Buffett's mind, you left yourself with little margin of safety.

To be sure, the company's yearly coupons stand a good chance of eventually beating bond yields. As long as yearly profits keep rising, the company will present a potentially better investment opportunity than a fixed coupon bond can. If you could hold this stock for several years, you are virtually assured of bond-beating results—your original goal. But to better ensure success, focus as much on the price you pay for the stock as on the company's earnings stream.

SIX RULES FOR COMPARING STOCKS TO BONDS

In my previous book, *Wall Street on Sale* (McGraw-Hill, 1999), I devised a set of rules that allow you to place bonds and stocks in their proper context. Because this context is crucial to understanding Warren Buffett's methodology, I summarize these rules here:

1. *Your overriding goal as a stock investor is to find companies whose returns can beat inflation.* Two hundred years of market history have proven that stocks offer a nearly guaranteed means of beating inflation.

2. *Your secondary goal is to beat the risk-free returns of government bonds, which are already priced to anticipate inflation.* If the stocks you select cannot beat a bond's return, you are better off putting your money into bonds.

3. *The proper way of comparing a stock's potential return to a bond's return is to compare their respective coupons, that is, the money that can be generated on your behalf each year.* When evaluating a bond, the relevant return is the yearly "coupon." When evaluating a stock, the relevant return is the "earnings" you predict the company can produce each year going forward.

4. *When possible, you should try to buy a stock whose current earnings yield, that is, current earnings divided by price, is near or above yields on a long-term bond.* If interest rates are 6 percent, you need an earnings yield close to 6 percent, that is, the stock's P/E ratio should be at or under 17. If rates are 8 percent, you should look for companies priced at 12.5 times earnings or less.

5. *The only time you should accept earnings yields that are lower than bond yields is when the company is growing and is expected to generate an earnings yield that would soon surpass bond yields.* A high growth rate compensates for a low earnings yield, but the company's coupon yield should still compare favorably to a bond within a few years. If you must wait 5 years or more for earnings to catch up to bond yields, you are likely overpaying for the company.

6. *Buying growth companies at the cheapest possible price is the best way to ensure that you can beat bond yields by a wide margin.* You should try to take advantage of the compounding effect of earnings growth, which provides a higher and higher rate of return on your initial investment. Continuous growth in earnings leads to continuous growth in the return on your investment, which should lead to higher and higher share prices over time.

EARNINGS YIELDS FOR BUFFETT'S MAJOR INVESTMENTS

Writers and analysts have speculated that Buffett performs detailed financial statement analysis to find all his winners, but what Buffett seemingly envies most is a consistently growing coupon that keeps him ahead of bond yields. Table 15.3 shows the coupon yields Buffett currently enjoys on some of his more publicized investments in the 1980s and 1990s. Viewed in this context, one can see why Buffett continues to hold onto his consumer stocks such as Coca-Cola, Gillette, and American Express. Each of his major holdings has consistently delivered coupon earnings far in excess of bond yields, giving him handsome returns he wouldn't want to give up. Despite the recent sluggishness in some of his key holdings, Buffett would be hard pressed to divest stocks that are still giving him huge returns on his *original* investment. To sell them would force Buffett to reinvest in other companies where the coupon returns, initially, would be quite low.

Table 15.3 compares earnings yields for several of Berkshire Hathaway's largest holdings during the 1990s. In calculating the returns, I assumed one could purchase each company outright starting January 1, 1990 and hold each investment through the end of 1999. As the sole owner, you would have been able to pocket all the net income the company generated each year. Table 15.3 also shows how price impacts earnings yields. If you had purchased American Express in 1990 at 15 times net income, the company's earnings yield would have been 48.8 percent by the end of 1999. That is, the net income generated by American Express constituted 48.8 percent of your original investment.

Had you paid 20 times net income for American Express, net income for 1999 would have provided a 36.6 percent return on your original investment. You can see how difficult it would be for a buyer in 1990 to want to part with American Express's stock by the end of the decade. It's pretty difficult to walk away from a 48.8 percent yearly return on your money. A private business owner would be derelict to sell such an investment, especially as American Express's yearly earnings would likely rise further in subsequent years, increasing the yield each year.

TABLE 15.3 Earnings yields for select Berkshire Hathaway holdings.

	Price Paid	1990	1991	1992	1993	1994	1995	1996	1997	1998	1999
					Net income ($mil)						
American Express		$338	$789	$436	$1,478	$1,413	$1,564	$1,901	$1,991	$2,141	$2,475
Coca-Cola		1,382	1,618	1,884	2,188	2,554	2,986	3,492	4,129	3,533	2,431
Federal Home Loan Mortgage		414	555	622	786	1,027	1,091	1,258	1,395	1,700	2,218
Federal National Mortgage		807	1,173	1,455	1,649	2,042	2,141	2,156	2,754	3,069	3,444
Gannett		377	302	346	398	465	477	943	713	783	958
Gillette		368	427	513	427	698	824	949	1,427	1,428	1,260
Washington Post		175	119	128	154	170	190	221	282	223	226
Wells Fargo*		281	399	518	654	800	956	1,154	1,351	1,950	3,747
Bought in 1990 at 15 times net income											
					Earnings yield						
American Express	$5,070	6.7%	15.6%	8.6%	29.2%	27.9%	30.8%	37.5%	39.3%	42.2%	48.8%
Coca-Cola	$20,730	6.7%	7.8%	9.1%	10.6%	12.3%	14.4%	16.8%	19.9%	17.0%	11.7%
Federal Home Loan Mortage	$6,210	6.7%	8.9%	10.0%	12.7%	16.5%	17.6%	20.3%	22.5%	27.4%	35.7%
Federal National Mortgage	$12,105	6.7%	9.7%	12.0%	13.6%	16.9%	17.7%	17.8%	22.8%	25.4%	28.5%
Gannett	$5,655	6.7%	5.3%	6.1%	7.0%	8.2%	8.4%	16.7%	12.6%	13.8%	16.9%
Gillette	$5,520	6.7%	7.7%	9.3%	7.7%	12.6%	14.9%	17.2%	25.9%	25.9%	22.8%
Washington Post	$2,625	6.7%	4.5%	4.9%	5.9%	6.5%	7.2%	8.4%	10.7%	8.5%	8.6%
Wells Fargo	$4,215	6.7%	9.5%	12.3%	15.5%	19.0%	22.7%	27.4%	32.1%	46.3%	88.9%

183

continued on next page

TABLE 15.3 continued

	Price Paid	1990	1991	1992	1993	1994	1995	1996	1997	1998	1999
Bought in 1990 at 20 times net income											
American Express	$6,670	5.0%	11.7%	6.4%	21.9%	20.9%	23.1%	28.1%	29.5%	31.7%	36.6%
Coca-Cola	$27,640	5.0%	5.9%	6.8%	7.9%	9.2%	10.8%	12.6%	14.9%	12.8%	8.8%
Federal Home Loan Mortgage	$8,280	5.0%	6.7%	7.5%	9.5%	12.4%	13.2%	15.2%	16.8%	20.5%	26.8%
Federal National Mortgage	$16,140	5.0%	7.3%	9.0%	10.2%	12.7%	13.3%	13.4%	17.1%	19.0%	21.3%
Gannett	$7,540	5.0%	4.0%	4.6%	5.3%	6.2%	6.3%	12.5%	9.5%	10.4%	12.7%
Gillette	$7,360	5.0%	5.8%	7.0%	5.8%	9.5%	11.2%	12.9%	19.4%	19.4%	17.1%
Washington Post	$3,500	5.0%	3.4%	3.7%	4.4%	4.9%	5.4%	6.3%	8.1%	6.4%	6.5%
Wells Fargo	$5,620	5.0%	7.1%	9.2%	11.6%	14.2%	17.0%	20.5%	24.0%	34.7%	66.7%

*Wells Fargo's 1999 results include more than $1 billion in venture capital gains.

184

WHEN ARE BONDS PREFERRED TO STOCKS?

With the examples above, you can determine whether a stock offers a better or worse potential return than a bond. *Stocks are most attractive when their earnings yields exceed bond yields.* Conversely, bonds are most attractive when their yields far surpass the average earnings yields of stocks. By late 1999, for example, a 30-year government bond yielded around 6.3 percent, but the average S&P 500 company traded at 30 times earnings, a yield of 3.3 percent. Even presuming that corporate earnings rise at healthy rates in 2000 and 2001, bonds still looked more attractive than stocks, a reason Buffett avoided new common stock investments in 1999. It would take a combination of events—falling interest rates and rapidly rising corporate earnings—for earnings yields to catch up to and surpass bond yields.

You can get a feel for how bonds are being valued in relation to stocks by visiting the website of economist Edward Yardeni of Deutsch Bank Securities (www.yardeni.com). Yardeni uses the bond yield to stock yield relation to gauge whether stocks are generally overvalued or undervalued. To make his assessment, Yardeni compares the current yield on 10-year government bonds to the expected earnings yield of the S&P 500 (derived by taking analysts' consensus estimates of earnings for the upcoming year). As Figure 15.1 shows, there has been a direct, close correlation between the two yields over the past 20 years. A decline in bond yields should translate into a proportionate decline in stock yields (rising P/E ratios), and vice versa. Markets get out of balance when wide discrepancies exist between the two yields. Yardeni's model showed the stock market to be in an extremely over-valued state by the end of 1999 (Figure 15.1).

Another way to capture this relationship is to compare earnings growth to bond yields and measure whether a company's stock can generate a return that beats a bond. For example, Oracle traded at about $82 in the spring of 2000, or 160 times its trailing earnings. In contrast, analysts were projecting that Oracle's earnings would grow at 30 percent annual rates for the next 5 years. Thus, the stock traded at more than five times its presumed growth rate. Using these few bits of data, you can quickly determine whether Oracle stands a good chance of beating bond yields going forward.

Let's say you had the option of buying $82 in Oracle stock or paying $82 for a U.S. Treasury bill that offered a 5.5 percent compounded

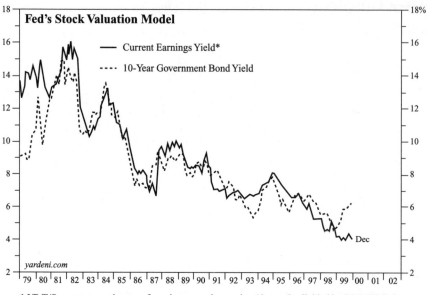

* I/B/E/S consensus estimates of earnings over the coming 12 months divided by S&P 500 Index.

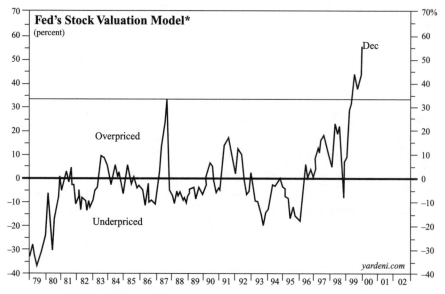

* Ratio of S&P 500 Index to I/B/E/S consensus estimates of earnings over the coming 12 months divided by the 10-year US Treasury bond yield minus 100.

FIGURE 15.1   Fed's stock valuation model.

annual yield. Which would you buy? If you bought the Treasury bill and rolled it over at then end of each year, your $82 investment would grow to $107.17 at the end of 5 years. Thus, for Oracle to beat a Treasury bill, it must trade for at least $107.17 in 5 years. Seems simple, but, in actuality, Oracle may not win this race. Let's say Oracle's beginning earnings were $0.50 per share and compounded at 30 percent annual rates. By the end of the fifth year, Oracle would earn $1.86 per share (the 5-year earnings stream would be $0.65, $0.85, $1.10, $1.43, and $1.86) (Table 15.4).

Recall that Oracle needed to trade about $107.17 in 5 years to beat a Treasury bill. That means it needs to trade for about 58 times earnings by 2005 ($107.17 divided by $1.86) just to match the returns of the Treasury bill. There's the rub. For Oracle to beat a bond, it must trade at high valuations consistently—for 5 more years. To make money, you must hope that investors pile onto the stock after you and keep bidding it up to higher and higher unsustainable prices (the Greater Fool Theory).

Of course, there's always a chance that Oracle's stock jumps above $107.17 in the first year and gives you instant gratification, but odds favor an eventual decline in Oracle's stock by the fifth year. No stock can consistently trade at such high earnings multiples for very long. If

TABLE 15.4   Oracle's earnings yields.

Year	EPS	Return on $82
2001	$0.65	0.8%
2002	$0.85	1.0%
2003	$1.10	1.3%
2004	$1.43	1.7%
2005	$1.86	2.3%
2005 price at:		
30× EPS	$55.80	
40× EPS	$74.40	
50× EPS	$93.00	
60× EPS	$111.60	

you intend to hold Oracle the full 5 years, you would not want to buy at $82 because you are inheriting too much downside risk. If the market decides to value Oracle at just 30 times earnings in 5 years (a reasonable assumption), the stock would trade for just $55.80 at the end of those 5 years. Not only would Oracle fail to beat the returns of a Treasury bill, you would also lose 32 percent of your principal.

P A R T

Avoiding Losses

C H A P T E R

THE BENEFITS OF AVOIDING LOSSES

HRONICLERS OF BUFFETT'S ACHIEVEMENTS have commented that his sterling track record, when gauged from a rear-view mirror, seems relatively straightforward. Anyone with the patience, mathematical knowledge, and diligence to screen stocks could have roughly approximated Buffett's results, they say. Indeed, knowing what we know now—and having Buffett's entire career sliced and diced over 1,000 or more news articles—much of what he attained seems elementary in retrospect.

Buffett would be the first to acknowledge that, although he possesses unusual mathematical gifts and is "wired a little differently" than most, thus permitting him to glean relevance from information others would overlook, the principles he applied could be mastered by virtually anyone with a grounding in finance. After all, how difficult can it be to find, say, a stock trading at one-half the value of its balance sheet cash; or a takeover deal that guaranteed a 50 percent annualized return; or a stock such as Coca-Cola trading at 12 times earnings; or a convertible preferred that could potentially double one's money within a few years. These types of situations, like lava from Mt.

Kilauea, bubble to the surface every day on Wall Street, waiting to be exploited by any investor who can find and understand them.

Make no mistake, every great investor's motives, strategies, and results look crystal clear in retrospect. Peter Lynch's marvelous years running the Magellan Fund appear much less incredible judged from the sky box of history. He bought and sold common stocks like the rest of us, including many of the same types of stocks you probably placed in your own portfolio. Why, then, did Lynch attain vastly superior results?

We tend to overlook the fact that the success of investors such as Lynch and Buffett derived from thousands of critical decisions they made over the course of decades, many of which were made on the fly; but the majority of which were correct. In our quest to find shortcut answers to how they did it, we tend to look at only the beginning—that Buffett started with $100—and at the end—his $30 billion fortune— and dismiss the daily rituals that got him from point A to point B. Those rituals, however, are what pushed Buffett's returns well above those of the crowd. "If everybody had seen what he had seen, he wouldn't have made huge gains from his visions," *Forbes* magazine once wrote.[1]

A typical investor who spreads his or her money over a basket of stocks can expect to achieve 10 to 12 percent annualized gains over great periods. That's a well-known platitude. The same investor who focuses on the types of stocks Buffett owns—Coca-Cola, Gillette, Capital Cities, Wells Fargo, etc.—could expect to gain perhaps a few percentage points more each year. These stocks have shown a tendency to outperform the market over long periods because they exhibited growth rates greater than the average U.S. corporation. A shrewd, full-time investor who focused on Buffett-like stocks and made sure to buy them at wonderfully cheap prices could add a couple of extra percentage points of gain a year. But the combined effects of these strategies still don't come close to producing the 33 percent compounded annual gain Buffett attained between the mid-1950s and the late 1990s. There's got to be more to the story.

THE POWER OF AVOIDING LOSSES

Buffett once summarized the essence of successful investing in a simple quip:

Rule number 1: Don't lose money.

Rule number 2: Don't forget rule number 1.

Losses occur for three primary reasons:

1. You took bigger risks and exposed yourself to a higher probability of loss.
2. You invested in an instrument that failed to keep pace with inflation and interest rates.
3. You didn't hold the instrument long enough to let its true intrinsic value be realized.

There aren't many ways an investor can avoid periodic losses. The best way is to invest all of your assets in bonds and hold them to maturity. You would, of course, experience an erosion in the value of the bond due to inflation. If interest rates rise during your holding period, the intrinsic value of the bond would fall and the yearly coupon wouldn't fully compensate you for inflationary pressures.

To reduce the chance of losses, you must minimize mistakes. The fewer errors made over your investing career, the better your long-term returns. We've already seen the advantage of adding extra points of gain to your yearly returns. Earning an extra 2 percentage points a year on your portfolio compounds into tremendous amounts. Beating the market's presumed 11 percent yearly return by 2 percentage points would translate into hundreds of thousands of dollars of extra profits over time.

The same holds true if you can avoid a loss. When you lose money, even if for just a year, you greatly erode the terminal value of your portfolio. You consume precious resources that must be replaced. In addition, you waste precious time trying to make up lost ground. Losses also reduce the positive effects of compounding.

Consider three portfolios, A, B, and C, each of which normally gains 10 percent a year for 30 years. Portfolio B, however, obtains zero gains (0%) in years 10, 20, and 30. Portfolio C suffers a 10 percent loss in years 10, 20, and 30. A $10,000 investment in portfolio A would return $174,490 by the 30th year. Portfolio B's would return considerably less—only $131,100—because of three break-even years (Table 16.1). The portfolio never actually lost money, but will forever lag far behind portfolio A by virtue of having three mediocre years.

TABLE 16.1   The effects of avoiding losses.

Portfolio A*			Portfolio B†			Portfolio C‡		
Year	Gain	Portfolio	Year	Gain	Portfolio	Year	Gain	Portfolio
		$10,000			$10,000			$10,000
1	10%	$11,000	1	10%	$11,000	1	10%	$11,000
2	10%	$12,100	2	10%	$12,100	2	10%	$12,100
3	10%	$13,310	3	10%	$13,310	3	10%	$13,310
4	10%	$14,641	4	10%	$14,641	4	10%	$14,641
5	10%	$16,105	5	10%	$16,105	5	10%	$16,105
10	10%	$25,937	10	0%	$23,579	10	–10%	$21,222
15	10%	$41,772	15	10%	$37,975	15	10%	$34,177
20	10%	$67,275	20	0%	$55,599	20	–10%	$45,035
25	10%	$108,347	25	10%	$89,543	25	10%	$72,530
30	10%	$174,494	30	0%	$131,100	30	–10%	$95,572

Investor A gains 10 percent every year.
†*Investor B has zero gains in years 10, 20, and 30.*
‡*Investor C loses 10 percent in years 10, 20, and 30.*

Historically speaking, portfolio B's returns aren't all that bad, for the investor managed to avoid losses every year.

Portfolio C, by contrast, loses 10 percent in years 10, 20, and 30. The effects of those three not-so-unreasonable years is to lop nearly $79,000 off the final value of the portfolio. That's what compounding can do. The actual loss in the 10th year was only $2,357. The loss in the 20th year was just $5,004; the final year loss was $10,619. But the power of compounding turned $17,980 in total yearly losses into $79,000 of lost opportunities.

THE LOSER'S GAME

It's a sad fact that most day traders *lose* money over time, as do most bond, options, futures, and commodities traders. Research has clearly shown that long-term returns are tied to your holding periods and to the price you pay. Excessive trading and a disregard for fundamental risks serve as a weighty anchor that keeps short-term oriented investors from consistently performing well. They strive so hard to compete at what are essentially "zero-sum" games that they unwittingly tax their performance into obscurity. Over time, their winning trades likely equal their losing trades, but they will continually lose a fraction of their money to taxes, commissions, and dealer spreads.

Analyst and author Charles Ellis, in a 1975 article published in the *Financial Analysts Journal*, was the first to label investing a "loser's game." He foresaw how the field of investing, particularly at the institutional level, would ultimately degenerate into a momentum-based tournament where tens of thousands of individuals claw over one another trying to buy "undiscovered" stocks ahead of their peers. A game with so many participants, all trained to look at information the same way, would naturally tempt investors to make "unforced errors," to borrow a term from tennis.

Ellis neatly summed up his findings in a formula that showed how the pursuit of market-beating gains naturally led to inferior returns among fund managers. To beat the market, fund managers first had to beat each other and had to increasingly engage in short-term momentum trading to do so. Ultimately, these managers predetermined their own poor results and occasionally caused huge losses.

Ellis concluded that the most successful investors are not necessarily the smartest people or those with million-dollar research budgets. Nor are they the ones who luckily scored 1,000 percent gains on a single stock. Rather, they are the ones who make the fewest mistakes during their careers.

> The belief that active managers can beat the market is based on two assumptions: 1) liquidity offered in the stock market is an advantage, and 2) institutional investing is a Winner's Game. [My] unhappy thesis can be briefly stated: Owing to important changes in the past 10 years, these basic assumptions are no longer true. On the contrary, market liquidity is a liability rather than an asset, and institutional investors will, over the long term, underperform the market because money management has become a Loser's Game.[2]

Golf provides an excellent example of a loser's game. The winner of a PGA tournament on Sunday is not necessarily the longest hitter, the best putter, nor has the best short game. The winner is the one who makes the fewest mistakes during the four rounds. That fact alone differentiates golf from most contact sports such as football or hockey. In contact sports, and even in tennis, the outcome of the game is determined by the winner, who presumably overpowers the opponent with skill and muscle to score the most points.

In golf, the actions of the loser determine the outcome. Tiger Woods wins tournaments mostly because all his opponents, who never compete directly with Tiger during the weekend, make more mistakes than he does. Tiger could shoot 10 under par and lose the tournament if one of the 64 other players happens to make fewer mistakes and shoots 11 under par. The final outcome is really outside Tiger's control—he must rely on others to make more mistakes on the fairways than he does. Bowling operates under similar rules of engagement. Each contestant starts with a theoretical perfect score of 300 and loses points as more pins are missed. The final outcome of the match is determined by the loser—the person who misses the most pins.

If you understand the rules of loser's games, you have taken a critical first step toward success in investments. Warren Buffett sits atop the financial world because he has made the fewest mistakes over his 40-year career. His most common mistakes, he admits, are "sins of omission," in which he failed to buy a stock that rallied, or sold a stock too soon. Neither type of mistake costs Buffett cash. They are simply lost opportunities.

If I polled 1,000 investors and asked them to list their top five rules for success, their answers would differ from Buffett's. Here is what they would probably say:

Rule 1: Take a long-term perspective.
Rule 2: Keep adding money to the market and let the magic of compounding work for you.
Rule 3: Don't try to time the market.
Rule 4: Stick to companies you understand.
Rule 5: Diversify.

I would venture to say that few investors would think to mention Buffett's cardinal "don't-lose-money" rule. Some investors, sadly, refuse to believe that losses can occur, so accustomed are they to the unprecedented rally in the major indexes since 1987. Surveys done by mutual fund companies during the past few years indicate that a high percentage of individual investors still don't believe that mutual funds can lose money or that the market is capable of dropping more than 10 percent anymore. Other investors see losses as temporary setbacks or as opportunities to add to their positions. Still others, acting out a psychological defense mechanism, try to avoid losses by violating their own rules. They let the ticker tape infect decision making and trade in and out of winners and losers to avoid the psychological trauma of having to report a loss.

Avoiding losses is probably the most important tool for long-term success in investing. No investor, even Buffett, can avoid periodic losses on individual stocks. Even if you resigned yourself to buying only at incredibly cheap prices, occasional mistakes will still occur. What differentiates Buffett from nearly all other investors is his ability to avoid yearly losses in his *entire portfolio.*

Diversification alone can't prevent losses. All diversification can do is minimize the chances that a few stocks implode and drag the performance of the portfolio with them. Even if you hold 100 stocks, you are forever vulnerable to "market risk," the risk that a declining market causes nearly all stocks to drop together.

Most investors use the market as their mechanism for avoiding losses. They simply sell when a stock falls below its break-even point, no matter the fundamentals. One highly touted strategy of the 1990s, espoused by *Investor's Business Daily,* implores investors to sell any issue that falls more than 8 percent below its purchase price, irrespective of events. Market timers rely on similar strategies. They make short-term bets on the direction of individual stocks and are prepared to exit quickly if the market turns against them.

These strategies ultimately degrade into a form of gambling, where the odds of success shrink because the investors' holding period is too short. Other investors avoid losses by continuing to hold poor-performing stocks, sometimes for years, until they rally back above their original cost. To profit from this strategy, you must pin your hopes on the market's ultimately validating your decision. Warren Buffett would rather not place his faith in the hands of investors and traders. The methods he uses to lock in yearly gains take the market out of the equation. He reckons that if he can guarantee himself returns, even in poor markets, he will ultimately be way ahead of the game.

Chapters 17 and 18 focus on how Buffett best avoids losses.

C H A P T E R

AVOIDING LOSSES II
Market Timing, Convertibles, and Options

KEEPING ABREAST OF MARKET CONDITIONS

GAIN AND AGAIN, Warren Buffett will tell you that he is not concerned about day-to-day fluctuations in the stock market. It doesn't matter to him whether the Dow Industrials rises 300 points in a single day or falls by the same amount. He doesn't care whether interest rates rose or fell for the day, or whether his portfolio declined $200 million in value (a frequent occurrence in 1999, by the way). "The market is there only as a reference point to see if anybody is offering to do anything foolish," he was quoted saying in 1988. "When we invest in stocks, we invest in businesses."[1]

However, Buffett—whether by accident or calculation—must be recognized as one of the most astute market timers in history. His ability to sense great perils in the market or see great opportunity when others see peril sets him apart from even the legendary market timers such as George Soros or Michael Steinhardt. It is also a chief reason he rarely suffers a yearly loss in his portfolio. His ability to find bargain stocks is well documented. Less known is his success in gauging market conditions and profiting from them. When Buffett begins talking up or down the market, it pays to listen.

His form of market timing is similar to Wayne Gretzsky's approach to hockey—don't go where the puck *is*, go where it's going to be. The great investors of the twentieth century all seemed to have a penchant for discovering undervalued securities, but they also were forward looking. When a recession was under way, they didn't brood. They looked for signs that a recovery was at hand. And when the economy was strong, they stayed mindful of the risk of a slowdown and planned accordingly. When playing the market, they looked for catalysts that could propel an industry ahead, even when Wall Street had turned negative on the sector. Conversely, they wouldn't wait for boom times to end but would sell ahead of others.

Warren Buffett owes his success through the years as much to what he *didn't* buy as to what he did. Likewise, what he sold—and *when* he sold it—played just as prominent a role in his returns as did decisions to buy and hold Coca-Cola, GEICO, or Gillette. Whitney Tilson of Tilson Capital Partners in New York, a frequent columnist to The Motley Fool website, reminds us that Buffett made no fewer than four distinct market-timing calls in his career, each of which proved correct and highly profitable.

MARKET CALL 1: SELLING OUT BEFORE
THE EARLY 1970s BEAR MARKET

Beginning in 1968, Buffett began to express sincere worries over stock prices. Writing near the peak of the go-go market of the 1960s, Buffett seemed to sense imminent danger to investors. Unable to find enough quality stocks at reasonable prices, he folded his investment partnership in 1969, acknowledging that his form of diligent, research-intensive stock-picking couldn't compete in a momentum-fed, short-term oriented market. "Spectacular amounts of money are being made by those participating in the chain-letter type stock-promotion vogue," he wrote his clients. "The game is being played by the gullible, the self-hypnotized, and the cynical."

"I believe the odds are good that, when the stock market and business history of this period is being written, [this] phenomenon will be regarded as of major importance, and perhaps characterized as a mania." Frustrated by the lack of sensible pricing and the inability of value-oriented managers to make headway amid a sea of momentum-hungry fund managers, Buffett liquidated clients' accounts, put most of his personal wealth into Berkshire Hathaway stock, and stayed mostly out of the money-management business for almost 5 years. He stayed on the sidelines while Americans experienced the most brutal bear market since the crash of 1929 to 1933.

MARKET CALL 2: GOING LONG IN 1974

Five years after the market had peaked, most Americans had turned disillusioned by the stock market. The average portfolio had dropped 40 percent or more in value. Investors holding the great blue chips of the day—Xerox, Walt Disney, IBM, General Motors, and Sears Roebuck, for example—saw their portfolios decline more than 60 percent during the crash of 1973 to 1974. To investors caught in the middle, it seemed like there was no end to the panic selling. Some individuals tried holding their stocks, waiting for a rebound that never took place. Exhausted, they gave in and sold after watching their portfolios lose 50 percent of their value. The rest took their cues from the market itself. Daily declines reinforced a selling mentality: Selling begat selling, and an orderly market turned into a vicious cycle of losses.

At the bottom, in 1974, few investors could be coaxed to reenter the arena. But Buffett, refreshed from a 5-year hiatus and sitting on plenty of cash, dove headlong into the same stocks the market could no longer tolerate. Like a boy in a candy store, Buffett found more values than he could possibly digest. An investor who plunged into the market at the 1974 low made a 74 percent return within 2 years.

MARKET CALL 3: SEEING THE OPPORTUNITIES
THAT WOULD OPEN UP IN THE 1980s

By 1979, the Dow Jones Industrial Average traded no higher than it did in 1964—15 years without a single point gain! Pessimism hit extreme levels. The public had gradually shifted their portfolios into bonds, real estate, and precious metals, and brokers found it difficult to peddle even stocks with 15 percent dividend yields. Leading market strategists of the day, predicting more of the same financial morass, implored investors to buy bonds and avoid stocks. Buffett saw things differently. From his perspective, quality blue-chip stocks were being given away; some sold for less than their book values, despite the fact that economic prospects for the United States still appeared bright. Corporate returns on equity remained healthy, blue-chip earnings were advancing at double-digit rates, and the speculative frenzy that had destroyed the integrity of the late-1960s markets had finally been removed from the equation.

"Stocks now sell at levels that should produce long-term returns superior to bonds," he told shareholders. "Yet pension managers, usually encouraged by corporate sponsors that must necessarily please, are pouring funds in record proportion into bonds. Meanwhile, orders for stocks are being placed with an eyedropper." How right Buffett was. As Tilson pointed out, the stock market has returned an annualized 17.2 percent since Buffett penned those words. Bonds returned 9.6 percent.

MARKET CALL 4: AVOIDING THE 1987 CRASH

By the mid-1980s, Buffett's buy-and-hold philosophy had been carved in stone. He maintained large stakes in his three favorite companies— GEICO, Washington Post Co., and Capital Cities/ABC (which later merged with Walt Disney)—and pledged to hold these "inevitables," as he called them, forever. He didn't share the same convictions about the rest of the stock market. At the Berkshire Hathaway annual meeting in 1986, Buffett lamented that he could not find suitable companies trading at low prices. Rather than dilute his portfolio with short-term stock investments, and given the fact that Buffett's stock holdings had already provided him tens of millions of dollars in gains, Buffett opted to take profits and shrink his portfolio.

"I still can't find any bargains in today's market," he told shareholders. "We don't currently own any equities to speak of." Just 5 months before the 1987 crash, he told shareholders of his inability to find any large-cap stocks offering a high rate-of-return potential: "There's nothing that we could see buying even if it went down 10 percent."

In retrospect, Buffett's comments about a 10 percent decline ultimately proved conservative. Five months after telling shareholders of his dilemma, the stock market lost 30 percent within a matter of days.

His decision to whittle away his portfolio slowly before the crash undoubtedly kept Berkshire's stock portfolio from imparting too big a negative influence on book value. As Table 17.1 shows, Buffett entered the 1980s energetic, ready to dive into a market he saw as woefully underappraised. As the market rose in value without pause, Buffett's conservatism got the better of him. By 1987, he was holding large stakes in just three stocks. When the decade began, Buffett had amassed large positions in 18 different companies.

Warren Buffett does not possess a magic formula for determining when the stock market is grossly overvalued or undervalued. By all accounts, his decisions to plunge into or escape from the market are based on several commonsense factors.

The relationship between stock yields and bond yields.   Recall from chapter 15 that Buffett covets stocks that offer earnings yields that can surpass bond yields over time. When bond yields are rising and threaten to overtake stock yields, the market is generally overvalued. When stocks fall to the point where their earnings yields (the inverse of P/E ratios) are above bond yields, they are most attractive.

The rate of climb in the market.   History tells us that the stock market cannot outperform the economy for very long. That is, you shouldn't expect corporate sales, earnings, or share prices to rise at rates in excess of economic output. If stock prices are rising at, say, four times the rate the economy is expanding, the market is primed for a fall at some point. Conversely, if stock prices are falling while the economy is surging, an undervalued condition may be opening up.

Earnings multiples.   In 1982, the P/E ratio of the S&P 500 index was just 7 (Americans were willing to pay just $7 for every $1 corporations earned on their behalf). By mid-1999, Americans were willing to pay $34 for every $1 of earnings generated by these same companies. What explained the disparity? Falling interest rates accounted for some of the increase in P/E ratios. Declining rates make every $1 of earnings worth more to an investor.

Improved profitability also accounted for some of the increase in P/E. By the late 1990s, corporate returns on equity and assets had reached 70-year highs. It stood to reason that $1 of earnings carried

TABLE 17.1   Buffett's shrinking portfolio of the 1980s: major holdings listed in Berkshire Hathaway's annual report.

	1980	1981	1982	1983	1984	1985	1986	1987
Affiliated Publications	x	x	x	x	x	x	x	
ALCOA	x	x						
Arcata		x						
Beatrice Co.						x		
Capital Cities/ABC					x	x	x	x
Cleveland Cliffs Iron	x	x						
Crum & Forster			x					
Exxon					x			
GATX		x						
GEICO	x	x	x	x	x	x	x	x
General Foods	x	x	x	x	x			
Handy & Harman	x	x	x	x	x	x	x	
Interpublic Group	x	x	x	x	x			
Kaiser Aluminum	x							
Lear Siegler							x	
Media General	x	x	x	x				
National Detroit	x							
National Student Marketing	x							
Northwest Industries					x			
Ogilvy & Mather	x	x	x	x				
Pinkerton's	x	x						
R.J. Reynolds	x	x	x	x				
SAFECO	x	x						
Time			x	x	x	x		
Times Mirror	x							
Washington Post	x	x	x	x	x	x	x	x
Woolworth (F.W.)	x							
Stocks revealed	**18**	**15**	**11**	**10**	**10**	**7**	**6**	**3**

more value because corporations could reinvest earnings at high rate. Yet the majority of the climb in stock prices can be attributed to emotion—the sheer willingness of investors to pay higher and higher prices without regard to value. When P/E ratios are expanding faster than what could be expected, given changes in interest rates and corporate profitability, investors must be on the alert for a correction.

The state of the economy.   When the economy is running full throttle and there seems to be little chance of its sustaining present growth rates, investors should ponder whether to decrease their exposure to the stock market and find alternatives. Likewise, during tough economic times, stocks usually fall to bargain levels and offer high rate-of-return potential. Using Buffett's 15 percent rule outlined in Chapter 12, you can quickly gauge whether stocks are worthy of holding. The general rule is to buy during a recession (when P/E ratios are at their lowest) and to sell when the economy can't get any stronger (and P/E ratios are their highest).

The big picture.   Because Buffett endeavors to hold a stock for several years or more, he must take a more holistic view of companies, industries, and the entire market before buying. Buffett won't buy or sell a stock in response to near-term changes in a company's profitability, nor will he pin his hopes on a sector "catching fire" on Wall Street to sell at a higher price. Instead, he assesses longer-term fundamentals in the economy and the market and examines whether those fundamentals can support higher stock prices. If a stock doesn't offer the potential rate of return he seeks, he is likely to sell the security or avoid buying. As Table 17.1 indicates, Buffett prefers to play an economic cycle to the fullest, whenever possible. During a recession, when nearly all U.S. industries are experiencing a downturn, Buffett is apt to load up on numerous stocks, knowing that several consecutive years of improved profitability lie ahead. When the economy peaks and odds favor an eventual slowdown, selling is the prudent course.

CONVERTIBLES

Some of Buffett's most lucrative investments in the late 1980s and early 1990s involved convertibles, which are hybrid securities that possess features of a stock and an income-producing security such as a bond or preferred stock. He made five publicized convertible investments starting in 1987: Salomon Brothers in 1987, Gillette in 1989, American Express in 1991, (all three profiled below) Champion International in 1989, and USAir Group in 1989. Combined, the five convertibles have provided more than $5 billion in gains and prompted Buffett to take larger stakes in three of the companies. He still holds all the common shares of Gillette and American Express that converted and dovetailed his Salomon Brothers investment to obtain large stakes in Travelers Group and Citigroup.

When you buy a convertible issued by, say, Gillette you get a fixed income stream, just as you would with a bond, but you also posses the right to convert your bond into a fixed number of shares of common stock. The conversion feature makes these investments most attractive, despite the fact that the convertible price is usually 15 to 25 percent above the common stock's price and the coupon rate on the bond is usually below prevailing bond rates. Say you pay $1,000 for XYZ Corporation's bond and have the right to convert it to 20 shares of XYZ stock (a conversion price of $50 per share). XYZ's shares sell for $40 each. Multiply $40 by 20 and you get $800. You're paying a premium of $200. The income component (whether in the form of a bond coupon or a preferred dividend) defrays the premium paid.

With a convertible, you're betting on the appreciation of the common stock to kick up your returns. If XYZ's shares rise to $50 or above, the convertible is said to be "in the money" ($50 per share × 20 shares = $1,000). Each $1 advance in the common stock should lead to $1 increases in the value of the convertible. You can choose to convert and sell your common shares for a profit. You also have the option of converting but holding onto your common stock or letting profits ride by holding the convertible. Because there is a bond component to the security, a convertible shouldn't decline as much as the common stock. Theoretically, the security won't fall below the face value of the underlying bond, no matter how low the common stock drops (unless the company faced financial distress).

Buffett will invest in convertibles when the combination of dividends and stock appreciation potential offers a market-beating return. "Under almost any conditions, we expect these preferreds to return us our money plus dividends," he wrote in his 1989 annual report. "If that is all we get, though, the result will be disappointing, because we will have given up flexibility and consequently will have missed some significant opportunities [elsewhere]. The only way Berkshire can achieve satisfactory results from...preferred issues is to have the common stocks of the investee companies do well."

SALOMON BROTHERS

With the corporate merger wave in full swing in the mid-1980s and the stock market soaring, Buffett's ability to profit squarely from new purchases was getting limited. As Table 17.1 showed, Buffett had clearly turned defensive by 1987, limiting new stock purchases to smaller "sure-thing" deals while he slowly sold most of the stocks in Berkshire's portfolio. The merger wave presented both a source of unpredictability to an investor and a potential source of profit. Stocks of many large-cap companies were bid up to reflect the possibility of a takeover, thereby limiting their rate-of-return potential. And deals were being announced at such huge premiums to prevailing prices that buyers were left with extraordinary downside price risk if the deal terminated.

One way to play this situation, Buffett surmised, was to adopt the role of "white knight": He would assist a select group of companies in their efforts to thwart a hostile bid. Buffett figured he could exact concessions from the companies and obtain convertible securities offering high rates of return (which the market no longer promised). The convertibles gave Buffett a security blanket—a rich dividend—that protected him from a decline in stock prices.

One month before the 1987 crash, Buffett stunned his shareholders by announcing he had bought $700 million of newly issued convertible preferred stock of Salomon Brothers, the investment banker and brokerage. Salomon Brothers later merged into Travelers Group and later became part of Citigroup (the merged result of Travelers and Citicorp).

At the time of the purchase, Salomon's stock traded for roughly $32; the preferred dividends converted into 18.4 million common shares at $38 per share. Once Salomon's stock rose above $38, Buffett could book a paper profit from the ultimate conversion. Meanwhile, the preferred paid a 9 percent annual dividend ($63 million on a $700 million investment). Figuring the investment banking company could generate sufficient earnings and returns on assets over time, Buffett saw the Salomon investment as an opportunity to profit with little downside risk to his wallet. As biographer Robert Hagstrom Jr. wrote, Salomon's stock had peaked in 1986 at $59. If the stock could inch its way up to $59 within 3 years, Buffett's total return (assuming he converted) would be 88 percent. If Salomon's stock didn't rebound to $59 until 1992—5 years after the purchase—Buffett could still walk away with an appealing 17.6 percent annual return. If Buffett did not convert, Salomon could redem the security over a 5-year period beginning in 1995.

At the time of Buffett's purchase, Salomon was trying to fend off a hostile takeover from Revlon chairman Ronald Perelman, who later would make a bid for Gillette. Perelman had been negotiating to obtain Salomon shares from the Oppenheimer family, whose South African mining concern, Mineral Resources, held a 14 percent stake in the investment banker. When news broke of Buffett's convertible purchase, Perelman dropped his takeover plans, and Salomon later repurchased Mineral Resources' stake.

All was well from Salomon's perspective. Buffett's interest was less clear. It was the largest investment he had ever made to date in a company, and this time he was staking Berkshire money on an industry (investment banking) Buffett had shunned and derided through the years. Buffett seemed to hold his nose and evaluate the deal on mathematics alone. Few good investment ideas presented themselves, and this one promised a rate of return that could beat a weak market.

But within a month of Buffett's purchase, the stock market dived, taking Salomon's stock down to $16. Perhaps Buffett saw a crash coming because, if he had simply bought Salomon common shares, he would have quickly lost half his money. In fact, it took nearly 4 years before Salomon's stock recovered to Buffett's original $32 entry price. The convertible provision was still worthless, although Buffett was making do with the $63 million yearly dividend.

It would take a few more years for Buffett's giant bet to finally pay off. In August 1991, just as the common stock was rebounding to the $38 conversion price, Salomon acknowledged it had engaged in illegal bond-trading activity (it nearly cornered an auction of 2-year Treasury notes in violation of Treasury Department rules). Senior executives knew of the transgression but had failed to notify authorities until a federal investigation began. These executives were forced to resign, Salomon's stock plummeted, and Buffett was asked to step in and temporarily assume the chairmanship.

This proved to be a most difficult period for Buffett, who had to fire senior managers, slash costs, restore credibility and profitability (which would aid his convertible holdings), handle myriad lawsuits filed against Salomon Brothers, deal with a federal investigation into the bond-trading activities, and try to persuade Congressional committees to allow Salomon to continue participating in Treasury bond auctions, without which Salomon would have gone belly up.

Buffett stepped down as interim chairman in June 1992, after the firm had agreed to pay a $290 million settlement to the federal government. It took until 1993, 6 years after Buffett had purchased the convertible, for Salomon's stock to rise above the $38 conversion price and put the security "in the money" for Buffett. In a show of confidence in Salomon's new management, Buffett began purchasing common shares of Salomon in 1993 and eventually lifted his total stake in the company (including common stock and preferred) to more than 20 percent.

He cashed in 20 percent of the preferreds in 1995, the first year in which they could be redeemed, and converted another 20 percent into common shares in 1996. Later that year, to hedge the remaining bet, Berkshire issued $440 million of exchangeable notes, which allowed buyers to convert Berkshire bonds into Salomon common stock. In 1997, he swapped his Salomon stock for stock in Travelers Group, which was buying Salomon.

GILLETTE

Buffett's interest in razor king Gillette harkens back a few decades but was never so acute than when the company found itself the target of several hostile takeover bids in the 1980s. The last bid, by raider Coniston Partners, was especially costly to Gillette. It barely won the proxy fight, and only after promising to buy back 19 million shares of stock from investors. The buy-back was financed with a debt offering that, overlaid with previous bond issues, was becoming burdensome for the company.

In stepped Buffett, who saw a way to profit from the turnaround of Gillette, provided it could stay independent. Buffett saw to it that Gillette would not fall into hostile hands. In July 1989 he proposed injecting $600 million of capital into Gillette. In return, the company issued him convertible preferred stock that paid an 8.75 percent yearly dividend. The preferred stock would convert into 12 million common shares at $50 per share, about 20 percent above Gillette's prevailing price. Buffett couldn't convert for 2 years, but Gillette reserved the right to force conversion if its common stock rose above $62.50.

On paper, the transaction favored Buffett more than Gillette, although it assuredly rescued the company from a takeover. Gillette used the $600 million cash infusion to pay down debt. Buffett obtained a high-yielding instrument that gave him a cushion against falling share prices. The equity component of the preferred stock allowed Buffett to piggyback off any increase in the price of Gillette's common stock. Further, Buffett was given a seat on Gillette's board and was buying a significant stake (11 percent) in an established company that seemingly had its best years ahead of it.

As it happened, the deal worked for Buffett as well as could be expected. After the release of its Sensor line of razors, Gillette's profitability soared. Sales jumped from $3.8 billion in 1989 to nearly $6.1 billion by 1994. The recession between 1990 and 1991 temporarily depressed Gillette's stock price, but by February 1991 the stock traded around $73, well above the $62.50 floor, and Gillette forced Buffett to convert. This gave Buffett an estimated $275 million paper profit (not counting the dividends) in less than 2 years. He has never parted with the original 12 million common shares, which subsequently split three times to become 96 million shares.

AMERICAN EXPRESS

Another of Buffett's interesting convertible deals surfaced in August 1991, when investors learned he had invested $300 million in charge-card giant American Express. Coming out of the recession, American Express was not the financial powerhouse it is today. Losses at its Shearson Lehman Brothers unit dragged down corporate performance, and gains from charge-card operations were deployed to prop up the ailing brokerage unit. American Express needed cash, Buffett knew it, and the two sides quickly assembled a deal that would benefit American Express and give modest upside potential to Berkshire.

The security offered Buffett was not a typical convertible preferred stock like the ones purchased for Salomon or Gillette. This one offered an 8.85 percent dividend ($26.55 million a year in dividends) and converted into American Express common shares at American Express's discretion and at a price based on the value of those common shares at the time of redemption. American Express traded around $25 when the deal was announced. Buffett's security had to be converted into a maximum 12,244,898 shares of common stock (which implied a conversion price of $24.50 per share). If the common stock traded below $24.50 in 3 years, Buffett could extend the conversion period 1 more year. If American Express' stock fell to, say, $18, Buffett would still get just 12,244,898 shares, giving him a $79.6 million loss on his principal. American Express also had the right to redeem the convertible shares if the common stock rose to $37.53.

In essence, this was a way to play the stock's 1-year to 3-year appreciation potential and lock in nearly $80 million in dividends before mandatory conversion. According to Buffett, American Express seemed to possess decent upside potential, and the 8.85 percent dividend was clearly superior to prevailing bond yields. Because Berkshire Hathaway could claim an exemption on 70 percent of the dividends, the convertible offered the equivalent of more than 11 percent on a pre-tax basis.

Buffett converted the investment on schedule in 1994 and took advantage of a weak market period to accumulate more American Express common stock. By the first quarter of 1995, Buffett had quietly amassed more than 48 million shares of the company, giving him a 9.8 percent stake. American Express went on to become one of Buffett's most profitable investments of the 1990s. As the decade ended, Buffett's stake (he later bought 2 million more shares) was worth $8.4 billion.

"This holding had proved extraordinarily profitable thanks to a move by your Chairman that combined luck and skill—110 percent luck, the balance skill," he wrote in the 1997 annual report. In fact, Buffett was prepared to sell his entire stake when the stock converted in 1994 but was talked out of it by the CEO of Hertz, Frank Olson, over a round of golf.

OPTIONS

On a number of occasions, Buffett has expressed his disdain for derivative securities such as futures and options contracts. Because these securities are bets on shorter-term price movements within a market, they fall under the definition of "gambling" rather than of "investing." An investor in put or call an option, for example, is making a timing bet on the near-term direction of a stock and is trying to magnify the gains through leverage, that is, not having to put up the full amount.

For example, an investor who thinks that shares of America Online, priced at $50, will rise may buy a call option with a strike price of $50. That gives him the right to buy the stock from the option seller for $50 per share regardless of America Online's price at the time, before the options contract expires. Let's say the investor paid a premium of $5 for the right to exercise this option. His total outlay is $500 (each contract covers 100 shares) that he cannot recover.

If America Online rises above $55 (the $50 strike price plus the $5 premium paid) by expiration, the contract will make money. Should the stock reach $60, the option would be valued at $10 ($60 minus the $50 strike price), a doubling of the investor's principal. At a price of $70, the option is worth $20. All it took was a 16.6 percent increase in the stock to cause a doubling of the option's value.

An investor in a put option attempts to do the opposite. Rather than obtain the right to buy the stock at a fixed future price, the put buyer wants the right to sell the stock at a later date and seeks to lock in the price up front. He'll pay a premium for the right to sell the stock that will make money if the stock falls enough to more than cover the cost of the premium.

If Warren Buffett does dabble in options, and few doubt he could dabble successfully, he does so quietly. He once acknowledged writing put options on Coca-Cola's stock; at the time he was thinking of adding to his stake in the soft-drink company. This occurred in April 1993, when Coke's stock hovered around $39 per share (before splits). Buffett was out to acquire several million more shares of Coca-Cola (he already owned 93.4 million shares) but was fearful that the stock would rally and run away from him. He wrote puts covering 5 million shares at an exercise price of $35. Buffett collected a $7.5 million premium ($1.50 per option).

By using options, Buffett was attempting to get more shares of Coke on the cheap and, in the process, collect a premium to defray his costs. It worked this way. If Coca-Cola's stock crashed before the option expired, the buyers would "put" the stock to Buffett, forcing him to take 5 million Coke shares off their hands for a net price of $33.50 per share (the $35 strike price minus the $1.50 premium). That suited him fine because he wanted the shares anyway and hoped they would fall in price when it came time to buy.

However, had Coke's stock risen in price, the buyer would have let the option expire worthless. No stock would have changed hands, but Buffett would have pocketed the $7.5 million premium, which is exactly what happened. The stock rose past the point at which Buffett wanted to buy and he walked away with $7.5 million, but knowing that he did not overpay for Coca-Cola.

Buffett would have to wait another year for the chance to buy Coca-Cola again. In 1994, he increased his then 93.4 million share stake to an even 100 million, which split in 1996 to become 200 million. This was the only time the press has made note of Buffett's foray into options, although he probably has used options numerous times in his career. It's likely he hedges future purchases of stock by selling put options ahead of his purchase. This gives him a locked-in premium and a chance to buy his favorite stocks while they are in decline. Mathematically speaking, the use of options in trying to obtain Coca-Cola stock represented a win–win situation for a value hunter such as Buffett. It would not be surprising to learn that Buffett tries to obtain many of his new stocks in this manner.

18

WARREN'S SECRET WEAPON

Arbitrage

GIVEN THE SECRECY surrounding Buffett's early career and the scant press attention paid to his activities, few understood just how this young, waggish crew-cut figure from Omaha consistently beat the Dow Jones Industrial Average. Buffett's chums from the Graham school of investing knew, of course, that the market was beatable; not just because Graham said it was, but because some of them were proving it with their own money. But the outside world, with nothing more to go on except the "efficient-market" dogma that crept into business schools, could ascribe Buffett's year-after-year successes to nothing more than chance. It's as if they secretly wished that the Nebraska prodigy would stumble one year to prove his mortality—and the market's invincibility.

It didn't happen. Not only did Buffett continue to beat the major market averages, but he suffered few single-year declines along the way. That second accomplishment is, by far, the more remarkable. Statistics tell us that any investor who buys and sells hundreds of stocks over a period of decades and leaves himself vulnerable to the near-term vagaries of the market has a perfect 100 percent chance of posting some yearly losses. It stands to reason that, no matter how well-chosen one's portfolio, profits will be vulnerable to factors outside the investor's control. On October 19, 1987, when the Dow Industrials fell 508 points, more than 97 percent of all stocks fell in price. Perhaps 1 in 1,000 ordinary investors made money that day; perhaps 1 in 10 made money the whole year.

Because the market has a tendency to fall 1 every 4 years or so, an average investor can expect 10 yearly losses over a 40-year period. A great investor might be able to reduce the number of yearly losses to five or six. Buffett's scorecard shows that he has increased the book value of Berkshire Hathaway's stock 35 consecutive years. In only four years did the S&P 500 Index beat the growth of Berkshire's equity. This is similar to 40 years of par golf or better.

There are only three ways an investor can attain a long-term, loss-free track record:

1. Buy short-term Treasury bills and bonds and hold them to maturity, thereby locking in 4 to 6 percent average annual gains.
2. Concentrate on private-market investments by buying properties that consistently generate higher profits and that can sell for greater prices each year.
3. Own publicly traded securities and minimize your exposure to price fluctuations by devoting some of the portfolio to unconventional "sure things."

STRINGING SMALL GAINS TOGETHER WITH TAKEOVERS

Right from the start of his investment management career, Buffett resorted extensively to *takeover arbitrage* (the trading of securities involved in mergers) to keep his portfolio results positive. In poor market years, arbitrage activities have greatly enhanced Buffett's performance and kept returns positive. In strong markets, Buffett has exploited the profit opportunities of mergers to exceed the returns of the indexes. Benjamin Graham, Buffett's mentor, had made arbitrage one of the keystones of his teachings and money-management activities at Graham-Newman between 1926 and 1956. Graham's clients were informed that some of their money would be deployed in shorter term situations to exploit irrational price discrepancies. These situations included reorganizations, liquidations, hedges involving convertible bonds and preferred stocks, and takeovers.

One of Graham's first investments was a classic arbitrage. In 1915, at the age of 21, he bought shares of Guggenheim Exploration Company, a holding company priced at around $69 per share. Guggenheim owned minority stakes in four copper-mining companies, Kennecott, Chino Copper, American Smelting, and Ray Consolidated. The Guggenheim stakes combined were worth more than $76 per share. Therefore on paper, an investor was getting $76 worth of assets for just $69. Graham reckoned that this situation could not continue indefinitely because Guggenheim's stock had to rise to at least $76, which would give him a locked-in $7 per-share profit.[1]

The word *arbitrage*, in the strict sense, refers to the simultaneous buying and selling of a security (or related security) in two different markets to capture irrational price movements. For example, if Hewlett-Packard's stock was selling for $80 on the New York Stock Exchange and for $82 on the Pacific Stock Exchange, an *arbitrageur* would buy all the Hewlett-Packard stock he could get his hands on in New York and make arrangements to sell it on the Pacific Exchange, locking in a $2 profit each time. The rub is that these opportunities, when they arise, don't last very long. Systematic purchases of Hewlett-Packard's stock in New York would drive up the price on that market, while concurrent selling on the Pacific Exchange would drive Hewlett-Packard's quote down. Both markets would quickly reach parity again.

Takeover arbitrages operate in roughly similar ways. In effect, you are trying to capture the "spread" between the market price of a stock and the deal price, that is, the price at which one company has agreed to pay for another. Merck, for example, might offer $85 per share in cash to buy Pfizer. If Pfizer's stock trades at, say, $80, an investor has the opportunity to lock in a guaranteed $5 profit by buying Pfizer and holding his shares until the deal is approved and then tendering them to Merck. The $5 profit represents a 6.25 percent gain on your $80 investment. If Pfizer's stock dropped below $80, the potential gain widens.

The trick in takeover arbitrage is to maximize your *annualized* gain and minimize your chances of loss. Companies usually disclose up front how fast they think they can consummate the merger, which has a big impact in determining your returns. In the Merck example, a $5 profit translates into a 12.9 percent annualized gain if the deal closes exactly 6 months after your purchase. If the deal closes in 4 months, your annualized gain turns into a more attractive 20 percent. Once the deal closes and you have received your money from Merck, deploy the proceeds into another deal offering similar profit opportunities.

By stringing together a succession of arbitrage trades, an investor can turn small percentage gains on each transaction into huge annual gains, providing all the deals work in your favor. If you can make 10 percent on consecutive deals that close in 3 months, your compounded return, assuming you reinvest all the profits from the previous deal, will be an astounding 46.4 percent for an entire year (Table 18.1).

There's no shortage of these opportunities. Between 10 and 20 mergers are announced every day on Wall Street, some of which have opened up fabulous profit-making bonanzas for investors sharp enough to spot them. Buffett has spoken sparingly of his arbitrage activity, except to say that he does it (especially when he has trouble finding good bargains), continues to do it, and has done pretty well at it.

TABLE 18.1   Compounded annualized return of an arbitrage deal.

	Time Until Deal Closes			
Discount (%)	1 month	2 months	3 months	6 months
2	26.8%	12.6%	8.2%	4.0%
3	42.6	19.4	12.6	6.1
4	60.1	26.5	17.0	8.2
5	79.6	34.0	21.6	10.3
6	101.2	41.9	26.2	12.4
7	125.2	50.1	31.1	14.5
8	151.8	58.7	36.0	16.6
9	181.3	67.7	41.2	18.8
10	213.8	77.2	46.4	21.0
11	249.8	87.0	51.8	23.2
12	289.6	97.4	57.4	25.4
13	333.5	108.2	63.0	27.7
14	381.8	119.5	68.9	30.0
15	435.0	131.3	74.9	32.3

"(We) sometimes engage in arbitrage as an alternative to holding short-term cash equivalents," he wrote in his 1988 annual report to shareholders. "We prefer, of course, to make major long-term commitments, but we often have more cash than good ideas. At such times, arbitrage sometimes promises much greater returns than Treasury bills and, equally important, cools any temptation we may have to relax our standards for long-term investments. [Charlie's signoff after we've talked about an arbitrage commitment is usually: 'Okay, at least it will keep you out of bars.']"[2]

Truth be told, there are more than a few investment advisers behind bars for attaining (however illicitly) the gains Buffett scored legally playing takeovers. Buffett wrote that Graham attained a 20 percent annual return from arbitrage activities between 1926 and 1956, a result that would have destroyed the returns of the Dow Industrials.[3] In 1988, Buffett claimed that his own returns from arbitrage, to date, had "averaged well over" Graham's 20 percent.

While running his private partnership in the 1950s and 1960s, Buffett invested in arbitrage situations dozens of times. He recognized the superior returns possible from stringing together small percentage gains over and over. Most important, Buffett seems to have used arbitrage to protect his clients' portfolios from the vagaries of the stock market. By putting a large portion of their money into takeover situations (what Buffett routinely called "workouts"), he could reap abnormal gains without worrying about the general conditions of the market. Indeed, in a poor market, Buffett could expect his arbitrage positions to gain in value, or at least not decline.

Knowing that he could insulate a good portion of clients' portfolios from losses, Buffett was free to concentrate the rest of their holding into just a few stocks. Writing to his clients in February 1960, Buffett said that 35 percent of their money was tied up in one stock (which he declined to name); the rest was invested in undervalued stocks and workouts: "To the extent possible, I continue to attempt to invest in situations at least partially insulated from the behavior of the general market."[4]

In general, workouts constituted the second largest component of Buffett's partnership portfolios. Whereas Buffett rarely told investors about the types of arbitrage situations he played, he openly acknowledged the volume of deals he transacted and that he borrowed money to make purchases.

At any give time, we may be in 10 to 15 of these; some just beginning and others in the late stage of development. I believe in using borrowed money to offset a portion of our workout portfolio since there is a high degree of safety in this category in terms of both eventual results and intermediate market behavior.[5]

At the 1999 Berkshire Hathaway annual meeting, Buffett was asked whether he believed he could beat the market consistently were he to start his career again with a fresh partnership. Naturally, Buffett said he could, by playing small-cap stocks and engaging in arbitrage. "I can think of about a dozen people [himself included] who could compound $1 million at 50 percent a year," he told the audience.

Buffett views arbitrage like most other endeavors, as a mathematical exercise, where the potential prize is the "weighted expected return" from the investment, taking into account the upside and downside risks. "If I think an event has a 90 percent chance of occurring and there are 3 points on the upside, and there is a 10 percent change that it will fall through, and there are 9 points on the downside, then that's $0.90 off of $2.70, leaving $1.80 mathematical expectation," Buffett was quoted saying in 1990.[6]

Assume, for example, that PeopleSoft is being acquired for $20 per share and its stock trades for $17—a 3-point discount to the deal price. Using Buffett's analogy, let's further assume that the deal had a 90 percent chance of consummating (which earns $3) and $9 of potential loss if the deal falls through. The weighted expected return is $1.80 [$(0.9 \times \$3) - (0.1 \times \$9)$]. This constitutes a 10.6 percent return on a $17 investment. If the deal takes 1 year to complete, your annualized return is 10.6 percent. If it takes only 6 months, the annualized return is 22.3 percent (1.106×1.106).

Double-digit, short-term gains are often available when playing takeovers. In April 1999, Global Crossing made a tender offer for the stock of Frontier Corp. in a bid to expand its telecommunications services coast to coast. The deal called for Frontier shareholders to receive the equivalent of $62 worth of Global Crossing's stock at completion. Yet, Frontier often traded at discounts of between 10 and 20 percent to the $62 price. Traders' anxiety that the merger would collapse outweighed the attractions of the protective collars Global Crossing attached to the deal. The merger closed successfully in September 1999, and investors who took full advantage of the periodic price swings in Frontier locked in triple-digit annualized gains.

It is during such periods of irrationality that people such as Buffett step in. An astute investor who was watching developments could have swooped in, bought Frontier for $45, and locked in a potential $17 return within 3 to 4 months. That translated into a 38 percent return on $45 and an *annualized* return of between 162 and 262 percent depending on when the deal closed.

Case exhibited equally irrational price movements after receiving a $55 per share cash takeover offer from New Holland NV in May 1999. Two months later, after rumors began swirling on Internet chatrooms that the deal would collapse, Case's stock plunged to $44. A savvy investor had a chance to lock in an $11 return on a $44 investment—a 25 percent return for someone willing to wait just a few months for the deal to conclude.

Experience shows that most takeover deals get plagued by irrationality. The target company's stock usually rises quickly on the day of the announcement, reaching a level 4 to 6 percent below the bid price. In the ensuing days or weeks, the stock likely falls in price again, as many mom-and-pop investors lose patience, decide not to tender their shares, and take their profits instead. Their selling opens up the types of high returns Buffett covets. Keep in mind that it doesn't take much of a decline in price to make an arbitrage deal very sweet. If company X wants to buy company Y for $20 per share in cash and company Y's stock trades at $19, your potential gain will be just 5.3 percent. If company Y's stock falls just 50 cents to $18.50, the arbitrage profits jump to 8.3 percent. If the deal closes in 3 months, your annualized gain will be 37.6 percent.

In 1990, *Forbes* unearthed financial filings made to state regulators by Berkshire Hathaway's insurance subsidiaries in an attempt to stitch together Buffett's yearly arbitrage activities. They sought out insurance records because Berkshire's insurance companies provide most of the cash Buffett needs to make new investments. *Forbes* found, for example, that Buffett used takeover arbitrage extensively in 1987 to keep Berkshire's investment portfolio rising in a highly volatile market. Interestingly, Buffett was significantly cutting the number of common stocks Berkshire held in its portfolio. Thus, at a time when ordinary investors were losing money on common stocks, Buffett was relying heavily on nontraditional investments to stay in the black. That year, Buffett played takeovers involving Kraft, RJR

Nabisco, and Philip Morris, in addition to lesser known companies such as Marine Midland, Federated, and Interco. He turned a $2.7 million bet on Southland into $3.3 million in 10 days for an annualized gain of more than 700 percent. In all, *Forbes* estimated that Buffett's arbitrage activities earned *90 percent* in 1987, whereas the S&P 500 returned 5 percent.[7]

In 1988, Buffett bet on 20 different takeovers, netting a gain of 35 percent, more than twice what the S&P 500 gained. The following year, Buffett was not as fortunate, *Fortune* magazine reported. He lost 31 percent on takeover deals. He did not reveal this loss to shareholders, but had warned them the previous year that he planned to take fewer arbitrage stakes in 1989 because of "extraordinary excesses" in the takeover arena. "The less the prudence with which others conduct their affairs, the greater the prudence with which we should conduct our own affairs," he wrote.[8] Nevertheless, that year Buffett tendered part of his arbitrage stake in RJR Nabisco to takeover specialists Kohlberg Kravis Roberts & Co. and sold the rest of his shares in the market for a combined $64 million profit.[9]

THE ROCKWOOD COCOA BEAN BONANZA

In 1954, his first year working for Graham, Buffett plunged into one of the more "offbeat" of his numerous arbitrage trades, and one of the few about which he has spoken freely. Rockwood & Co., a barely profitable chocolate maker, found itself in a squeeze when the price of cocoa temporarily soared 10-fold and the company tried to liquidate its inventory for a profit. The catch was that Rockwood faced a nearly 50 percent income tax on the sale.

Luckily, that same year, the Internal Revenue Service allowed companies to avoid taxes on inventory sales if they sold their material to shareholders as part of a restructuring of the business. Taking advantage of the rule change, Rockwood announced it would sell its cocoa butter business and assigned 13 million pounds of beans to that division's inventory. As part of the deal, Rockwood announced it would repurchase stock from shareholders and give them 80 pounds of beans per share. With cocoa beans selling for 60 cents a pound, Rockwood was essentially repurchasing stock at $48 per share. Just before the announcement, Rockwood's stock traded for just $15.

Buffett seized the opportunity. He bought Rockwood's shares on the open market, sold the shares back to Rockwood, and then sold beans he received in the exchange and used the proceeds to purchase more Rockwood shares. This enabled Buffett to profit continuously until the spread between bean prices and Rockwood's stock price evaporated. "For several weeks I busily bought shares, sold beans, and made periodic stops at Schroeder Trust to exchange stock certificates for warehouses receipts. The profits were good and my only expense was subway tokens," Buffett said.[10]

ARCATA CORP.

In September 1981, takeover specialists Kohlberg Kravis Roberts & Co. (KKR) offered to purchase all assets of Arcata Corp., a paper, printing, and forest-products concern. At the time, Arcata was locked in a dispute with the federal government over the valuation of its land. The government had taken title to 10,700 acres of Arcata's timberland in 1978 to expand Redwood National Park. In return, it paid Arcata $97.9 million, which the company contested as inadequate. This dispute complicated the takeover by KKR, which, in the end, offered to pay $37 per share for Arcata plus two-thirds of any incremental awards paid by the government for the timberlands.

"We had to ask ourselves what would happen if the KKR deal did fall through, and here we also felt reasonably comfortable," Buffett wrote several years after the fact. "Arcata's management and directors had been shopping the company for some time and were clearly determined to sell. If KKR went away, Arcata would likely find another buyer, though, of course, the price might be lower. Finally, we had to ask ourselves what the redwood claim might be worth. Your chairman, who can't tell an elm from an oak, had no trouble with that one: He coolly evaluated the claim at somewhere between zero and a whole lot." Buffett said.[11]

The deal was expected to be completed by January 1982, and Buffett bought 655,000 shares at prices between $33.50 and $38. All along, Buffett was under the impression he would receive a minimum $37 per share plus a share of any future settlement with the government. The deal hit a snag when KKR's lenders expressed worries about the timber industry, and the vote to approve the deal was delayed several months. Finally, KKR agreed to pay $37.50 per share, which netted Buffett a $1.7 million profit over a 6 month period.

Five years later, a trial judge determined that the federal government woefully underpaid Arcata for its redwood land and ordered the government to pay $519 million. "We received an additional $29.48 per share, or about $19.3 million," Buffett reported.[12]

MGI PROPERTIES

Capturing small crumbs in a short period of time is nothing to sneeze at. If tiny gains attract someone as prosperous as Buffett, they should also attract you. In early 1999, for example, Buffett revealed that he was accumulating a stake in MGI Properties, a real estate investment trust (REIT) with a portfolio of office buildings and apartment complexes. The press immediately assumed that Buffett had tuned his radar toward REITs, an out-of-favor group whose stocks were yielding an average of 3 percentage points more than 30-year Treasury bonds.

To the contrary, MGI was a typical Buffett workout. In October 1998, directors of MGI approved a plan to liquidate the entire portfolio of properties and return the proceeds to shareholders as a special dividend. They estimated that the sale of properties would fetch between $29 and $30 per share for investors. At the time of the announcement, the stock sold for around $24. As MGI went to work arranging the sales, it became apparent that the liquidation had a 100 percent chance of being completed. At that point, it was just a matter of calculating how long it would take investors to get their $29 to $30. Buffett began buying tens of thousands of shares of MGI, even as the stock gradually rose closer to $29. He committed upward of $50 million of capital in the hopes of culling an average gain of $1 to $3 per share.

Once again, mathematics made the decision for Buffett. There was no chance that the deal would fall through, so there was zero downside risk to an investor. MGI's liquidation, in fact, proceeded smoothly—the company signed deals to sell more than 80 percent of its office space by May 1999, a time when Buffett was eagerly buying shares. If he paid an average price of $27.50 per share and the liquidation fetched $30, Buffett would enjoy a 10.9 percent *guaranteed* gain in just a few months.

What investors may find odd about the MGI transaction was that Buffett bought these shares for his private account rather than through

Berkshire Hathaway. In addition to his Berkshire stock, Buffett keeps a sizeable portfolio on the side, which becomes his "play" money, so to speak. At the time Buffett bought MGI's shares, his Berkshire stock was worth about $38 billion. This begs the question: Why did Buffett bother to dabble in a liquidation arbitrage that could, at best, increase his net worth by a few million dollars? Here was another example of Buffett seizing an opportunity, no matter how small, for guaranteed gains. The move shows that, no matter how wealthy Buffett becomes, he will not pass up a chance to extract a few free percentage points when the situation presents itself.

GENERAL DYNAMICS

One of Buffett's most profitable investments (on a dollar basis) resulted from a routine arbitrage deal that turned to gold. In July 1992, defense contractor General Dynamics, then in the midst of a restructuring, announced that it would repurchase up to 30 percent of its stock in a Dutch auction at prices between $65.37 and $72.25 per share (General Dynamics has since split two for one twice). In previous months, the company had sold off three of its nondefense-related divisions (Data Systems, Cessna Aircraft, and Hughes Aircraft) and had raised $1.25 billion. As the U.S. military was gradually paring down and reducing orders to contractors, General Dynamics opted not to plow the $1.25 billion in proceeds back into the company. Instead, it made a bold move to reduce the number of shares outstanding and substantially raise per-share earnings for investors who wouldn't tender.

Sensing an opportunity to make a few dollars' profit, Buffett, buying through Berkshire Hathaway, accumulated 4.3 million shares of General Dynamics at prices averaging $72 ($18 post split). "I had paid little attention to the company until last summer, when it announced it would repurchase about 30 percent of its shares," Buffett wrote in his 1992 annual report. "Seeing an arbitrage opportunity, I began buying the stock for Berkshire, expecting to tender our holdings for a small profit."[13]

It was only after purchasing the shares that Buffett began studying General Dynamics and saw the unique turnaround being engineered by CEO William Anders. Anders had been wringing tens of millions of dollars of costs out of the company's operations by laying off several thousand employees, closing manufacturing facilities, and slicing research and development expenditures. Wall Street seemed elated with Anders' moves. General Dynamics stock had more than doubled off its bottom before the company announced the Dutch auction. Still, the stock traded below the company's book value, a point that caught Buffett's attention.

Rather than tender his 4.3 million shares, Buffett hung on, believing that the stock had further rallying power. Over the next 5 years, the shares Buffett continued to hold would nearly quadruple in price. In addition, General Dynamics declared three special dividends in 1993 amounting to $50 per share ($12.50 post split). Buffett's 4.3 million share purchase would have turned into 17.2 million shares after the splits, but Buffett sold 20 percent of his stake in April 1994 and then another 14 percent stake in August. He disposed of another 20 percent over the next 2 years.

By 1998 Berkshire Hathaway held 7,693,637 shares of General Dynamics that, at one point, were worth about $530 million. The $50 per-share dividends Buffett received and his pre-tax profits, including profits from shares sold between 1994 and 1997, totaled an estimated $450 million by mid-1999. "We were lucky," Buffett acknowledged after the fact.

ADDING ARBITRAGE TO YOUR PORTFOLIO

Investors who wish to enhance their yearly portfolio returns should seriously consider playing takeover deals. By reserving a portion of your portfolio to arbitrage, as Buffett has, you can potentially add several percentage points of gain to your yearly returns. Table 18.2 shows how an investor would have fared by setting aside 25 percent of her portfolio every year to engage in takeover transactions. I assumed that this investor achieved annualized gains of 20 percent on takeover picks. The rest of the portfolio (75 percent) was invested in S&P 500 stocks.

Starting in 1960 with $10,000, the investor would have increased his or her portfolio to $1,774,802 by the end of 1998. That's a compounded gain of 14.6 percent a year. In contrast, the investor who put 100 percent of his portfolio into the S&P 500 saw $10,000 grow into just $817,402, less than half as much. The compounded return was 12.3 percent.

Adding 2.3 percentage points a year to your returns has the added benefit of reducing the probability of yearly losses. In the example presented in Table 18.2, the investor who entrusted all of her money to S&P 500 stocks suffered losses in 8 of the 38 chosen years. The investor who devoted 25 percent of the portfolio to arbitrage lost money in just 5 of 38 years. The investor would have sustained no yearly losses over a 24-year period starting in 1975.

On paper, an extra 2.3 percent a year in gain doesn't seem like much, but, when compounded year after year, 2.3 percent adds up to significant, incremental results. These results become magnified with improved arbitrage abilities. If an investor averaged a 25 percent annualized return from arbitrage, a $10,000 portfolio would have grown to $2,719,955 by the end of 1998, a 15.9 percent compounded gain.

As I showed earlier, Buffett was devoting a considerable portion of his clients' portfolios to workouts and was *borrowing* money to buy shares. Borrowing money had the effect of multiplying his returns. It's no wonder the partnership defeated the Dow Jones Industrial Average every single year. In Table 18.2, I show how the returns of the Dow Industrials could have been enhanced by a money manager who put half of the portfolio in the index and the other half in arbitrage situations that netted a 20 percent annual return. In the third column, I assume the portfolio manager bought arbitrage securities on margin. As you can see, once margin is deployed, the returns come much closer to duplicating Buffett's accomplishment.

If such gains are possible, why isn't arbitrage practiced more often? Frankly, most investors are so coached to expect 20 to 30 percent yearly gains on their growth stocks that they scoff at the prospects of making a few percentage points at a time. They fail to realize that it's possible to earn higher yearly returns than the major market indexes by stringing these deals together (Table 18.3).

Buffett is by no means alone in what he does. Hundreds of professional investors worldwide make their living speculating on stocks involved in takeovers. They do little else but sit at terminals and watch news wires for announcements of a takeover. When one flashes across their screen, they quickly analyze the deal, form a strategy, and act. They may close the position within hours or days, depending on their goals. Some arbitrageurs will hold their stocks until the deal is consummated and they receive their cash or shares.

TABLE 18.2 How arbitrage would have enhanced the Dow Jones Industrial Average (DJIA).

	DJIA	DJIA + 50% Arbitrage	DJIA + 50% Arbitrage on Margin	Buffett
1957	–8.4%	5.8%	8.7%	**10.4%**
1958	38.5%	29.3%	43.9%	**40.9%**
1959	20.0%	20.0%	30.0%	**25.9%**
1960	–6.2%	6.9%	10.4%	**22.8%**
1961	22.4%	21.2%	31.8%	**45.9%**
1962	–7.6%	6.2%	9.3%	**13.9%**
1963	20.6%	20.3%	30.5%	**38.7%**
1964	18.7%	19.4%	29.0%	**27.8%**
1965	14.2%	17.1%	25.7%	**47.2%**
1966	–15.6%	2.2%	3.3%	**20.4%**
1967	19.3%	19.7%	29.5%	**35.9%**
1968	7.7%	13.9%	20.8%	**58.8%**
1969	–11.6%	4.2%	6.3%	**6.8%**
Annual. Return	**7.4%**	**14.0%**	**20.9%**	**29.5%**

From all indications, however, none has been as successful at capturing returns from deals as Buffett because he focuses only on "sure-thing" deals, which these days represent a smaller and smaller fraction of the mergers announced. Buffett also has the luxury of patience on his side. "Arbs," in contrast, need to justify their existence by trading. They tend to react quickly to as many deals as possible, sometimes before the companies release all the details of the merger. Buffett, however, picks and chooses a few deals a year from among hundreds already announced. He is more likely to research the deal thoroughly and wait for a temporary dip in the target's stock to lock in a guaranteed high return.

Buffett also differs from other "arb" specialists in that he almost always enlists on the side of the common shareholder. He takes positions *after* mergers are announced rather than use his clout and financial backing to force deals to occur (which was typical of takeover specialists in the 1980s). He never invests based on rumored takeovers,

TABLE 18.3   How arbitrage can add to returns.

	S&P 500 Portfolio		25% Arbitraged Portfolio*	
		$10,000		**$10,000**
1960	0.5%	$10,050	5.4%	$10,538
1961	26.9%	$12,753	25.2%	$13,190
1962	–8.7%	$11,644	–1.5%	$12,989
1963	22.8%	$14,299	22.1%	$15,860
1964	16.5%	$16,658	17.4%	$18,615
1965	12.5%	$18,740	14.4%	$21,291
1966	–10.1%	$16,847	–2.6%	$20,743
1967	24.0%	$20,891	23.0%	$25,514
1968	11.1%	$23,210	13.3%	$28,914
1969	–8.5%	$21,237	–1.4%	$28,516
1970	4.0%	$22,086	8.0%	$30,798
1971	14.3%	$25,245	15.7%	$35,640
1972	19.0%	$30,041	19.3%	$42,501
1973	–14.7%	$25,625	–6.0%	$39,940
1974	–26.5%	$18,835	–14.9%	$33,999
1975	37.2%	$25,841	32.9%	$45,185
1976	23.8%	$31,991	22.9%	$55,510
1977	–7.2%	$29,688	–0.4%	$55,288
1978	6.6%	$31,647	10.0%	$60,789
1979	18.4%	$37,470	18.8%	$72,217
1980	32.4%	$49,611	29.3%	$93,377
1981	–4.9%	$47,180	1.3%	$94,614
1982	21.4%	$57,276	21.1%	$114,531
1983	22.5%	$70,163	21.9%	$139,584
1984	6.3%	$74,584	9.7%	$153,159
1985	32.2%	$98,599	29.2%	$197,805
1986	18.5%	$116,840	18.9%	$235,140
1987	5.2%	$122,916	8.9%	$256,068
1988	16.8%	$143,566	17.6%	$301,136
1989	31.5%	$188,789	28.6%	$387,336
1990	–3.2%	$182,748	2.6%	$397,406

continued on next page

TABLE 18.3   continued

	S&P 500 Portfolio		25% Arbitraged Portfolio*	
1991	30.4%	$238,303	27.8%	$507,885
1992	7.7%	$256,653	10.8%	$562,610
1993	9.9%	$282,061	12.4%	$632,514
1994	1.3%	$285,728	6.0%	$670,307
1995	37.5%	$392,876	33.1%	$892,346
1996	23.0%	$483,238	22.3%	$1,090,893
1997	33.4%	$644,639	30.1%	$1,418,707
1998	26.8%	$817,402	25.1%	$1,774,802
Return	12.3%		14.6%	

Assumes annualized returns of 20% on arbitrage activities.

either. Buffett's cardinal goal is to profit from the spread in price, not to take a controlling interest in the company and force a turnover of management. Nor is he interested in acquiring properties for the sake of busting them up into pieces. His role, as he sees it, is merely to exploit the attractive mathematics these deals offer. The deal itself is of no consequence to Buffett because he rarely cares about the companies in play. He simply senses opportunities for abnormal profits and pounces.

Those looking for evidence that the market can be beaten need look no farther than the impressive arbitrage record of Buffett and Graham starting in the 1920s. In Buffett's case, it is clear that takeover arbitrage has been an important artifice that propelled his yearly returns beyond what could have been expected by a practicing value investor. What made this record all the more remarkable was its innocence: Virtually any investor could have reaped similar, market-beating gains from arbitrage activity, Buffett noted in his 1988 annual report:

> In my opinion, the continuous 63-year arbitrage experience of Graham-Newman Corp., Buffett Partnership, and Berkshire illustrates just how foolish [efficient market theory] is. The results are not skewed by a few fortunate experiences; we did not have to dig for obscure facts or develop keen insights about products or managements—we simply acted on highly publicized events.

RULES FOR ENGAGING IN ARBITRAGE

Invest in "cash" deals rather than "stock deals" and only invest in deals that have already been announced.   An offer of $50 in cash is preferable because the deal has a fixed unit of exchange that limits the downside potential of the target stock. Avoid deals where there's a chance that the amount you eventually get is less than the original offer. Say a company whose stock trades at $50 offers 1.5 shares of its stock. The deal is worth $75 per share to you on the day of the offer. If the stock declines to $30 by the time the deal is consummated, you'll get only $45.

Determine your expected rate of return up front.   Before taking a position in a merger, calculate the potential profits and losses and the probabilities of each occurring. Then determine the time needed to complete the deal and your potential annualized return. Avoid deals that can't offer an annualized return of 20 to 30 percent or better.

Make sure the deal will be consummated.   The target's stock could drop unexpectedly if the deal falls through. Any number of reasons can kill a deal, including antitrust concerns expressed by regulators, a sharp decline in the acquirer's stock, a tiff between CEOs over compensation, or a vote by either company's shareholders to nix the merger. Some mergers, including those involving utilities or foreign companies, can take more than a year to complete, which can tie up your money for a considerable time.

If you decide to play a "stock merger" (the target company's shareholders receive shares of the acquirer), look for deals with protective "collars."   The merger should include mechanisms for keeping the target stock's price from falling after the deal is announced. Typically, the acquirer will offer a variable number of shares of stock based on the trading range of its stock.

Don't rely exclusively on arbitrage for your profits.   The market tends to make as many correct as incorrect judgments about a stock's price. Randomly selecting deals to play will likely result in ordinary returns over time. You must exercise discipline and review all relevant facts carefully. When a large spread develops between the market price and takeover price, market participants are expressing worry that the deal may fizzle. Someone may have obtained information indicating that the deal won't proceed.

Don't be afraid to buy arbitrage stocks on margin (that is, with borrowed money) if you believe the deal is a sure thing. You can enhance your portfolio returns further if you regularly borrow money to finance the purchase of arbitrage shares. Your major risk, of course, is that the deal falls through, in which case your margin purchase will accelerate your losses. But with broker loan rates hovering between 7 and 8 percent annually, investors should considering borrowing if they see opportunities to obtain annualized gains (adjusted, of course, for risk) far exceeding loan rates.

P A R T

CHICKEN SOUP
FOR THE INVESTOR

BUFFETT'S THOUGHTS ON FORMING GOOD HABITS

I
N HIS BEST-SELLING BOOK, *Emotional Intelligence*, Daniel Goleman proposed that human beings are, at their root, a species of animal that came into its own just 10,000 years ago, barely enough time to adapt to our circumstances. Dinosaurs had more than 150 million years to adapt and evolve, both physically and intuitively, to their environment. In contrast, the 500 or so generations modern man has existed on earth and the accomplishments we have squeezed within that setting have hardly been sufficient for us to maximize our potential.

For example, our motor skills—the ability to walk, run, manipulate our fingers, or carry objects—hardly differ from the skills possessed by early humans. Perhaps in 1 million years we will be able to run 35 miles an hour, throw a baseball 125 miles an hour, or lift 2,000 pounds on our backs. For now, humans must accept that such quantum leaps in genetic makeup do not happen overnight. By the same token, Goleman argued, there has been little change in our *cognitive* makeup. Our abilities to reason, to express emotion, and to make decisions aren't much different from the aptitudes shown by early civilizations: "The slow deliberate forces of evolution that have shaped our emotions have done their work over the course of a million years. The last 10,000 years…have left little imprint on our templates for emotional life."[1]

Michael Mauboussin of Credit Suisse First Boston, a leading researcher in the growing field of behavioral finance, says Goleman's theories of cognitive evolution have particular relevance for investors. Most of the sweeping developments in the fields of economics and finance, Mauboussin noted, were tested, applied, and taught within the past 40 years, about 1/50,000th of the time humans have existed.

From a genetic perspective, humans have not been exposed long enough to these theories to adapt themselves cognitively, and there's the rub. Academics can preach until they're blue in the face on how to act rationally with money, diversify a portfolio, or analyze information, but our cognitive capacities (which have not evolved much in 2 million years) prevent us from acting reasonably all the time. "If it takes tens of thousands of years for us to catch up with our environment, it is fair to say that humans have no mental basis, or context, to understand how to invest in capital markets rationally," Mauboussin argues.

"Humans are not hard-wired to rationally weigh risk and reward. We are still better suited to run like hell when we see a sabre-toothed tiger than to consider potential returns of intangible assets."[2] This awareness of our limitations can help us avoid common stock-picking errors. According to Mauboussin, investors tend to make seven common errors of judgment:

1. We have an innate desire to be part of a crowd and feel safer making mistakes with others than striking out on our own.

2. We suffer from overconfidence in our abilities.

3. We are unable to assess probabilities rationally.

4. We are easily lured by storytelling, especially when the story attempts to provide answers to pressing questions.

5. We want to rely on "rules of thumb" even in the absence of rigorous proof.

6. We ignore statistical truisms regarding chance and probability.

7. We believe that the intuitive skills possessed by some humans (successful stock pickers, for example) are readily transferable.

Emotions and habits play a vital role in the investment process. If you can corral irrational behavior and channel it into a logical thought process, you will be a better stock-picker. This is the untold parable of Warren Buffett—his lack of emotion with regard to money. He comes as close to being the perfectly rational investor as any you'll read about. Granted, even he has made mistakes, and huge ones, from time to time. But he sits atop the investing world primarily because of his ability to keep passion outside the sterile proverbs of mathematics.

Any individual wishing to duplicate Buffett's results must first try to understand his personal stock-picking habits. For the rest of the section, I've let Buffett do the talking, by reprinting his comments and those of other financial titans on a number of topics relating to behavior and emotion.

Follow your own counsel, not the advice of others.

You have to think for yourself. It always amazes me how high-IQ people mindlessly imitate. I never get good ideas talking to other people.[3]

Full-time professionals in other fields, let's say dentists, bring a lot to the layman. But in aggregate, people get nothing for their money from professional money managers.[4]

Have the courage of your knowledge and experience. If you have formed a conclusion from the facts and if you know your judgment is sound, act on it—even though others may hesitate or differ. You are neither right nor wrong because the crowd disagrees with you. You are right because your data and reasoning are right. Similarly, in the world of securities, courage becomes the supreme virtue after adequate knowledge and a tested judgment are at hand."[5]

Never be a price taker or assume the market is always right.

Naturally the disservice done students and gullible investment professionals who have swallowed Efficient Market Theory has been an extraordinary service to us and other followers of Graham. In any sort of a contest—financial, mental, or physical—it's an enormous advantage to have opponents who have been taught that it's useless to even try."[6]

Ben [Graham]'s Mr. Market allegory [reprinted as Appendix 1] may seem out-of-date in today's investment world, in which most professionals and academicians talk of efficient markets, dynamic hedging and betas. Their interest in such matters is understandable, since techniques shrouded in mystery clearly have value to the purveyor of investment advice. After all, what witch doctor has ever achieved fame and fortune by simply advising "Take two aspirins"?[7]

Common sense and a knowledge of business is more important to the investment process than academic formulas.

To invest successfully, you need not understand beta, efficient markets, modern portfolio theory, option pricing or emerging markets. You may, in fact, be better off knowing nothing of these. That, of course, is not the prevailing view at most business schools, whose finance curriculum tends to be dominated by such subjects. In our view, though, investment students need only two well-taught courses—How to Value a Business, and How to Think About Market Prices.[8]

I have seen no trend toward value investing in the 35 years I've practiced it. There seems to be some perverse human characteristic that likes to make easy things difficult.[9]

I am a better investor because I am a businessman, and a better businessman because I am an investor.[10]

We are enormously indebted to those academics: What could be more advantageous in an intellectual contest—whether it be bridge, chess or stock selection—than to have opponents who have been taught that thinking is a waste of energy?[11]

Ignore day-to-day fluctuations in the market: They're often meaningless to the bigger picture.

I never attempt to make money on the stock market. I buy on the assumption that they could close the market the next day and not reopen it for five years.[12]

For some reason, people take their cues from price action rather than from values. What doesn't work is when you start doing things that you don't understand or because they worked last week for somebody else. The dumbest reason in the world to buy a stock is because it's going up.[13]

Avoid relying on forecasts because most prove to be wrong and are made to entice you to trade.

I have no use whatsoever for projections or forecasts. They create an illusion of apparent precision. The more meticulous they are, the more concerned you should be. We never look at projections but we care very much about, and look very deeply, at track records. If a company has a lousy track record, but a very bright future, we will [pass on] the opportunity.[14]

We essentially spend no time thinking about macroeconomic factors. In other words, if somebody handed us a prediction by the most revered intellectual on the subject, with figures for unemployment or interest rates, or whatever it might be for the next two years, we would not pay any attention to it. We simply try to focus on businesses that we think we understand and where we like the price and management. If we see anything that relates to what's going to happen in Congress, we don't even read it. We just don't think it's helpful to have a view on these matters.[15]

We try to *price*, rather than *time*, purchases. In our view, it is folly to forego buying shares in an outstanding business whose long-term future is predictable, because of short-term worries about an economy or a stock market that we know to be unpredictable. Why scrap an informed decision because of an uninformed guess? We purchased National Indemnity in 1967, See's in 1972, Buffalo News in 1977, Nebraska Furniture Mart in 1983, and Scott Fetzer in 1986 because those are the years they became available and because we thought the prices they carried were acceptable. In each case, we pondered what the business was likely to do, not what the Dow, the Fed, or the economy might do. If we see this approach as making sense in the purchase of businesses in their entirety, why should we change tack when we are purchasing small pieces of wonderful businesses in the stock market?[16]

Thousands of experts study overbought indicators, oversold indicators, head-and-shoulder patterns, put-call ratios, the Fed's policy on money supply, foreign investment, the movement of the constellations through the heavens, and the moss on oak trees, and they can't predict markets with any useful consistency, any more than the gizzard squeezers could tell the Roman emperors when the Huns would attack.[17]

Remember that you are buying a piece of a company and trying to share in its fortunes. Don't adopt the view that investing is about shuffling stock certificates.

Investment is an activity of forecasting the yield on assets over the life of the asset...speculation is the activity of forecasting the psychology of the market.[18]

If you are an investor, you are looking at what the asset—in our case, business—will do. If you are a speculator, you are primarily forecasting on what the price will do independent of the business.[19]

Investing is found in the attitude towards stock-price movements. The speculator's concern is anticipating and profiting from stock-price fluctuation. The investor's primary interest is in acquiring and holding suitable securities at suitable prices. Market fluctuations are important to the investor because they create low price levels to buy and, alternatively, high price levels to refrain from buying. The investor with a portfolio of great businesses should expect prices to fluctuate and should neither be concerned by sizable declines nor be wildly excited by sizable advances.[20]

We do not need more people gambling on the nonessential instruments identified with the stock market in the country, nor brokers who encourage them to do so. What we need are investors and advisers who look at the long-term prospects for an enterprise and invest accordingly. We need the intelligent commitment of capital, not leveraged market wagers. The propensity to operate in the intelligent, prosocial sectors of capital markets is deterred, not enhanced, by an active and exciting casino operating in somewhat the same arena, utilizing somewhat similar language, and serviced by the same workforce.[21]

Arrogance will always get the best of you in finance.

Five centuries before Christ, Demosthenes noted that: "What a man wishes, he will believe." And in self-appraisals of prospects and talents, it is the norm, as Demosthenes predicted, for people to be ridiculously over optimistic. For instance, a careful survey in Sweden showed that 90 percent of automobile drivers considered themselves above average. And people who are successfully selling something, as investment counselors do, make Swedish drivers sound like depressives. Virtually every investment expert's public assessment is that he is above average, no matter the evidence to the contrary. Smart, hard-working people aren't exempted from professional disasters from overconfidence. Often, they just go aground in the more difficult voyages they choose, relying on their self-appraisals that they have superior talents and methods.

It is, of course, irritating that extra care in thinking also introduces extra errors, but most good things have undesired "side effects," and thinking is no exception. The best defense is that of the best physicists, who systematically criticize themselves to an extreme degree, using a mindset described by Nobel laureate Richard Feynman as follows: "The first principle is that you must not fool yourself and you're the easiest person to fool.[22]

Let time be the natural friend of your portfolio.

There is also another alternative: Don't do anything. More fortunes are made by sitting on good securities for years at a time than by active trading.[23]

Even the most thoughtful and steadfast investor is susceptible to the influence of skeptics who yell "Sell" before it's time to sell. We've all been taught the same adages: "Take profits when you can," and "A sure gain is always better than a possible loss." But when you've found the right stock and bought it, all the evidence tells you it's going higher, and everything is working in your direction, then it's a shame if you sell. A fivefold gain turns $10,000 into $50,000, but the next five folds turn $10,000 into $250,000. Investing in a 25-bagger is not a regular occurrence even among fund managers, and for the individual, it may only happen once or twice in a lifetime. When you've got one, you might as well enjoy the full benefit.[24]

Time is the enemy of the poor business and the friend of the great business. If you have a business that's earning 20%–25% on equity, time is your friend. But time is your enemy if your money is in a low return business.[25]

And don't get bogged down overanalyzing things. You'll force yourself to make errors.

Based on my own personal experience—both as an investor in recent years and an expert witness in years past—rarely do more than three or four variables really count. Everything else is noise—attributed to Marty Whitman.

One of the most astute investors I've ever known was a remarkable example of long-term investing. He owned several hundred different securities accumulated in small increments over many years. He told me once that his job as a registered representative with a stock exchange firm had never paid him more than $10,000 a year in his life. And he started with little or no inherited money.

He liked to talk about his successes. One in particular was fascinating. In his 20s, he invested $1,400 in a relatively obscure company. Over the next 60 years, the stock was split repeatedly for a net of 360 shares for one. At that point, his $1,400 had grown to $2,000,000....He said at one time he checked the company by talking to the management. "They seemed to know what they were doing," he told me.

That is security analysis in a nutshell. If the figures look right and the management knows what it's doing, why does one need a 40-page report?[26]

Investors should remember that their scorecard is not computed using Olympic-diving methods: Degree-of-difficulty doesn't count. If you are right about a business whose value is largely dependent on a single key factor that is both easy to understand and enduring, the payoff is the same as if you had correctly analyzed an investment alternative characterized by many constantly shifting and complex variables.[27]

The stock market is a no-called-strike game. You don't have to swing at everything—you can wait for your pitch. The problem when you're a money manager is that your fans keep yelling, "Swing, you bum!"[28]

Stay within your strengths when evaluating businesses.

Intelligent investing is not complex, though that is far from saying that it is easy. What an investor needs is the ability to correctly evaluate selected businesses. Note the word "selected": You don't have to be an expert on every company, or even many. You only have to be able to evaluate companies within your circle of competence. The size of that circle is not very important; knowing its boundaries, however, is vital.

Your goal as an investor should simply be to purchase, at a rational price, a part interest in an easily-understandable business whose earnings are virtually certain to be materially higher five, ten and twenty years from now. Over time, you will find only a few companies that meet these standards—so when you see one that qualifies, you should buy a meaningful amount of stock. You must also resist the temptation to stray from your guidelines: if you aren't willing to own a stock for ten years, don't even think about owning it for ten minutes.[29]

The strategy we've adopted precludes our following standard diversification dogma. Many pundits would therefore say the strategy must be riskier than that employed by more conventional investors. We disagree. We believe that a policy of portfolio concentration may well *decrease* risk if it raises, as it should, both the intensity with which an investor thinks about a business and the comfort-level he must feel with its economic characteristics before buying into it.[30]

Judge a business by what it's worth to its owners and what it costs to maintain it.

The strange thing—it's a real contradiction—is that if a business is earning a given amount of money and everything else is equal, the less it has in assets, the more it's worth. You won't get that in an accounting book. The really desirable business is that one that doesn't take any money to operate because it's already proven that money will not enable anyone to get a position within the business. Those are the great businesses.[31]

The business is wonderful if it gives you more and more money every year without putting up anything—or very little. And we have some businesses like that. A business is also wonderful if it takes money, but where the rate at which you reinvest the money is very satisfactory. The worst business of all is the one that grows a lot, where you're forced to grow just to stay in the game at all and where you're reinvesting the capital at a very low rate of return. And sometimes people are in those businesses without knowing it.[32]

Don't trap yourself into believing a business or product is worth exactly what someone is willing to pay. Someday, you'll end up paying dearly for a business propped by perception only.

Maybe grapes from a little 8-acre vineyard in France are really the best in the whole world, but I have always had a suspicion that about 99 percent of it is in the telling and about 1 percent is in the drinking.[33]

Seek companies with franchise value. You'll know them when you see them.

If you own See's Candy, and you look in the mirror and say, "mirror, mirror on the wall, how much do I charge for candy this fall," and it says "more," that's a good business.[34]

The key to investing is not assessing how much an industry is going to affect society, or how much it will grow, but rather determining the competitive advantage of any given company and, above all, the durability of that advantage. The products or services that have wide, sustainable moats around them are the ones that deliver rewards to investors.[35]

Do your homework before purchasing a stock.

I don't think you can be a really good investor over a broad range without doing a massive amount of reading. You might think about picking out 5 or 10 companies where you feel quite familiar with their products, but not necessarily so familiar with their financials....Then get lots of annual reports and all of the articles that have been written on those companies for 5 or 10 years....Just sort of immerse yourself. And when you get all through, ask yourself, "What do I not know that I need to know?" Many years ago, I would go around and talk to competitors and employees....I just kept asking questions....It's an investigative process—a journalistic process. And in the end, you want to write the story....Some companies are easy to write stories about and other companies are much tougher to write stories about. We try to look for the ones that are easy.[36]

Never feel compelled to buy or sell just because it seems fashionable.

You do things when the opportunities come along. I've had periods in my life when I've had a bundle of ideas come along, and I've had long dry spells. If I get an idea next week, I'll do something. If not, I won't do a damn thing.[37]

We don't get paid for *activity*, just for being *right*. As to how long we'll wait, we'll wait *indefinitely*.[38]

A low price doesn't guarantee a bargain. The company must offer a combination of good value and improving fundamentals.

It doesn't have to be rock bottom to buy it. It has to be selling for less than you think the value of the business is, and it has to be run by honest and able people. But if you buy into a business for less than it's worth today, and you're confident of the management, and you buy into a group of businesses like that, you're going to make money.[39]

The investor cannot pinpoint just how much per share a particular company will earn two years from now. As a matter of fact, the company's top management cannot. Under these circumstances, how can anyone say with even moderate precision just what is overpriced for an outstanding company with an unusually rapid growth rate? If the growth rate is so good that in another ten years the company might well have quadrupled, is it really of such great concern whether at the moment the stock might or might not be 35% overpriced? That which really matters is not to disturb a position that is going to be worth a great deal more later.[40]

We have tried occasionally to buy toads at bargain prices with results that have been chronicled in past reports. Clearly our kisses fell flat. We have done well with a couple of princes—but they were princes when purchased. At least our kisses didn't turn them into toads. And, finally, we have occasionally been quite successful in purchasing fractional interests in easily-identifiable princes at toad-like prices.[41]

Volatility is your friend if you keep a business owner's perspective.

I consider there to be three basic ideas that if they are really ground into your intellectual framework, I don't how you could help but do reasonably well in stocks. None of them are complicated. None of them take mathematical talent or anything of the sort. [Benjamin Graham] said you should look at stocks as small pieces of the business. Look at [stock] fluctuations as your friend rather than your enemy—profit from the folly rather than participate in it. And [Graham] said the three most important words of investing: "margin of safety." I think those ideas, 100 years from now, will still be regarded as the three cornerstones of sound investing.[42]

[Many] investors who expect to be ongoing buyers of investments throughout their lifetimes...illogically become euphoric when stock prices rise and unhappy when they fall. They show no such confusion in their reaction to food prices: Knowing they are forever going to be buyers of food, they welcome falling prices and deplore price increases. (It's the seller of food who doesn't like declining prices.) Similarly, at the Buffalo News we would cheer lower prices for newsprint—even though it would mean marking down the value of the large inventory of newsprint we always keep on hand—because we know we are going to be perpetually buying the product.

Identical reasoning guides our thinking about Berkshire's investments. We will be buying businesses—or small parts of businesses, called stocks—year in, year out as long as I live (and longer, if Berkshire's directors attend the seances I have scheduled). Given these intentions, declining prices for businesses benefit us, and rising prices hurt us.

The most common cause of low prices is pessimism—some times pervasive, some times specific to a company or industry. We *want* to do business in such an environment, not because we like pessimism but because we like the prices it produces. It's optimism that is the enemy of the rational buyer.

None of this means, however, that a business or stock is an intelligent purchase simply because it is unpopular; a contrarian approach is just as foolish as a follow-the-crowd strategy. What's required is thinking rather than polling. Unfortunately, Bertrand Russell's observation about life in general applies with unusual force in the financial world: "Most men would rather die than think. Many do."[43]

Price fluctuations have only one significant meaning for the true investor. They provide him with an opportunity to buy wisely when prices fall sharply and to sell wisely when they advance a great deal. At other times he will do better if he forgets about the stock market and pays attention to…the operating results of his companies.[44]

MR. MARKET

Reprinted with the permission of Warren E. Buffett.

WARREN BUFFETT BELIEVES investors could greatly improve their stock-picking if they realize one simple fact about the financial markets: They exist to serve you, not guide you. The following passage, taken from Berkshire Hathaway's 1987 annual report, is necessary for understanding Buffett's feelings about stock prices.

Whenever Charlie (Berkshire Hathaway Vice-Chairman Munger) and I buy common stocks for Berkshire's insurance companies ...we approach the transaction as if we were buying into a private business. We look at the economic prospects of the business, the people in charge of running it, and the price we must pay. We do not have any time or price of sale. Indeed, we are willing to hold a stock indefinitely so long as we expect the business to increase in intrinsic value at a satisfactory rate. When investing, we view ourselves as business analysts—not as market analysts, not as macroeconomic analysts, and not even as security analysts.

Our approach makes an active trading market useful, since it periodically presents us with mouth-watering opportunities. But by no means is it essential: a prolonged suspension of trading in the securities we hold would not bother us any more than does the lack of daily quotations on World Book or Fechheimer [two companies that Berkshire Hathaway owns]. Eventually, our economic fate will be determined by the economic fate of the business we own, whether our ownership is partial or total.

Ben Graham, my friend and teacher, long ago described the mental attitude toward market fluctuations that I believe to be most conducive to investment success. He said that you should imagine market quotations as coming from a remarkably accommodating fellow named Mr. Market who is your partner in a private business. Without fail, Mr. Market appears daily and names a price at which he will either buy your interest or sell you his.

Even though the business that the two of you own may have economic characteristics that are stable, Mr. Market's quotations will be anything but. For, sad to say, the poor fellow has incurable emotional problems. At times he feels euphoric and can see only the favorable factors affecting the business. When in that mood, he names a very high buy-sell price because he fears that you will snap up his interest and rob him of imminent gains. At other times he is depressed and can see nothing but trouble ahead for both the business and the world. On these occasions he will name a very low price, since he is terrified that you will unload his interest on him.

Mr. Market has another endearing characteristic: He doesn't mind being ignored. If his quotation is uninteresting to you today, he will be back with a new one tomorrow. Transactions are strictly at your option. Under these conditions, the more manic-depressive his behavior, the better for you.

But, like Cinderella at the ball, you must heed one warning or everything will turn into pumpkins and mice: Mr. Market is there to serve you, not to guide you. It is his pocketbook, not his wisdom, that you will find useful. If he shows up some day in a particularly foolish mood, you are free to either ignore him or to take advantage of him, but it will be disastrous if you fall under his influence. Indeed, if you aren't certain that you understand and can value your business far better than Mr. Market, you don't belong in the game. As they say in poker, "if you've been in the game 30 minutes and you don't know who the patsy is, you're the patsy."

Ben's Mr. Market allegory may seem out of date in today's investment world, in which most professionals and academicians talk of efficient markets, dynamic hedging and betas. Their interest in such matters is understandable, since techniques shrouded in mystery clearly have value to the purveyor of investment advice. After all, what witch doctor has ever achieved fame and fortune by simply advising "take two aspirins"?

The value of market esoterica to the consumer of investment advice is a different story. In my opinion, investment success will not be produced by arcane formulae, computer programs or signals flashed by the price behavior of stocks and markets. Rather an investor will succeed by coupling good business judgment with an ability to insulate his thoughts and behavior from the super-contagious emotions that swirl about the marketplace. In my own efforts to stay insulated, I have found it highly useful to keep Ben's Mr. Market concept firmly in mind.

Following Ben's teachings, Charlie and I let our marketable equities tell us by their operating results—not by their daily or even yearly, price quotations—whether our investments are successful. That market may ignore business success for a while, but eventually will confirm it. As Ben said: "In the short run, the market is a voting machine but in the long run it is a weighing machine." The speed at which a business's success is recognized, furthermore, is not that important as long as the company's intrinsic value is increasing at a satisfactory rate. In fact, delayed recognition can be an advantage: It may give us the chance to buy more of a good thing at a bargain price.

Sometimes, of course, the market may judge a business to be more valuable than the underlying facts would indicate it is. In such a case, we will sell our holdings. Sometimes, also, we will sell a security that is fairly valued or even undervalued because we require funds for a still more undervalued investment or one we believe we understand better. We need to emphasize, however, that we do not sell holdings just because they have appreciated or because we have held them for a long time. (Of Wall Street maxims the most foolish may be "You can't go broke taking a profit.") We are quite content to hold any security indefinitely, so long as the prospective return on equity capital of the underlying business is satisfactory, management is competent and honest, and the market does not over value the business.

B

YOUR COMPETITIVE
ADVANTAGE OVER
BUFFETT

The Internet

A S A YOUNG MONEY MANAGER, Warren Buffett would spend 12 hours a day or more in his home reading annual reports and various stock-picking guides he had purchased. The activity consumed Buffett and naturally dovetailed into his love for detail and phenomenal memory for numbers. When he wasn't poring over reports at home, Buffett was at the city and university libraries in Omaha, reading investment books, academic studies, and financial newspapers.

Working virtually alone, he probably studied companies more thoroughly than the best analysts on Wall Street. Buffett's favorite reference materials have been *The ValueLine Investment Survey*, from where Buffett draws the majority of his investment ideas, and the voluminous company guides published by *Standard & Poor's* and *Moody's*. Each guide, which can still be found in local libraries, provides broad descriptions of hundreds of companies and their product lines and presents 10 to 15 years of financial data.

Buffett has found these sources extremely useful through the years. *ValueLine*, for example, acts as a great first screen for investors. It divides companies by their industries and gives you detailed statistical data on returns on equity, quarterly results, depreciation rates, shares outstanding, profit margins, debt levels, and yearly cash flow. "I started at page one [of these manuals] and went through every company that traded, from A to Z," he sometimes says at annual meetings. "When I was done, I knew something about every company in the book."

Buffett doesn't want to buy every company he studies. Instead, he tries to keep a mental file on companies that *might* interest him in the future. Thus, when a stock drops 20 percent or more in a short period, there's a good chance Buffett has already studied it and has formed some notion of its value. It's merely a matter of collecting old notes and quickly assessing whether the company is worth buying at a reduced price.

Spending 12 hours a day researching investment information is no longer *de rigeur*, thanks, in large part, to the Internet. With the speed of a mouse click, individual investors can assemble in a matter of a few hours the same information it used to take Buffett days, if not weeks, to gather. For the cost of a computer modem and a modest monthly phone fee, investors can hook up to the Internet and access data that once cost Wall Street's investment houses tens of thousands of dollars a year—if it was available at all.

> In my experience, there is little difference between a very high-priced business education and those available for a lot less money. I went to the University of Nebraska my last year in college. I went to Wharton a couple of years before that. I learned just as much at Nebraska as I did at Wharton. It's not necessary to pay $35,000 for an education. A lot of education is self-taught. With libraries and the Internet, there is all kinds of information out there to be taken.[1]

Given the massive amounts of data available on companies around the world, it almost behooves serious investing students to exploit the Internet fully to cut their research time. As with any other form of information, you must act as your own editor. The Internet tempts you with a lot of novelties—low-commission trading, free news services, up-to-the-minute quotes and charts, and earnings estimates—but you should never rely on the Internet to make a decision for you.

For investors wanting to use the Internet to sniff out bargains, I list numerous sites that provide great sources of information the Internet offers. The following website addresses were current as of April 2000.

ACCOUNTING INFORMATION

Accounting links—*www.cpalinks.com*

American Institute of Certified Public Accountants—*www.aicpa.org*

Andersen Consulting—*www.ac.com*

Arthur Andersen—*www.arthurandersen.com*

Deloitte & Touche—*www.dtonline.com*

Ernst & Young—*www.ey.com*

Financial Accounting Standards Board—
    www.rutgers.edu/Accounting/raw/fasb/

Grant Thornton—*www.gt.com*

KPMG Peat Marwick—*www.kpmg.com*

PricewaterhouseCoopers—*www.pwcglobal.com*

FINANCIAL INFORMATION AND EDUCATION

American Association of Individual Investors—*www.aaii.org*

Equity Analytics—*www.e-analytics.com*

Ibbotson Associates—*www.ibbotson.com*

Investment newsletters—*www.newsletteraccess.com*

Moody's Investor Services—*www.moodys.com*

Morningstar, Inc.—*www.morningstar.net*

Motley Fool—*www.fool.com*

Natl. Association of Investors Corp. (NAIC)—
    www.better-investing.org

Standard & Poor's—*www.standardpoors.com*

GOVERNMENT AGENCIES—FINANCIAL FILINGS

Bureau of Labor Statistics—*www.bls.gov*

Comptroller of the Currency—*www.occ.treas.gov*

Conference Board (The)—*www.crc-conquest.org*

Department of Commerce, STAT database—*www.stat-usa.gov*

Economic Statistics Briefing Room —
    www.whitehouse.gov/fsbr/esbr.html

Federal Deposit Insurance Corp.—*www.fdic.gov*

Federal Reserve Bank of New York—*www.ny.frb.org*

Federal Reserve Bank of St. Louis— *www.stls.frb.org*

Federal Reserve Board—*www.bog.frb.fed.us*

Government Accounting Office—*www.gao.gov*

Patent & Trademark Office—*www.uspto.gov*

Securities and Exchange Commission—*www.sec.gov*

SEC, EDGAR database—*www.sec.gov./cgi-bin/srch-edgar*
    www.edgar-online.com

Treasury Department—*www.ustreas.gov*

U.S. Census Bureau—*www.census.gov*

U.S. House of Representatives—*www.house.gov*

U.S. Senate—*www.senate.gov*

White House—*www.whitehouse.gov*

NEWSPAPERS AND MAGAZINES

Atlanta Journal-Constitution—*www.ajc.com*

Barron's—*www.barrons.com*

Boston Globe—*www.bostonglobe.com*

Business Week—*www.businessweek.com*

Chicago Sun-Times—*www.suntimes.com*

Denver Post—*www.denverpost.com*

Economist (London)—*www.economist.com*

Financial Times (London)—*www.ft.com*

Forbes—*www.forbes.com*

Fortune—*www.pathfinder.com/fortune*
Gannett Newspapers—*www.gannett.com/web/gan013.htm*
Houston Chronicle—*www.chron.com*
Inc.—*www.inc.com*
Individual Investor—*www.iionline.com*
Industry Standard—*www.thestandard.com*
Kiplinger—*www.kiplinger.com*
Knight-Ridder newspapers, database of articles—*newslibrary.infi.net*
Los Angeles Times—*www.latimes.com*
Miami Herald—*www.herald.com*
Money—*www.money.com*
Newsweek—*www.newsweek.com*
New York Times—*www.nytimes.com*
Philadelphia Enquirer, Philadelphia Daily News—
   www.phillynews.com
Red Herring—*www.redherring.com*
San Francisco Chronicle—*www.sfgate.com/chronicle*
Seattle Times—*www.seattletimes.com*
Slate—*www.slate.com*
SmartMoney—*www.smartmoney.com*
Time—*www.time.com*
Tribune Co.—*www.tribune.com*
Vanity Fair—*www.vanityfair.com*
Variety—*www.variety.com*
Wall Street Journal—*www.wsj.com*
Wall Street Transcript—*www.twst.com*
Washington Post—*www.washingtonpost.com*
Worth magazine—*www.worth.com*

NEWS SERVICES

ABC News—*www.abcnews.com*
British Broadcasting Corp.—*www.bbc.co.uk*
Bloomberg News Service—*www.bloomberg.com*

BusinessWire—*www.businesswire.com*
Canadian Broadcasting Corp.—*http://cbc.ca*
CBS Marketwatch—*http://cbs.marketwatch.com*
CNBC—*www.cnbc.com*
CNN Financial—*http://cnnfn.com*
C-Span—*www.c-span.org*
Daily Stocks—*www.dailystocks.com*
Dow Jones Interactive—*www.djnr.com*
Fox network—*www.foxnews.com*
Lycos Stock Find—*www.stockfind.newsalert.com*
Microsoft Investor—*www.moneycentral.msn.com*
NBC News—*www.nbcnews.com*
NewsEdge—*www.newspage.com*
PR Newswire—*www.prnewswire.com*
Reuters MoneyNet—*www.moneynet.com*
Streeteye—*www.streeteye.com*
Wall Street Journal Interactive—*www.wsj.com*
Yahoo finance—*http://quote.yahoo.com*

STOCK EXCHANGES

All world stock markets (links)—*www.qualisteam.com*
American Stock Exchange—*www.amex.com*
Chicago Board of Trade—*www.cbot.com*
Chicago Board Options Exchange—*www.cboe.com*
Chicago Mercantile Exchange—*www.cme.com*
Kansas City Board of Trade—*www.kcbt.com*
London Metal Exchange—*www.lme.co.uk*
London Stock Exchange—*www.londonstockex.co.uk*
NASDAQ stock market—*www.nasdaq.com*
New York Cotton Exchange—*www.nyce.com*
New York Mercantile Exchange—*www.nymex.com*
New York Stock Exchange—*www.nyse.com*
Pacific Stock Exchange—*www.pacificex.com*

Philadelphia Stock Exchange—*www.phlx.com*
Tokyo Stock Exchange—*www.tse.or.jp*
Toronto Stock Exchange—*www.tse.com*
Vancouver Stock Exchange—*www.vse.ca*
Yahoo links to foreign bourses—*www.finance.yahoo.com*

STOCK INFORMATION AND INVESTMENT ADVICE

Briefing Room—*www.briefing.com*
The Financial Center—*www.tfc.com*
Daily Rocket—*www.dailyrocket.com*
Daily Stocks—*www.dailystocks.com*
Data Broadcasting Corp.—*www.dbc.com*
Futures investing—*www.futuresweb.com*
Interquote—*www.interquote.com*
Investools—*www.investools.com*
Investor Links—*www.investorlinks.com*
Investors Edge—*www.stockpoint.com*
Market Mavens—*www.marketmavensreport.com*
Microsoft Investor—*www.moneynet.msn.com*
Quicken—*www.quicken.com*
Wall Street City—*www.wallstreetcity.com*
The Street—*thestreet.com*
The Syndicate—*www.moneypages.com/syndicate*
Thomson Investor Network—*www.thomsoninvest.net*
Yahoo—*www.quote.yahoo.com*

MISCELLANEOUS FINANCIAL TOPICS

Bonds: Corporate and Treasuries
www.bondsonline.com
www.convertbond.com

Business valuation
www.nvst.com

www.quicken.com/investments/stkeval/
www.appraisers.org

Company websites
www.investorama.com

Corporate profiles
www.hoovers.com

Earnings estimates
www.zacks.com
www.earningswhispers.com
www.vcall.com

Economic charts, links
www.yardeni.com
http://condor.depaul.edu/~dshannon

Executive pay
www.paywatch.org

Global investing
www.global-investor.com
www.ifc.com
www.tradershaven.com

Gold and silver
www.bullion.org
www.goldsheet.simplenet.com

Historical financial charts
www.globalfindata.com
www.pinnacledata.com

Insider trading
www.fedfil.com
www.biz.yahoo.com
www.insidertrader.com

www.dailystocks.com
www.cda.com

Merger announcements/arbitrage
www.nvst.com/rsrc/mergerstat
www.securitiesdata.com
www.madaily.com
www.mergerstat.com
www.moneycentral.msn.com
www.investhelp.com
www.takeovertarget.com

Portfolio tracking
www.investor.msn.com
www.yahoo.com
www.stockup.com
www.dailystocks.com
www.quicken.com/investments/

Proxy voting
www.proxyvote.com

Quote services
www.wwquote.com
www.itfa.com

Special situations
www.convertbond.com
www.donedeals.nvst.com
www.numa.com
www.gopublicentral.com

Stock buy-backs, splits, dividend announcements
www.dailyrocket.com

Stock charts
www.bigcharts.com

Stock options, executive options
www.cbot.com
www.cboe.com
www.biz.yahoo.com
www.nceo.org
www.e-analytics.com

Stock screening services
www.marketplayer.com
www.rapidresearch.com
http://www.stockscreener.com

ENDNOTES

CHAPTER 1

1 Roger Lowenstein, *Buffett: The Making of an American Capitalist*, New York, Doubleday, 1995, p. 20.

2 Martin Fridson, *How to Be a Billionaire*, New York, John Wiley & Sons, 2000, p. 216.

3 John Train, *The Money Masters*, New York, HarperBusiness, 1980, pp. 158–159.

4 John Neff, *John Neff on Investing*, New York, John Wiley & Sons, 1999, p. 45.

5 Neff, *John Neff on Investing*, p. 45.

6 Andy Kilpatrick, *Of Permanent Value: The Story of Warren Buffett*, AKPE, 1998, p. 56.

7 Lowenstein, *Buffett*, p. 22.

8 Kilpatrick, *Of Permanent Value*, p. 57.

9 Kilpatrick, *Of Permanent Value*, p. 69.

10 Kilpatrick, *Of Permanent Value*, p. 71.

CHAPTER 2

1 Letter to his partners dated October 9, 1969.

2 Charles Munger, Annual meeting of Wesco Financial, 1993.

3 From a 1998 appearance with Bill Gates before business students at the University of Washington, Seattle.

4 Andrew Kilpatrick, *Of Permanent Value: The Story of Warren Buffett*, AKPE, 1998, p. 333.

CHAPTER 3

1 Andrew Kilpatrick, *Of Permanent Value: The Story of Warren Buffett*, AKPE, 1998, p. 128.

2 Roger Lowenstein, *Buffett: The Making of an American Capitalist*, New York, Doubleday, 1996, p. 10.

3 Warren Buffett, Letter to partners, January 18, 1963.

4 "Warren Buffett—The Pragmatist," *Esquire*, June 1988, p. 150.

5 Annual report, 1998.

6 "Mr. Buffett on the Stock Market," *Fortune*, November 22, 1999. Reprinted with permission of the magazine.

CHAPTER 4

1 Benjamin Graham, *The Intelligent Investor*, 4th ed. New York, HarperBusiness, 1973, pp. 293–294.

2 Philip Fisher, *Common Stocks and Uncommon Profits*, New York, reprint of the 1958 ed., John Wiley & Sons, 1996, pp. 108–109.

3 Jim Rasmussen, "Buffett Talks Strategy with Students," *Omaha World-Herald*, January 2, 1994, p. 17.

4 Robert Hagstrom, Jr., *The Warren Buffett Portfolio*, New York, John Wiley & Sons, 1999, p. 58.

5 Linda Grant, "The $4 Billion Regular Guy," *The Los Angeles Times Magazine*, April 7, 1991.

CHAPTER 5

1 Janet Lowe, *Warren Buffett Speaks*, New York, John Wiley & Sons, 1997, p. 16.

2 This story was told to me by Buffett biographer Andrew Kilpatrick.

3 Andrew Kilpatrick, *Of Permanent Value: The Story of Warren Buffett*, AKPE, 1998, p. 23.

CHAPTER 6

1 Robert Dorr, "Newspaper Holdings Kind to Omaha Investor Buffett," *Omaha World-Herald*, April 16, 1978.

2 "Mr. Buffett on the Stock Market," a transcription of speeches Buffett gave privately to business leaders in 1999, which were collated by friend Carol Loomis and published in *Fortune*, November 22, 1999.

3 Special letter to shareholders, August 5, 1988, when the New York Stock Exchange was considering letting Berkshire Hathaway's stock trade on the exchange.

4 Lecture to business students at the University of North Carolina, Chapel Hill, 1995.

CHAPTER 7

1 Peter Bernstein, *Against the Gods—The Remarkable Story of Risk*, New York, John Wiley & Sons, 1996, p. 23.

2 Charles Munger, speech to the Foundation Financial Officers Group, October 14, 1998.

CHAPTER 9

1 John Burr Williams, *The Theory of Investment Value*, reprint of 1938 ed., Burlington, Fraser Publishing Co., 1997, p. 55.

2 Benjamin Graham and David Dodd, *Security Analysis*, reprint of 1934 ed., New York, McGraw-Hill, 1997, p. 493.

3 Annual report of Berkshire Hathaway, 1989.

4 Graham and Dodd, *Security Analysis*, p. 493.

5 Annual report of Berkshire Hathaway, 1996.

6 Benjamin Graham, *The Intelligent Investor*, 4th rev. ed., New York, HarperBusiness, 1973, p. 147.

CHAPTER 10

1 From the "Owners Manual" distributed to Berkshire Hathaway shareholders, 1996.

2 Marilyn Ostermiller, "Power Source," *Best's Review—Property-Casualty Insurance Edition*, June 1, 1999.

3 Annual report to shareholders, 1988.

4 Annual report to shareholders, 1982.

5 Annual report to shareholders, 1998.

6 Annual report to shareholders, 1982.

7 Annual report to shareholders, 1982.

CHAPTER 11

1 Annual report of Berkshire Hathaway, 1979.

2 Annual report of Berkshire Hathaway, 1977.

CHAPTER 12

1 Annual report of Berkshire Hathaway, 1996.

CHAPTER 13

1 Charles T. Munger, speech before the Foundation Financial Officers Group in Santa Monica, California, October 14, 1998.

CHAPTER 14

1 Annual meeting of Berkshire Hathaway, 1992.

2 Annual meeting of Berkshire Hathaway, 1999.

3 *Outstanding Investor Digest*, September 24, 1998, p. 41.

4 Andrew Kilpatrick, *Of Permanent Value: The Story of Warren Buffett,* Birmingham, APKE, 1994, p. 198.

5 Annual meeting of Berkshire Hathaway, 1999.

CHAPTER 15

1 Buffett, Warren E "How Inflation Swindles the Investor," *Fortune,* May 5, 1977, p. 250.

2 From the 1981 annual report to shareholders.

CHAPTER 16

1 T. Pouschine, "Will the Real Warren Buffett Please Stand Up," *Forbes*, March 19, 1990, p. 92.

2 Charles Ellis, "The Loser's Game," *Financial Analysts Journal*, July/August, 1975, p. 95.

CHAPTER 17

1 "Faces Behind the Figures," *Forbes*, January 4, 1988.

CHAPTER 18

1 Janet Lowe, *Value Investing Made Easy*, New York, McGraw-Hill, 1996, pp. 147–148.

2 Annual report of Berkshire Hathaway, 1988.

3 Annual report of Berkshire Hathaway, 1988.

4 Warren E. Buffett, Letter to partners dated February 20, 1960, p. 3.

5 Warren E. Buffett, Letter to partners dated January 24, 1962, p. 5.

6 *Outstanding Investor Digest*, April 18, 1990, p. 16.

7 T. Pouschine, "Will the Real Warren Buffett Please Stand Up," *Forbes*, March 19, 1990.

8 Annual report of Berkshire Hathaway, 1988.

9 Annual report of Berkshire Hathaway, 1988.

10 Annual report of Berkshire Hathaway, 1988.

11 Annual report of Berkshire Hathaway, 1988.

12 Annual report of Berkshire Hathaway, 1988.

13 Annual report to Berkshire Hathaway, 1992.

PART 5

1 Daniel Goleman, *Emotional Intelligence*, New York, Bantam Books, 1995, p. 5.

2 Michael Mauboussin, "What Have You Learned the Past 2 Seconds," Equity Research Paper, March 12, 1997, p. 2.

3 Linda Grant, "Striking Out at Wall Street," *U.S. News & World Report*, June 20, 1994, p. 58.

4 Grant, "Striking Out at Wall Street," p. 58.

5 Benjamin Graham, *The Intelligent Investor*, 4th ed., New York, HarperBusiness, 1973, p. 87.

6 Annual report of Berkshire Hathaway, 1988.

7 Annual report of Berkshire Hathaway, 1987.

8 Annual report of Berkshire Hathaway, 1996.

9 Janet Lowe, *Warren Buffett Speaks: Wit and Wisdom from the World's Greatest Investor*, New York, John Wiley & Sons, 1996, p. 100.

10 Forbes 400, October 18, 1993.

11 Andy Kilpatrick, *Of Permanent Value: The Story of Warren Buffett*, Burlington, AKPE, 1996.

12 "Buffett Listed by Fortune with Wall Street Winners," *Omaha World-Herald*, July 31, 1983.

13 L.J. Davis, "Buffett Takes Stock," *The New York Times Magazine*, April 1, 1990, p. 16.

14 Janet Lowe, *Value Investing Made Easy*, New York, McGraw-Hill, 1996, p. 61.

15 Annual meeting of Berkshire Hathaway, 1982.

16 Annual report of Berkshire Hathaway, 1994.

17 Peter Lynch, *One Up on Wall Street*, New York, Penguin Books, 1989.

18 Attributed to John Maynard Keynes.

19 Attributed to Warren Buffett.

20 Michael A. Lee-Chin, Chairman and Chief Executive Officer, AIC Limited.

21 Warren Buffett, Letter to U.S. Representative John Dingell of Michigan, Chairman of the House of Representatives Subcommittee on Oversight and Investigations, March 1982, from Lowe, *Warren Buffett Speaks*, pp. 107–108.

22 Charles T. Munger, speech before the Foundation Financial Officers Group in Santa Monica, California, October 14, 1998.

23 Interview with Philip Carret, *Outstanding Investor Digest*, October 31, 1990.

24 Lynch, *One Up on Wall Street*, p. 253.

25 Annual meeting of Berkshire Hathaway, 1998.

26 Interview with Philip Carret, *Outstanding Investor Digest*, October 31, 1990.

27 Annual report of Berkshire Hathaway, 1994.

28 Annual meeting, 1999.

29 Annual report of Berkshire Hathaway, 1996.

30 Annual report of Berkshire Hathaway, 1993.

31 Lecture to Stanford Business School, April 18, 1990.

32 Annual meeting of Berkshire Hathaway, 1998.

33 Lowe, *Warren Buffett Speaks*, p. 36.

34 Jim Rasmussen, "Billionaire Talks Strategy with Students," *Omaha World-Herald*, January 2, 1994, p. 17s.

35 *Fortune*, November 22, 1999.

36 Annual meeting of Berkshire Hathaway, 1999.

37 Gary Strauss, "Buffett a Buddy to Targeted Firms," *USA Today*, August 9, 1989.

38 Annual meeting of Berkshire Hathaway, 1998.

39 Warren Buffett, *Nightly Business Report*, PBS, December 13, 1994.

40 Philip Fisher, *Common Stocks and Uncommon Profits*, reprint of 1958 ed., New York, John Wiley & Sons, 1996, pp. 82–83.

41 Annual report of Berkshire Hathaway, 1981.

42 Speech to the New York Society of Security Analysts, December 6, 1994.

43 Annual report of Berkshire Hathaway, 1990.

44 Graham, *The Intelligent Investor*, p. 109.

APPENDIX B

1 "You Won the Lottery," *George*, April 2000, p. 39.

INDEX

Note: Boldface numbers indicate illustrations; italic t indicates a table.

ABOUT THE AUTHOR

Timothy P. Vick is the senior analyst with Arbor Capital Management, with offices in Jacksonville, Anchorage, and the Chicago area. He is the founder and former editor in chief of *Today's Value Investor*, a nationally distributed market newsletter devoted to value-oriented stock picking. Mr. Vick also serves as a consultant to small businesses on matters relating to valuation and strategic planning. He has appeared on CNBC and CNN and has been quoted by *The New York Times*, *The Wall Street Journal*, *The Los Angeles Times*, *The Washington Post*, *Barron's*, *The Chicago Tribune*, *Investor's Business Daily*, *Kiplinger's*, *Money*, *Financial World*, and *Futures*. Mr. Vick is a frequent guest on radio talk shows and is the author of *Wall Street on Sale—How to Beat the Market as a Value Investor*, a primer on the methods of Benjamin Graham and Warren Buffett. Mr. Vick holds a master's degree in management from Purdue University. He and his family reside in Munster, Indiana, a suburb of Chicago.